Stuart Hillard

SIMPLE SHAPES STUNNING QUILTS

PAVILION

CONTENTS

INTRODUCTION

I made my first piece of patchwork many years ago, at school. My teacher, Miss Jenkins, shared with me a partial quilt top she had worked on with students the previous year and taught me to sew little hexagons of fabric, wrapped around paper templates, to join with what she already had. In the coming weeks I sewed many tiny rosettes together with stitches that started clumsily but became neater. She let me loose on a bag of her precious fabric scraps that was kept in the art cupboard and I felt like a pirate, discovering buried treasure! Right there and then, I had learned a simple equation: 1 + 2 really did make 3, the three simple truths of quilting...

Truth 1: The shapes are simple
A triangle or square, circle or hexagon is all it takes to make a quilt. These were shapes I was familiar with, had drawn and coloured in in kindergarten – this was easy!

Truth 2: The process is simple
Easy enough for me at age six or seven to learn in a few hours. Yes, I would spend a lifetime exploring that process, of course, and learn many more techniques. I would refine and change the way I approached my quiltmaking and my skills would adapt, but in just a few hours I had learned enough to start that journey.

Truth 3: The results are extraordinary!
Those simple shapes and easy process had made this glorious 'new' fabric that was richer, wilder, more vibrant and exciting than any of the individual elements. This was alchemy and I had been entrusted with the secret of turning base fabrics into golden quilts!

That first project was never finished, of course – certainly not by me, anyway. My time in Miss Jenkins' class came to an end, and I moved up to the next classroom, but my hexagons remained behind, to be picked up and added to by many more generations. I never forgot those lessons learned and now I want to share them with you.

Within the pages of this book you will find the patterns for 100 quilts, all using simple shapes, organized into five chapters. There are twenty quilts in each chapter covering one-patch quilts, strips and squares, triangles, curves and finally foundation-pieced quilts. Every chapter has its share of easy, beginner-friendly designs, so if you're new to all of this, look out for these as a great place to start. You'll also find designs that require a little more experience or time to complete and some that are a challenge. Choose a design that makes your heart sing, use fabrics that you love and make a beautiful quilt of your own – it's as easy as 1, 2, 3!

WHAT IS A QUILT?

A quilt is usually thought of as a three-layered bed-covering made up of a quilt top, a layer of wadding (batting) in the middle and a backing fabric. The three layers are held together with stitching or 'quilting', and the edges generally have a binding attached to them.

THE TOP

This can be 'wholecloth' – one single piece of fabric, plain or patterned – but is more usually 'pieced' as patchwork blocks sewn together to make a larger pattern. Sometimes the top may be 'appliquéd', where shapes or motifs are stitched on top of a background to create the design. This book contains designs using both piecing and appliqué and some designs combine both techniques.

THE WADDING

This is the layer that provides warmth and 'bulk' to the quilt. Many different natural materials and blends are available: wool, cotton, bamboo, even silk, plus those made from man-made fibres.

THE BACKING

This is the underside of the quilt and can be a whole piece of plain or patterned fabric, made up of joined panels or pieced more decoratively. Although it isn't often seen, it's just as important as the top! Use good-quality cotton fabric for the backing of your quilt.

For me, quilts aren't just for beds. I love to use quilts as sofa and chair throws and to decorate the walls in my home as wallhangings. I make quilted cushions, table and bed runners, bags and wearables. I've presented the majority of the designs in this book as bed or wall quilts, but feel free to use them as you wish. One block makes a great cushion or bag front, two or three and you have a runner for a table and five is enough for the end of a bed.

MAKING COLOURS WORK TOGETHER

Whole books have been written about colour theory in general and for quiltmaking in particular. It's something that many quilters struggle with and the truth is they don't need to struggle at all! I spent many years as a primary school teacher and noticed a wonderful thing... the younger children had no fear of colour, no 'rules' to confuse their artistic vision, no inner voice telling them they were 'no good with colour'. They trusted their hearts, they did what felt right; in essence, they had an instinctive sense of colour. The fact is, you were born with that same sense of colour – maybe it's still there and you just 'forgot' how to use it? Trust me on this one, it is definitely still there! So how do you reconnect?

USE THE COLOUR WHEEL

The colour wheel is a thing of beauty and a useful tool to unlock combinations that will work. The simplest schemes are:

▪ Monochromatic

Take one colour from the wheel – say, blue – and choose your fabrics in different shades, from the very palest, lightest blue through to the very darkest. This is a very reliable and easy to use colour scheme, but it can be a little – how do I put this politely? – dull! Rather than use the same kind of blue, use all sorts of blues: those with a touch of yellow or green, the pinky blues, and the red-toned blues, as well as those with a white base. Using a wider variety of the same colour family is much more exciting and vibrant – and even if some of the blues are a bit 'off', they will work in mixed company!

Complementary colours

Simply put, colours that sit opposite each other on the colour wheel are 'complementary' and will enhance and blend beautifully with each other. Let's take blue again. Follow a straight line across the colour wheel and you will see that it sits opposite orange. Blue and orange are complementary and will work well together in a colour scheme, although this type of scheme is pretty 'high contrast'.

Split complementary schemes

These are a bit more exciting to me – they have more variety. To work a split complementary scheme, start with your main colour. Again, for this example we will use blue. Find the complementary colour – we know that's orange. Rather than using orange, we will instead use the colours either side of it; in this case, that is yellow-orange and red-orange – much more dynamic!

Triadic colour schemes

For these you'll need to use three colours, as the name suggests. Start by choosing a colour – you've guessed it, we'll use blue. Trace an equilateral triangle over the colour wheel – note the colours at the three points of the triangle: blue, yellow and red. This forms a triadic colour scheme.

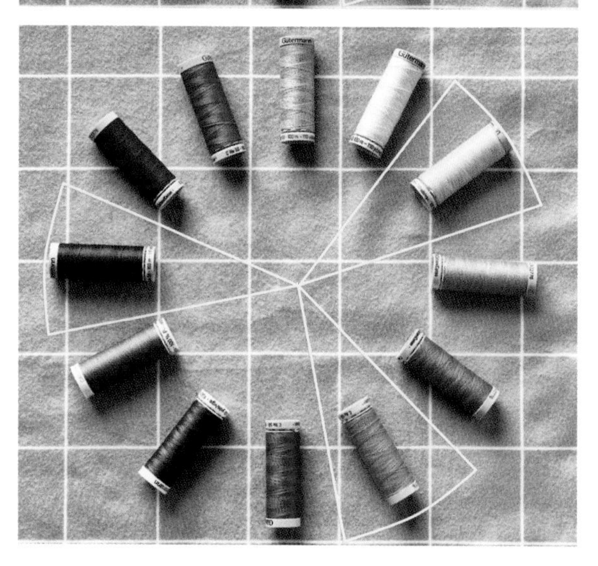

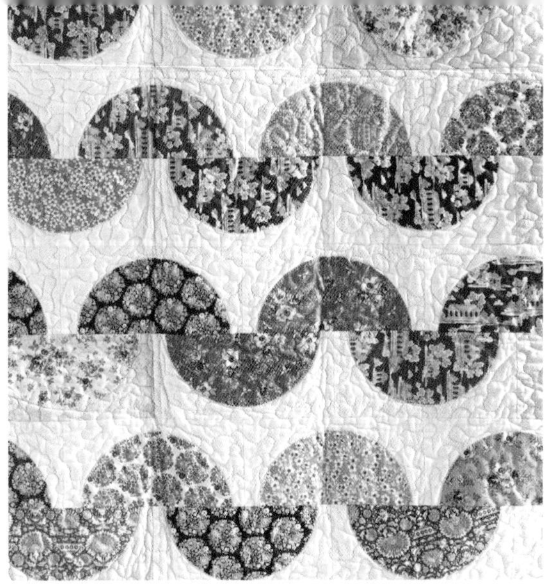

Colour choice is a very personal matter. Play around with your fabrics and use what feels right to you.

OR DON'T USE THE COLOUR WHEEL

As your colour confidence grows, you will learn to listen to your heart and follow your instincts. Colour combinations will start to 'feel' right. The more you use this 'colour sense', the more its strength will grow.

If you need inspiration, take a walk in the city, visit a different part of town and see how people have painted their houses or planted their garden, go to the park or visit the countryside and see how nature puts colours together.

You'll be inspired, I'm sure of it – don't forget your camera! Go to the grocers or vegetable market and take a look at the displays, especially the ones that make your mouth water. Be inspired by the colours and get your creative juices flowing! Above all, notice that nature doesn't always get it 'right'; the colours are almost always a little 'off'. Nature isn't a scientist in a lab mixing perfect quantities of dyes so that everything matches. Can you imagine how dull and predictable the world would be if it worked like that? Apply this same logic to your quiltmaking. By all means fall in love with that beautiful new fabric range. Delight in perfectly matched and co-ordinated fabrics – but then throw in some other fabrics that change the balance, even if it's just a little, and see the wonderful difference it makes.

Use neutrals to create negative space

The backgrounds, the spaces between, and the places your eyes can rest, are just as important as the focus, the features, the star turns. Traditional quilts tend to use white, cream, tan and black as their neutral colours and these indeed are the true 'neutrals', since they lack any 'colour' as such. Modern quilters have embraced mustard yellow, ochre, navy, grey and chartreuse and given greater emphasis to this 'space between' so that it becomes the focus. Use your design wall (see page 27) to audition different neutral fabrics and increase or decrease the negative space in your quilt until it 'feels' right. I like to live with potential designs on my wall for days, sometimes weeks. I walk past them and have a quick glance, or sometimes I study the colours more carefully. Sometimes I will absentmindedly rearrange the blocks and suddenly I know it's right.

Contrast

In most quilts, it's really important to have contrast – a variety of lighter and darker fabrics so that you can see the patterns you're stitching. Sewing a white triangle to a black triangle is as high contrast as possible and this extreme contrast makes the pattern really sharply defined. If you want your patterns to be highly contrasting, it's essential to use fabrics that are lighter and darker. We call these tints and shades. Tints are colours with white added to them and shades are those same colours with black added. It's easy to get distracted by the colour of a fabric and lose sight of how light or dark it is. Once you place one fabric next to another, this can also change how dark or light it appears. If in doubt, photograph your fabric selection and switch the picture digitally to black and white. Once the colours are gone, what you're left with is the relative lightness or darkness... easy!

TECHNIQUES, TOOLS AND MATERIALS

ROTARY CUTTING

For the majority of my quiltmaking, I use the rotary cutting system. When you know how, it's very accurate, fast and easy to do. You'll need what I like to call 'The Holy Trinity' of three very important pieces of equipment:

Rotary cutter Essentially a circular blade mounted on a handle. As you push away, the blade rotates and cuts through up to eight layers of fabric. Beginners should start with cutting one layer at a time and build up to more. My own cut-off is four layers; beyond that I get ruler slippage. The most useful size cutter to buy is one with a 1¾" (45mm) blade, although larger and smaller ones are available.

Rotary cutting ruler An ⅛" (3mm) thick perspex ruler made specifically to use with a rotary cutter, it is marked in a grid of inches with smaller increments. The fabric is measured and cut using the ruler – no marking on shapes is necessary! Most also have lines showing the 45 and 60 degree angles. The most useful size to buy is 24" x 6", although other sizes are available. Rotary cutting rulers are also available with centimetre markings if you prefer to use metric. Do not substitute any other kind of ruler, you must use one designed specifically for rotary cutters!

Self-healing mat This goes on your work surface, with the fabric and ruler on top, and then you cut. The mat protects your table from the blade and also has grid lines printed on it to help you measure and square up fabric. The most useful size to buy is 18" x 24" (45.7 x 61cm) – slightly bigger than a piece of A2 paper. Just a note here about storage: keep your mat flat at all times. Don't prop it up against a wall overnight or leave it in the boot of the car, as it will warp and will never go flat again. No one wants to try cutting fabric on a surface with more ripples than the ocean!

FIRST THINGS FIRST!

Get the iron out and press those fabrics! Even fabric that has come straight off the bolt needs to be pressed and those scraps that have been lingering in a pile will definitely need straightening out! Press well, and use steam. I like to use a spray of ordinary laundry starch, too, as it makes the fabric a little crisper for cutting and it's easier to piece.

STRAIGHTENING THE EDGE OF FABRIC

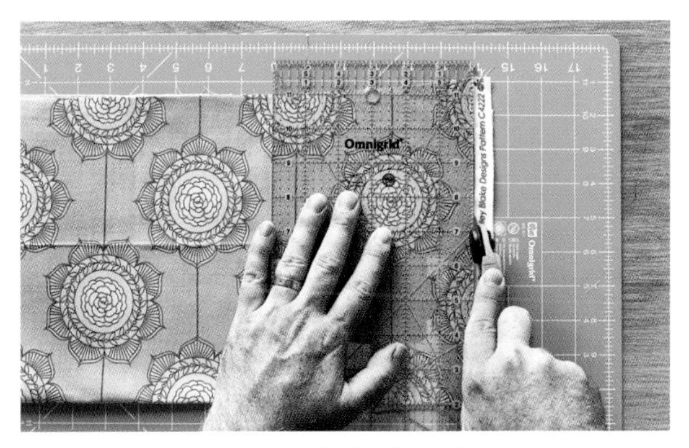

To straighten the edge, first fold the fabric if necessary, selvedge to selvedge, and place it on your mat with the fold at the bottom.

Align a straight line on your ruler with the fold and hold the ruler firmly down with your left hand. Stick out your little finger (pinky) and place it on the mat to help steady your hand. Push the blade of your rotary cutter out, position it against the ruler about 1" (2.5cm) below the start of your fabric on the right-hand side (if you are right handed; reverse for left handers) and push the blade firmly up the edge of the ruler.

Once you have cut about 6" (15.2cm), of fabric you will need to stop cutting and move your left hand up the ruler before continuing to cut, to prevent the ruler from slipping.

CUTTING STRIPS

Turn the mat so that the straightened edge of the fabric is on the left and the fold is at the top. Do it this way rather than turning the fabric – turning will disturb the straight edge you've just cut!

Position your ruler on the fabric with the top of the ruler lined up with the fold and the width of strip you require underneath. Use the grid lines on the ruler to measure the strip width. Position the cutter at the bottom of the ruler and push it up along the ruler edge. If you require more strips, simply move the ruler over to the right by the required width and cut again.

If the strip you require is wider than your ruler, turn the ruler on its side so that you now have 24" (61cm) of ruler to work with. Cut about 5" (13cm), move the ruler along and continue to cut.

CUTTING RECTANGLES, SQUARES AND TRIANGLES

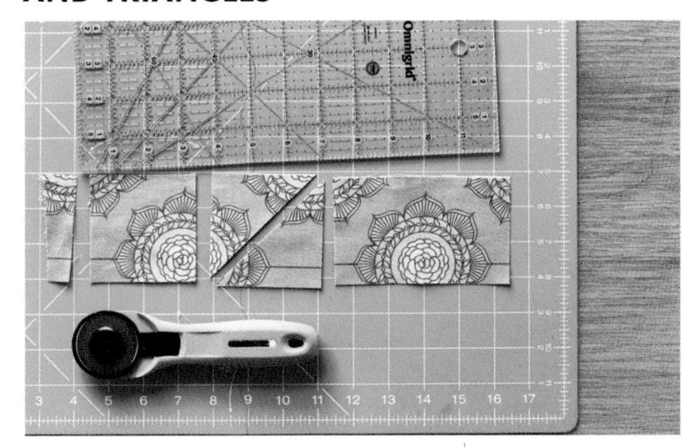

Cut strips to the required width, then sub-cut those strips into rectangles or squares; cut rectangles or squares on the diagonal to make triangles.

CUTTING PATCHES FROM IRREGULAR SCRAPS

You can cut squares, rectangles and all kinds of other patches from your irregular little scraps, too.

First determine the 'straight of grain'. That's easy on a full width of fabric, it runs parallel to the selvedge, but on a small scrap you'll need to look closer. You want the weave of the fabric to be as straight as possible when you make that first cut.

Straighten one edge, keeping the straight edge 'on grain', and then use that cut edge to line up your ruler for the second, third and subsequent cuts.

USING TEMPLATES

Some shapes can't be cut easily using a rotary cutter and ruler. Curves, circles and other 'odd' shapes require a slightly different approach – you need to make a template and cut with scissors. You can draw and cut templates for many simple shapes quickly and easily and this is particularly useful if you only have scissors.

My favourite template material is a wonderful thing called 'freezer paper'. You can get it from quilt shops and online. It's an American product and is used to wrap meat for the freezer. I would love to meet the quilter who discovered its many uses for patchwork – it really is wonderful! Freezer paper has a matte paper side and a shiny waxy side. Trace the desired shape carefully onto the matte paper side. Use a ruler for straight edges and make sure the template you are tracing has the ¼" (6mm) seam allowance added (all of the piecing templates in this book do, but appliqué shapes are always shown without a seam allowance; see pages 24–26). Cut the paper template out carefully with scissors.

If you only have a few shapes to cut, then simply iron the freezer paper, shiny side against the fabric, then cut out the shape. The paper will peel off when you're all cut out and can be re-used a number of times. If you need to cut hundreds of a shape, then it's worth ironing your freezer paper to thin card for a more durable template. You can also buy template plastic, but keep your iron away from it – it melts!

It's also possible to buy acrylic templates in many of the most commonly used shapes, including triangles, squares, hexagons and half-hexis and clamshells. These acrylic shapes can be placed on top of multiple layers of fabric and rotary cut around, speeding up the process considerably. You can also 'die cut' your shapes – and when it comes to traditional 'template territory', I prefer the die-cutting approach!

DIE CUTTING

Fabric cutting has experienced something of an evolution over the last few decades, with most of us shunning scissors for the faster and more accurate rotary cutting route. A few years ago I discovered fabric die cutting with my AccuQuilt Go cutter (pictured above), and it is now a favourite way for me to quickly and accurately cut and prepare my fabrics for quilting.

In a nutshell, die cutting works in much the same way as a cookie cutter, stamping through multiple layers of fabric in one go to create perfect shapes every time. Each 'die' cuts a particular shape in a particular size – and because quilters use a lot of the same size and shape pieces for almost endless variations, it isn't necessary to have a huge collection of dies in order to make great quilts!

Fabric is layered on top of the chosen die in a 'fan' or 'concertina' fold. Generally, these home-use dies will cut up to six layers of cotton fabric. A special self-healing mat is placed on top of the fabric and then the die/fabric/mat sandwich is sent through a die cutting machine, which is essentially a set of hand- or electric-cranked rollers that presses the blades through the fabric. Die cutting comes into its own when complex shapes are required or when a huge number of pieces are needed. Die cutting is also a great choice for quilters with mobility or strength issues in their hands or arms.

As a 'basic tool kit' for die cutting, I recommend the following:

- 6½" square (6" finished)
- 3½" square (3" finished)
- Half square triangle – 6" finished square
- Quarter square triangle – 6" finished square
- Half square triangle – 3" finished square
- Square on point – 4¾" (4¼" finished)
- Parallelogram 45° – 3 11/16" x 4 15/16" (3" x 4¼" finished)
- Rectangle – 3½" x 6 ½" (3" x 6" finished)

Dies can be purchased individually or in sets. I also get great use out of my 1½" and 2½" strip cutting dies.

Whenever I have a bunch of scraps left over at the end of a project, I run the remainders through my die cutter and cut a variety of these basic shapes and store them ready for future use.

PIECING

Patchwork is sewn with a ¼" seam and if everything is going to fit together easily and perfectly, then accuracy really counts! You may have a ¼" or 'patchwork' foot for your sewing machine. These are handy, but they don't guarantee accuracy - only you can control that! Try this handy exercise to see if you're sewing an accurate ¼" seam. If you work in metric you will need to use a 6mm seam allowance. Follow the same process as for imperial sewers, but use a metric ruler. Stick to one system, imperial (inches) or metric (centimetres). Don't mix the two!

THE PERFECT SEAM

Cut three pieces of fabric, each 2½" x 4½" (6.4 x 11.4cm). Using your ¼" foot, sew two of the strips together, then press the seam one way. Now add the last rectangle to the top. It should fit perfectly - but does it?

2½" + 2½" minus two ¼" seam allowances should equal 4½"

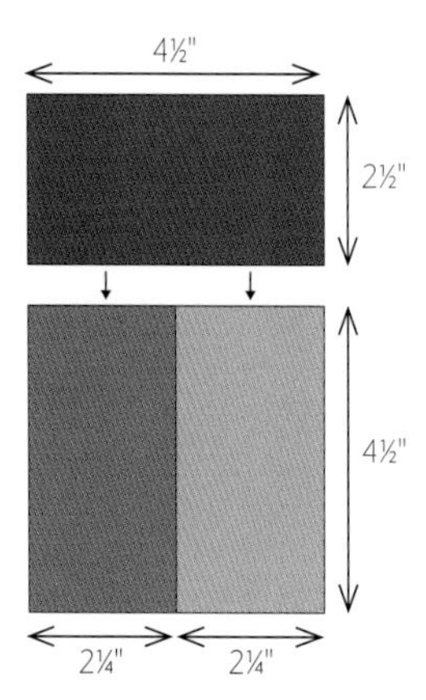

If the third strip is too long, your seam allowance is too big and needs slimming down. If it's too small, your seam allowance is a bit on the skinny side and needs fattening up. It's easy to make small adjustments now before you start on a project.

If you don't have a ¼" foot for your sewing machine but are able to move your needle position, you can use the regular foot to sew a perfect ¼" seam allowance. Generally, you need to move your needle position over to the right a bit... this is usually done by adjusting the stitch width while in straight stitch mode. Place your rotary ruler under the foot of your machine, with the edge of the ruler aligned with the edge of your presser foot. Hand crank the needle down until the tip just touches the ruler. Keep moving the needle position and hand cranking the needle down to touch the ruler until it is just on the ¼" mark. Take a note of the needle position for future reference. If you can't move the needle position, place your ruler as before, so that the needle just touches the ¼" mark, then place a strip of masking tape on the bed of your sewing machine. Use this tape as a guide for your fabric.

Check your ¼" seam allowance regularly! I like to make a unit - for example, a four-patch - then measure it and check that it is the correct size. Then make one block in its entirety and measure it. It's much better to know that adjustments are needed now, before you make the remaining 99 blocks!

SEWING PATCHES

1. Place the fabrics right sides together.
2. Match the ends first and pin.
3. Sew the seam using a stitch length of approximately 2.2–2.6.
4. Clip the threads as you go.
5. Press the seams one way, usually towards the darker fabric to avoid show-through.

STRIP PIECING

Construction can be made faster by sewing strips of fabric together and then cutting segments from this panel. This really speeds the process of patchwork up, particularly when sewing units with squares and rectangles.

1. Place two strips right sides together and pin.
2. Sew the seam using a slightly shorter than normal stitch length - a stitch length of 2 is perfect.
3. Press the seam one way, usually towards the darker fabric.
4. Continue to add strips and press until your strip-pieced panel is complete.
5. Cross-cut your panel into suitably sized segments. These can then be pieced with other strips.

PIECING

STRING PIECING

Some of the quilts in this book use 'string piecing', which is a technique whereby thin strips and scraps are pieced together to form a larger piece of fabric that is then cut to the correct size.

1. Sew your first two strips together using a ¼" (6mm) seam allowance.
2. Press the seam one way.
3. Continue to add strips and press the seams until your panel is large enough or you have used up all the available fabric.
4. If a strip of fabric is not long enough to add to the panel, sew several together to make the required length. Join this 'pieced strip' to the panel and continue.
5. Cut your patches from this newly made 'fabric'.

Make the most of your leftovers by rejoining and cutting more shapes.

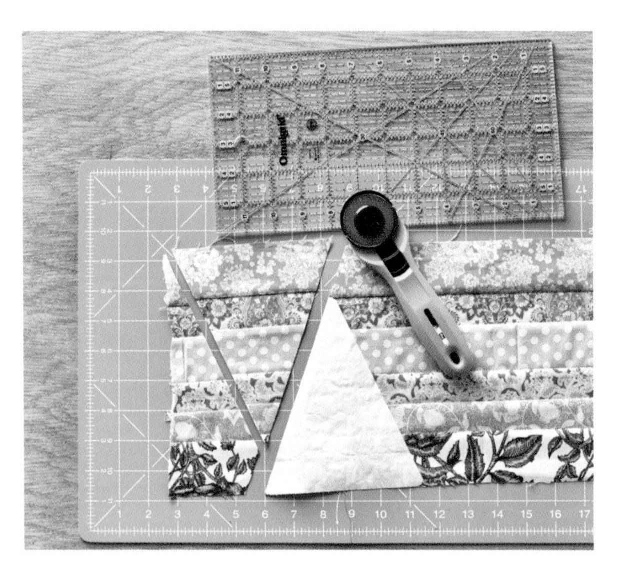

BASIC PATCHWORK UNITS

There are a few basic patchwork units that crop up all the time. Here are my favourite methods to produce these quickly and accurately.

HALF SQUARE TRIANGLE (HST) UNITS

To calculate the size of fabric you need to cut for the HST, start with the finished size – for example, 3" (7.6cm) finished. Add ⅞" (2.2cm) and cut two squares to this size – i.e. ⅞" (9.8cm). Proceed as follows.

1. Pair two squares right sides together and mark one diagonal with a pencil. Sew ¼" (6mm) either side of the pencil line.
2. Cut apart on the drawn line. Open up the HST units and press the seams one way.
3. Trim the seams neatly, as shown.

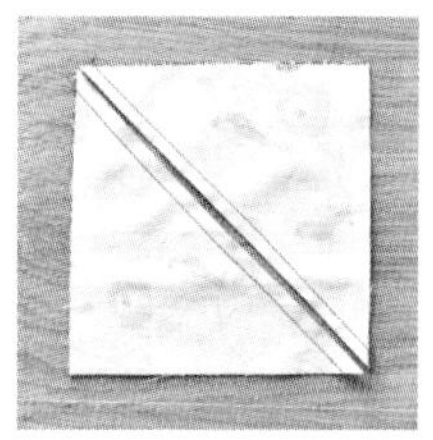

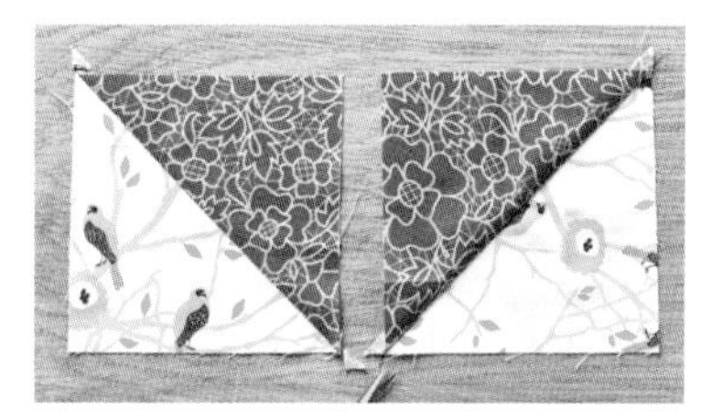

QUARTER SQUARE TRIANGLE (QST OR HOURGLASS) UNITS

To calculate the size of fabric you need to cut for the QST, start with the finished size – for example, 3" (7.6cm) finished. Add 1¼" (3.2cm) and cut two squares to this size – i.e. 4¼" (10.8cm). Proceed as follows.

1. Pair two squares (usually one dark and one light) right sides together, pin together, and mark both diagonals with a pencil.
2. Sew ¼" (6mm) away from the pencil line to the centre, on the same side of each quarter triangle, as shown.
3. Cut apart on the drawn lines.
4. Open up the pieces and press the seams one way.
5. Rejoin the units in pairs to yield two units.

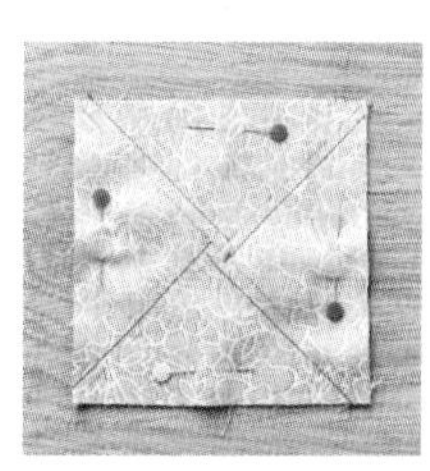

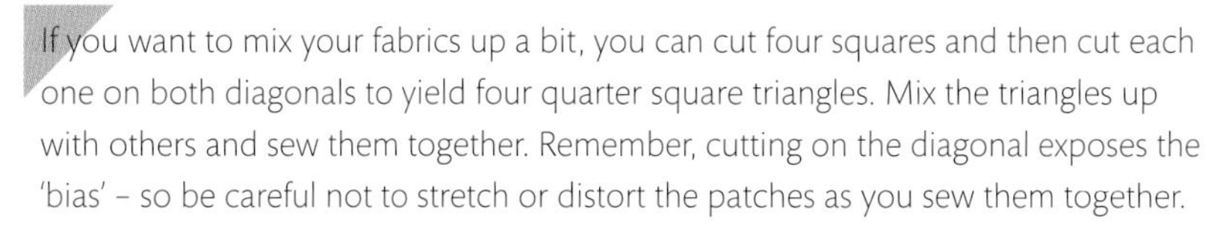

If you want to mix your fabrics up a bit, you can cut four squares and then cut each one on both diagonals to yield four quarter square triangles. Mix the triangles up with others and sew them together. Remember, cutting on the diagonal exposes the 'bias' – so be careful not to stretch or distort the patches as you sew them together.

STITCH AND FLIP

This is a great method for adding triangles to larger blocks and is sometime referred to as 'snowballing'. It is also a very accurate method for making 'square in a square' units and is used in blocks such as the Pineapple Log Cabin (see page 160).

1. Take one small square (this will become the triangle corner) and lightly mark the diagonal on the wrong side with a pencil. Place this small square, right sides together, on the top of the larger square, with the diagonal line running across the corner. Stitch on the marked diagonal line or even a thread's width inside the line.
2. Flip the small square back and press it. If the flipped square lines up exactly with the background, all is well and you can flip it back, trim the underside away and press again. If the results aren't as accurate as you'd like, unpick, have another go and re-check.
3. Repeat with a second small square on the opposite corner.
4. To create a 'square in a square', add two more small squares in the same way.

FLYING GEESE UNIT (FG) – 'NO-WASTE' METHOD

To calculate the size of fabric you need to cut for the FG, start with the finished size (for example, 6" x 3" /15.2 x 7.6cm).

Fabric A (goose): finished width of FG unit + 1¼" (3.2cm). For example, 6" (15.2cm) finishe size plus 1¼" (3.2cm) = 7¼" (18.4cm). Cut one square for four units.

Fabric B (sky): finished width of FG unit + ⅞" (2.2cm). For example, 3" (7.6cm) finished size plus ⅞" (2.2cm) = 3⅞" (9.8cm). Cut four squares for four units.

Proceed as follows:

1. Cut one square of fabric A and four squares of fabric B.
2. Place two of the smaller squares on top of the larger square, right sides together, as shown. The small squares will overlap slightly in the centre. Mark the diagonal, through the two small squares, with a pencil. Sew ¼" (6mm) either side of the pencil line. Cut along the drawn line.
3. Working on one of the halves, flip back the two small square halves and press. Add another small square, right sides together, as shown. Mark the diagonal, and sew ¼" (6mm) either side of the pencil line. Cut along the drawn line, flip the small triangle over and press again. Repeat with the remaining pieces half created in step 2.

You will have four flying geese units.

Often, I cut and piece my flying geese individually, and instructions are given for this method in some of the patterns. Where large numbers of the same combinations are required, the no-waste method is usually faster.

PAPER FOUNDATION PIECING

This is one of my favourite patchwork techniques and once you try it, I'm sure it will become one of yours, too. Don't confuse paper foundation piecing with English paper piecing (EPP) – that's a hand-sewn technique and not the same thing at all! So what is paper foundation piecing? Essentially, it involves machine sewing fabric directly to a sheet of paper printed with the patchwork block pattern. Fabric is placed on the non-printed side of the pattern and you sew on the printed side, following the lines. It's easy when you know how!

Let's start with an easy block, the square in a square.

1. Download and print (see page 220 for link) or photocopy one copy of the Square in a Square foundation (also page 220). Make sure that you print it actual size and then measure the printed foundation. It should measure 4½" x 4½" (11.4 x 11.4cm) up to the dotted outer line.
2. Pre-cutting your fabric patches makes sewing the block much easier. I cut out shapes that are at least ½" (12mm) bigger on all sides than the finished size. Using a rotary cutter means that you can cut multiple blocks in one go.
3. Gather your supplies. You'll need some fairly fine (60wt) cotton or polyester thread in a neutral colour for piecing, an open-toed foot for your sewing machine, pins, your sewing machine and a pair of scissors. You'll also need a piece of card – a postcard is ideal!

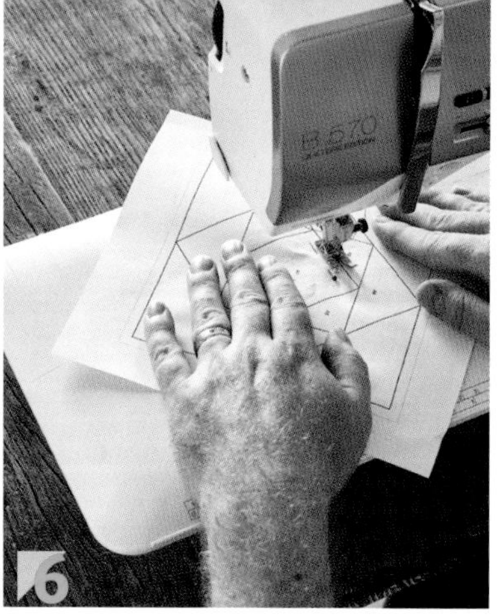

4. Set up your sewing machine: neutral thread in the top and bobbin, a new needle (size 75 Microtex is my favourite). Then set your stitch length to shorter than normal – between 1 and 1.5 is perfect for paper foundation piecing. Try sewing a piece of paper... the paper should perforate and come apart easily when pulled, but it shouldn't disintegrate as you're sewing.

5. Place your first piece of fabric on the back of the paper foundation (here, the middle square), right side facing UP. It should cover patch number 1 completely and overhang the surrounding patches by at least ¼" (6mm). Hold the foundation up to a light source and check! Pin in place. Place patch number 2 on top of patch 1, right side DOWN, raw edges lined up. Pin in place.

6. Turn the foundation over so that the printed side is facing up and sew on the line between patches 1 and 2. Make sure that you start and finish sewing at least ¼" (6mm) over the end of the patch.

7. Flip the foundation so the fabric is facing you, and press patch number 2 back. Hold it up to the light and make sure that is has properly covered number 2 and extends into the surrounding patches by at least ¼" (6mm).

8. Add patches 3, 4 and 5 in the same manner, one at a time, sewing, flipping back and pressing each time.

If your fabric pieces are too big, you can trim away the excess. Place a postcard on top of the foundation against the next seam line and fold the paper back against it. This will reveal the overhanging fabric underneath. Place your rotary ruler on top and trim the excess away, leaving a ¼" (6mm) seam allowance. This makes lining the next patch up very easy!

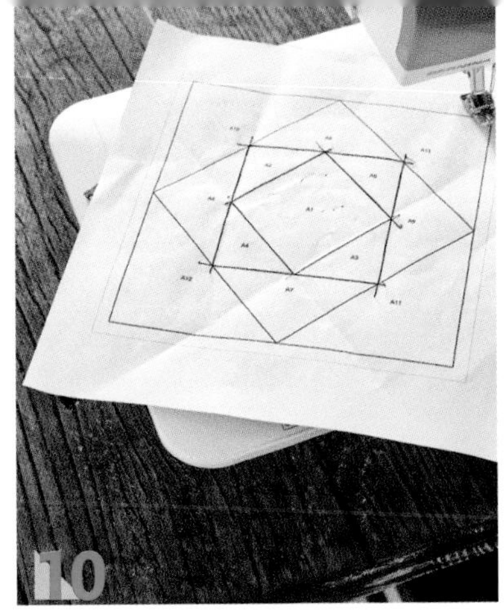

9. Add patches 6, 7, 8 and 9 in the same way.
10. Turn the foundation over so that the paper side is facing up.
11. Use a rotary cutter, ruler and mat to trim the block along the outside lines. Be careful here! Use the outer line to trim so that the final ¼" (6mm) seam allowance is included.
12. Leave the paper intact until all sides of the block have been sewn to something else. Remove the paper by tearing along the sewn lines. The paper should come away very easily, but if it doesn't you can lightly spritz with water and leave to soften for 30 seconds. A pair of tweezers is handy for removing tiny pieces of paper left in the seam intersections.

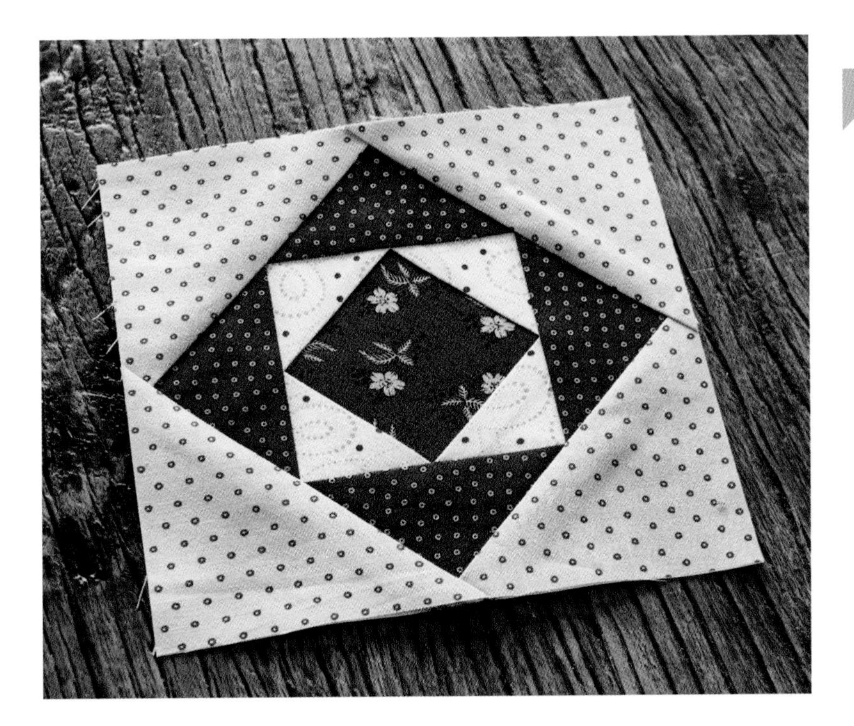

Some blocks require you to make several different foundations (labelled A, B, C etc.). If that's the case, sew the foundations separately, then trim the blocks to the outer dotted line (this includes the ¼"/6mm seam allowance). Place foundations A and B right sides together, then sew along the final printed line. I like to use a very long machine basting stitch (stitch length 5 or 6) for doing this. I can then check for correct alignment. If I'm out at all, I can easily remove the basting stitches and have another go.

If everything is perfect, I re-sew the seam using a very short stitch length (1–1.5).

APPLIQUÉ

Appliqué is the process whereby one fabric is laid on top of another and sewn down (or 'applied'), and is a perennial favourite for quilters. Appliqué can be 'raw edge' or 'turned edge' and both techniques are easy to learn.

RAW EDGE OR FUSED APPLIQUÉ

For this technique you will need a background fabric, fabric for the appliqués and fusible web. This is available from a variety of manufacturers and in several different weights, including a heavy weight that does not need sewing at all. Make sure you are using fusible web designed for appliqué (as opposed to fusible interfacing). You'll also need thread to match or contrast with your appliqué fabrics.

1. Trace the shape to be appliquéd onto the paper side of the fusible web. Keep in mind that your finished appliqué will be the reverse of your traced image, so letters and numbers (for example) should be reversed for tracing.
2. Roughly cut the shape out of fusible web, leaving approximately ½" (12mm) allowance around your traced image.
3. Fuse the web to the wrong side of your chosen appliqué fabric. It is a good idea to protect the sole plate of your iron from the fusible web by covering the appliqué fabric with baking parchment.
4. When the fabric has cooled, cut the appliqué shape out accurately on your drawn line.
5. Remove the paper backing and lay the appliqué shape on your chosen background fabric in its final position.
6. Iron the appliqué shape in place. Refer to the manufacturer's instructions for the correct heat setting.
7. Sew around the edge of your appliqué with matching or contrasting thread to neaten the raw edges and provide more durability. You can use a small zigzag stitch or a blanket stitch to do this.

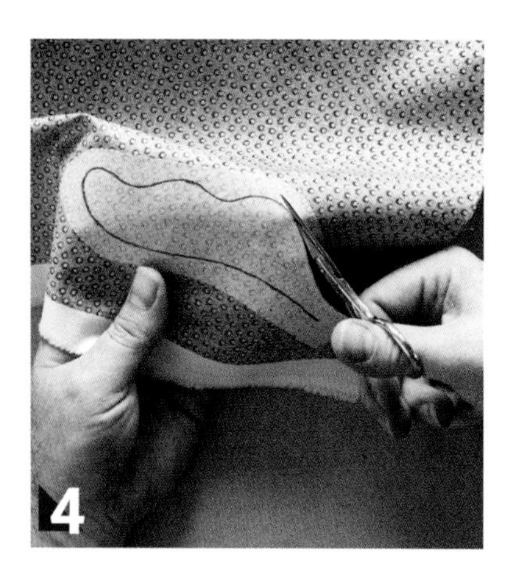
4

6

7

TURNED EDGE APPLIQUÉ

Turned edge appliqué is a great choice for quilts that will be used and washed a lot, since the raw edges are turned under before stitching. Traditionally this is done by 'needle turning', but this is a slow and laborious process. I have two methods that I prefer to use to turn the edge.

'SOFT-EDGE' TURNED APPLIQUÉ

1. Trace the appliqué shape onto the smooth side of a piece of lightweight fusible interfacing (the kind used for dressmaking) and cut it out roughly.

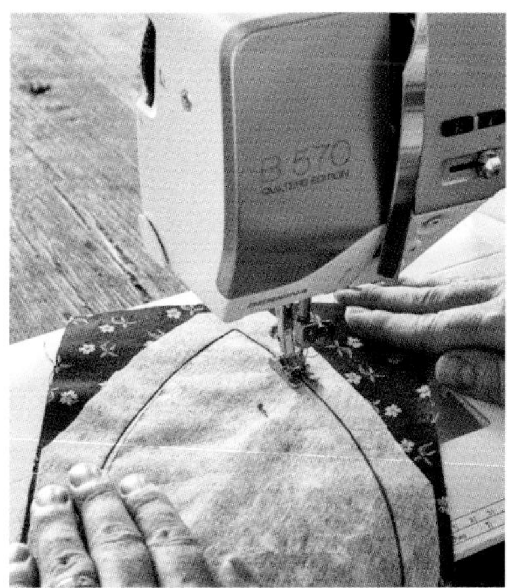

2. Place the glue side of the interfacing on the right side of your chosen appliqué fabric and sew around the traced shape, on the drawn line. Use a slightly smaller stitch than normal (2.0 is spot on!).

3. Trim the seam down to a scant ¼" (6mm) and clip the curves. Make a small slip in the back of the interfacing and turn through to the right side.

4. Run the tip of your scissors or a blunt tool, such as a chopstick, around the edge of the shape and flatten with your hand.

5. Place the appliqué shape on your chosen background fabric and iron in place, then sew around the shape by hand or machine.

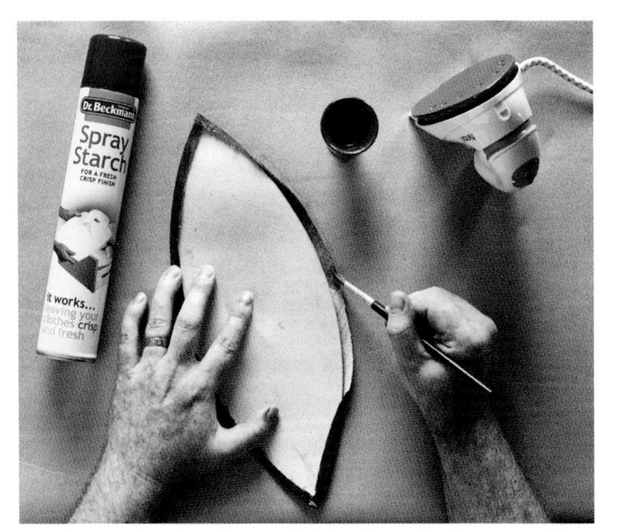

STARCH AND PRESS APPLIQUÉ

1. Trace the appliqué shape onto thin card... a piece of cereal box is ideal. Cut out neatly, following your drawn line.

2. Cut your chosen appliqué fabric ¼" (6mm) bigger than the card shape on all sides.

3. Paint the ¼" (6mm) of extra fabric with liquid starch. Just spray starch from a can into a small cup and wait till the bubbles settle. Dip a fine paintbrush into the liquid and 'paint' the edges of your appliqué. You want them fully wetted but not dripping!

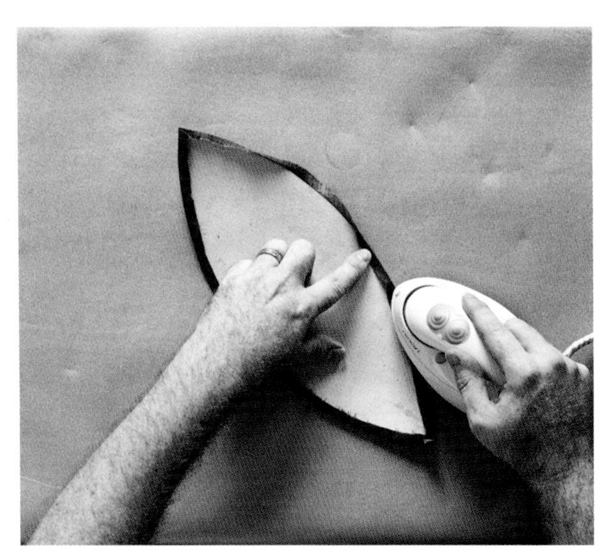

4. Place the card template on top of the wrong side of the fabric, then use a small iron (a travel iron works for me!) to lift the wetted edge up and over onto the card. Press in place for a few seconds to dry the starch and fix your turned edge in place.

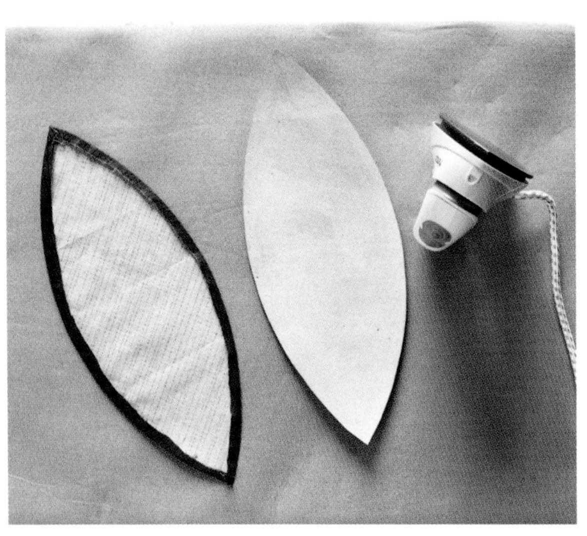

5. When all of the edge has been turned, remove the card template and re-use.

6. Place the prepared appliqué on your chosen background and pin or tack (baste) it in place. Sew in place by hand or machine.

MAKING AND USING A DESIGN WALL

I am a huge fan of the design wall – a space where I can audition fabrics, try blocks in different positions or simply see how my quilt is progressing before it all gets stitched together. I used to lay blocks out on the floor or on a bed, and that is an option, but having a design wall allows you to literally stand back and view your work – it's so much better!

If you have the option of a permanent design wall in your sewing space, simply cover large rectangles of insulation board (bought from a DIY store) with either quilt wadding (batting) or flannel fabric. Pull the edges of the wadding or fabric to the back of the board and staple in place, then fix the covered boards to the wall with screws. The 'fluffiness' of the wadding or flannel will cause the blocks or fabrics pieces to 'stick', allowing you to stand back and assess their positions.

If a permanent design wall isn't an option, then you could still make the design wall as described above, but attach picture hooks and hang and take down as necessary. You could even simply prop it against the wall. A simpler solution would be to attach a flannel sheet or large piece of wadding to the wall with painters' tape and simply take it down and fold away when it's not in use (pictured, left).

Once you've used a design wall, I know you'll see the value!

ADDING BORDERS

Quilts often have one or more borders around them. Borders can be simple or complex, plain or fancy, 'whole' or pieced: the choices are endless! Borders can really make a quilt when they are well chosen and well applied. Follow my tips for border success!

1. Keep a sense of scale. A border is usually there to frame and draw attention to the centre of the quilt, so take care to keep the proportions of the border sympathetic. Frames that are proportionate to the blocks in the centre look pleasing to the eye – so, for example, if the blocks are 10" (25cm), then a 5" (12.5cm) border will inevitably look more 'right' than a 6" (15cm) border. If you're adding multiple borders, it's a good idea to keep the total width no bigger than one of the blocks. For example, choose 2" (5cm), 6" (15cm) and 2" (5cm) borders for a quilt with 10" (25cm) blocks.

2. Create 'natural-fit' borders for your quilt by using elements from the pieced blocks as a border. They will allow borders to enhance rather than overpower the design.

3. Use a multi-coloured border fabric to create 'sense' out of a myriad of scraps. Quilters often find a patterned border fabric first and choose their colours from this, but sometimes we have to work in reverse. Finding a border fabric that is just right can be a challenge, so I prefer to pick the border fabric before the blocks are joined together. That way, if I need to introduce an extra colour or two into the quilt to make the border 'work', I can!

4. Add borders to increase the size of a quilt without having to make a huge number of extra blocks. For example, if you're using 6" (15cm) blocks and you want a 66" x 72" (168 x 183cm) quilt, you are going to need to piece 132 blocks. To make that quilt 6" (15cm) bigger on all sides, you'll need either an extra 50 blocks, or a simple 6" (15cm) border!

5. Use a folded or 'flange' border (see page 30) to add a pop of colour to your quilt. Sometimes that's all that's needed to create harmony in a quilt.

The Crossing Borders quilt (left, and on page 130) is a frame quilt that makes a real feature out of the borders themselves.

Like a lot of things, there's a right way to add a border and a wrong way... let's look at the wrong ways first.

THE VERY WRONG WAY TO ADD A BORDER

1. Sew a long strip of fabric to the side of the quilt.
2. Chop the ends of the strip off, level with the quilt centre.
3. Hope and pray that the quilt stays square.

Why is this so wrong? Well, the outer edges of a quilt top generally flare out slightly. Fabric can stretch as it's sewn, so the outer edge can become very distorted and will 'ripple' and 'frill' instead of being perfectly straight and square.

THE SLIGHTLY LESS WRONG WAY TO ADD A BORDER

1. Measure the side of the quilt.
2. Cut a piece of fabric to this length.
3. Sew the strip to the side of your quilt.
4. Repeat on all four sides.

Why is this still a bit wrong? Well, we are assuming that the edges of the quilt are straight and square, and generally they are not. Our borders are still likely to ripple – although not as much as the 'very wrong' way to add a border method.

THE RIGHT WAY TO ADD A BORDER

1. Measure through the centre of your quilt top, from top to bottom, and make a note of the measurement.
2. Repeat the measuring process at a quarter and three-quarters of the way along the quilt.
3. Add the measurements together and divide by three; in other words, take several measurements and find the average.
4. Cut two side border pieces to this length.
5. Find the centre of the border and place a pin. Find the quarter positions, too, and again place pins.
6. Find the quarter, half and three-quarter positions on the side of your quilt and match up the pinned border.
7. Match the ends and pin, too.
8. Pin well in between, easing any slight fullness throughout the seam.
9. Sew the border in place.
10. Press the border back, then add the opposite border in the same way.
11. Repeat the measuring process through the width of the quilt and border to find the required length for the remaining two sides.

Yes, it takes longer than methods 1 and 2. Yes, it's worth it!

In this example, I have measured my quilt (in inches) through the centre (1) at 94", at the quarter point (2) at 96" and at the three-quarters point (3) at 95". So the average measurement, and the required length of my side border pieces, is 95": 94 + 96 + 95 divided by three.

ADDING A FOLDED OR 'FLANGE' BORDER

1. Measure your quilt for the side outer border pieces and cut those pieces to size. For example, for a 4" (10.2cm) finished border cut two border strips at 4½" (11.4cm) x length of your quilt top and two at 4½" (11.4cm) x width of your quilt top plus the width of the borders.
2. Also cut four strips of your 'flange' fabric to the same length, then fold this narrow strip in half, wrong sides together, and press.
3. Pin and tack (baste) these folded strips to the edges of your quilt, with the raw edges aligned and the folds pointing inwards towards the quilt centre. At the corners, simply overlap the folded strips.
4. Pin your first outer border strip (in this case, the 4½"/11.4cm strip) to one side of the quilt, overlapping the folded flange.
5. Sew the border on with a ¼" (6mm) seam.
6. Press the border back to reveal a 4" (10.2cm) finished border with a narrow folded flange captured in the seam.
7. Repeat on the opposite side, and then on the top and bottom edges of the quilt.

A flange is a strip of fabric that goes between the quilt centre and the border. It can be any width – just choose the finished width and double it, then add a ½" (12mm) seam allowance to find the width of the strip you need to cut. For example, for a ¾" (19mm) flange you would double ¾" (19mm). That makes 1½" (3.8cm) and then add ½" (12mm) for seam allowances. So cut strips at 2" (5.1cm) wide by however long your quilt side is.

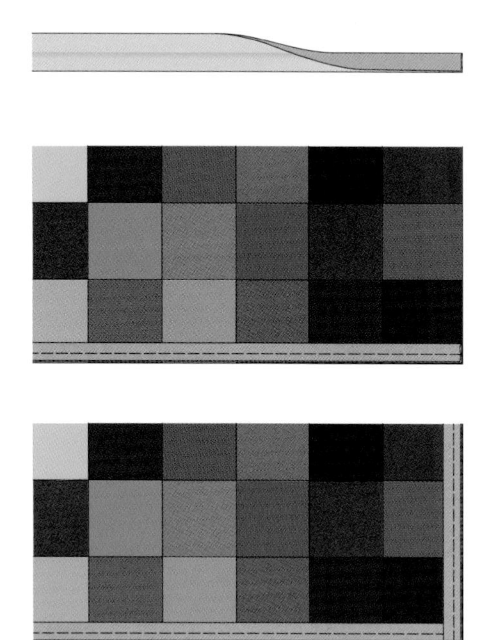

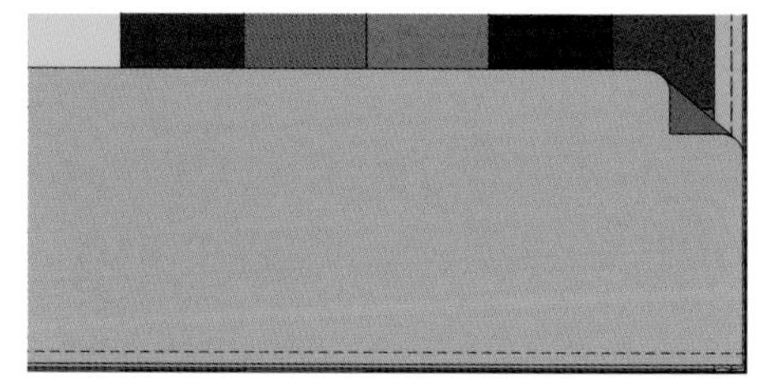

LAYERING

Once your quilt top is completed, you're almost ready to layer and quilt... I said 'almost'! Before you layer your quilt top, there are a few jobs to be done.

1. Clip any threads that are hanging loose on the back or front of your quilt top.
2. Make sure that seams are well pressed and are lying flat. If any seams are twisted, unpick the twisted part, flatten and re-sew.
3. Sew around the outer edge of your quilt top about ⅛" (3mm) in from the raw edge to stabilize it.
4. Give your quilt top a final press.

Cut a piece of backing fabric for your quilt. It needs to be at least 2" (5.1cm) bigger on all sides than the quilt top. Piece the backing if necessary to get the required size. Make sure that these seams are pressed open to reduce bulk and avoid a ridge.

Cut a piece of quilt wadding (batting) to the same size as the backing fabric. It's a really good idea to open out your batting 24–48 hours before layering to allow the wrinkles to 'relax'. Just lay it out over a spare bed for a day or so.

1. Lay your backing fabric down, wrong side up. Smooth out and tape at the edges with masking tape.
2. Lay your wadding on top and smooth from the centre out to make sure it is flat and wrinkle free.
3. Lay your quilt top on top, right side facing up, centring the top on the wadding and backing and placing it 2" (5.1cm) down from the top.
4. Use curved safety pins to hold the layers together. As a general rule. I try to make sure there is no more than a fist's width between the pins.

Alternatively use 505 quilt basting spray to temporarily hold the layers of your 'quilt sandwich' together while you quilt. Follow the manufacturer's instructions to do this.

The quilt wadding and backing don't need to be cut square at this stage; just make that sure you have at least 2" (5.1cm) extra on all sides.

QUILTING

There's a saying amongst quilters – 'It's not a quilt until it's quilted' – and this is certainly true in my book! A quilt consists of three layers: the top, the backing and a layer of wadding (batting) in between. Machine or hand stitches through all three layers hold them together – this is the 'quilting'.

Your chosen wadding will recommend how far apart your lines of stitches need to be in order to hold the quilt together properly, but as a general guide quilting should be evenly spread across the whole quilt surface to be aesthetically pleasing and functional.

Quilting can be done by hand or by machine, and nowadays it can also be done by credit card. I shall explain!

QUILTING BY HAND

Using a short 'betweens' (or quilting) needle and a 16" (40cm) length of strong thread, sew a running stitch through the layers of the quilt. Start and finish with a small knot that can be pulled into the middle of the quilt to hide it. Aim to keep your stitches even on the front and back. 'Big stitch' hand quilting is another popular choice and involves using cotton perle thread and a larger than usual running stitch to add decorative hand quilting to certain parts of your quilt.

QUILTING BY MACHINE

Use a 'walking foot' for straight lines and a 'darning foot' for free-motion swirls, shapes and stipples. Machine quilting can be as simple as sewing slightly to one side of all of the main blocks and pieces in a quilt, or it can form an integral part of the overall design. The choices are yours. There are a number of great books specifically on this important skill and it's worth considering this as a separate skill to patchworking.

QUILTING BY CREDIT CARD

'Longarm quilting' is a very useful service offered by a number of professionals and is well worth considering if you do not enjoy or are daunted by the task of quilting on your domestic sewing machine. You send the top to a 'longarmer', who then professionally quilts your top for a fee and sends it back to you for binding. Make sure you discuss what you would like before sending your precious top away and follow the longarm quilter's directions for preparation to the letter!

ADDING A HANGING SLEEVE

If you want to display your quilt on a wall or at a quilt show, you will need to add a hanging sleeve to the back. This is most easily done before you bind the quilt.

1. Cut a strip of fabric that is 8½" (21.6cm) wide x the width of your quilt. For example, if your quilt is 80" x 80" (203.2 x 203.2cm), the strip should be 8½" x 80" (21.6 x 203.2cm).
2. Fold the raw ends of the strip in by ½" (12mm) and press. Repeat to neaten the ends. Stitch in place. Fold the sleeve in half, wrong sides together, and press. The sleeve will now be 2" (5.1cm) shorter than the quilt and 4¼" (10.8cm) wide.
3. Align the raw edges of the sleeve with the top raw edge of your quilt, centring the sleeve, and tack (baste) it in place.
4. Attach the binding to your quilt, simultaneously attaching the binding and the top of the sleeve in one step.
5. Hand sew the binding to the back of the quilt.
6. Hand sew the bottom edge of the hanging sleeve to the back of your quilt. Use small stitches and make sure your stitches do not show on the front of your quilt.
7. Pass a rod or wooden batten through the sleeve to allow hanging.

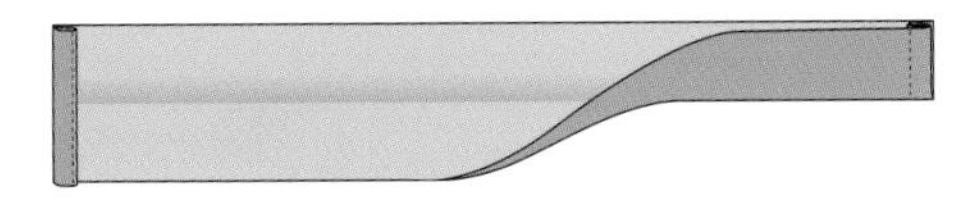

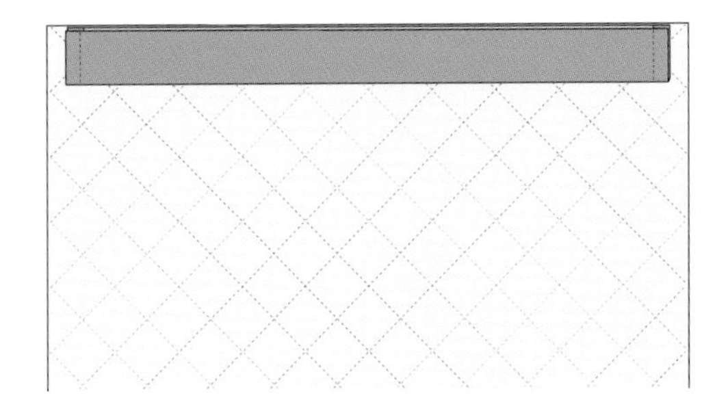

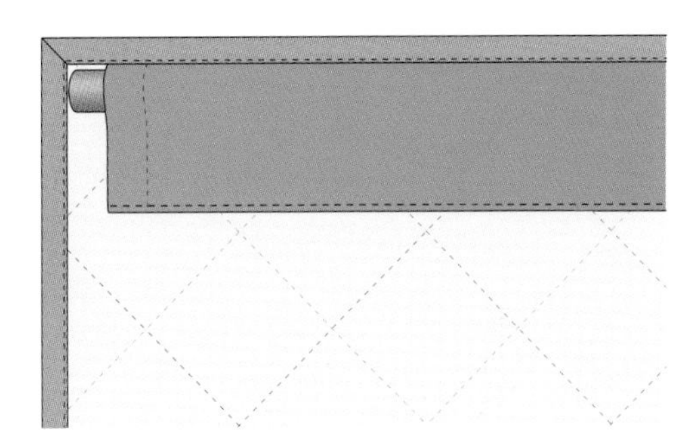

BINDING

I like to bind my quilts with double fold binding cut at 2½" (6.4cm) on the straight of grain. This gives a sturdy binding and is the most commonly used type of quilting.

1. Measure the four sides of your quilt, add together and add 10" (25.4cm) extra for corners and overlap. Cut strips of fabric from the widthwise or lengthwise grain of your fabric and piece them together to give this length. Use straight or diagonal seams and press the seams open to reduce bulk.
2. Fold the binding strip in half to create a strip that is 1¼" (3.2cm) wide, with the right sides of the fabric on the outside. Also fold 1" (2.5cm) in on the lead end and press to neaten it.
3. Starting on the right side of the quilt and approximately 6" (15cm) down from a corner, pin the neatened end of the binding to the raw edge of the quilt.
4. Using a ¼" (6mm) seam allowance and starting approximately 3" (7.6cm) down from the neatened edge, sew the binding to the first side of the quilt, finishing exactly ¼" (6mm) from the corner and backstitching to secure your thread.
5. Take the quilt out from under your machine and clip your threads.
6. With the newly bound edge of your quilt at the top and the next edge to be bound on the right-hand side, fold your binding strip up until it is in line with the next edge to be bound.
7. Fold the binding back down on itself and align the raw edges of the binding with the raw edge of the quilt. Pin at the corner.

8. Start sewing ¼" (6mm) in from the edge of the quilt and sew with a ¼" (6mm) seam until you get to ¼" (6mm) off the next corner. Backstitch, remove your quilt from the machine and clip the threads. Repeat for each side of the quilt.
9. When you get back to the first edge, make the last corner and sew approximately 2" (5cm) down. Backstitch and clip threads.
10. Trim the end of your binding strip, allowing about 1" (2.5cm) to tuck inside the neatened lead edge. Pin in place and sew the remaining binding in place.

Once the binding has been machine sewn to the front of your quilt, you can turn the folded edge to the back of your quilt and slipstitch it in place by hand. It's a fairly slow process to do well, but you will be left with an immaculate binding that will really finish your quilt to perfection!

USEFUL EQUIPMENT

If you're already a quilter, then you will almost certainly have everything you need to start your quilting adventure. If this is your first foray into patchwork, then you are in for a treat! You will need some basic equipment. Don't be put off by the list - these things can last a lifetime!

THE HARD STUFF

SEWING MACHINE You'll need a sewing machine that sews a good straight stitch and for the majority of quiltmaking it need be nothing more complex than that! A zigzag stitch and blanket stitch are both useful for machine appliqué.

SCISSORS For cutting both fabric and paper. I like a large pair of shears for cutting yardage and small pointed embroidery scissors for cutting out appliqués and finer detail.

THREAD SNIPS Because nothing dulls a pair of scissors' blades like snipping thread!

PINS I like fine, long pins for piecing and shorter, fine pins for appliqué. Lace, lingerie or bridal pins are most suitable.

HAND SEWING NEEDLES I like milliners/sharps for appliqué and hand sewing binding. For hand quilting I use a 'between'.

MACHINE NEEDLES I love Microtex needles for my machine piecing, appliqué and quilting and generally use a 75 for everything if I can get away with it. Use a larger needle if you are having issues with thread breakage and, of course, match your needle to your thread type, particularly if you use embroidery or metallic threads. Change your needles regularly. I recommend every 6–8 hours of sewing time or before if you notice skipped or poorly formed stitches or the needle is bent.

ROTARY CUTTER, RULER AND SELF-HEALING MAT The Holy Trinity of cutting! Always use these three items together for accuracy and safety. I like a trigger grip cutter, a 6" x 24" (15.2 x 61cm) Perspex ruler and an A2 cutting mat.

OTHER RULERS A 12" (30.5cm) or 15" (38.1cm) square is wonderful for cutting larger pieces easily and quickly and for trimming quilts after quilting. A smaller rotary cutting ruler, say 6" x 12" (15.2 x 30.5cm) or 3" x 12" (7.6 x 30.5cm), is useful for cutting smaller pieces and trimming.

TEMPLATE PLASTIC Perfect for cutting templates for curved shapes, appliqués and for those who prefer to cut with scissors. Cereal box cardboard is another option, particularly if only a few shapes are required.

DIE CUTTING MACHINE AND DIES Cut accurately, quickly and without the associated hand and arm strain of scissors and rotary cutting methods by using a die cutting system.

CURVED SAFETY PINS Ideal for pinning the layers of a quilt together in preparation for quilting. Buy in bulk, as many hundreds will be needed to pin baste a large quilt.

505 QUILT BASTING SPRAY A temporary adhesive spray used to hold the layers of a quilt together, eliminating the need for pinning or traditional thread tacking (basting). Always use in a well-ventilated room or outdoors, and away from pets.

THE SOFT STUFF

FABRIC For quilting, I generally only use 100% cotton quilt-weight fabric. It's easy to piece, presses well and is available in a fabulous array of colours and patterns. I don't mix fabrics of different weights and types in a quilt, but if you want to it's a good idea to fuse lightweight interfacing to the back of the lighter fabrics in order to 'bring them up' to the same weight as the heavier fabrics. Do this also if you are mixing fabrics with stretch.

Some quilters like to pre-wash their fabrics, others do not. I'm in the 'not' camp and prefer to wash my finished quilts. This way any shrinkage is spread through the finished quilt and lends my quilts a gently 'wrinkled' look, which I like. I always put half a dozen colour-catching sheets into the wash and use a 30°C cycle and colour liquid. Follow these same guidelines for pre-washing fabrics, but always test fabrics for colourfastness before washing.

BACKING FABRIC I like to use a fabric of similar quality and weight to the fabrics used on the front of my quilt. This generally means that I have to piece my backings to get the required size, although extra-wide quilt backing fabrics are available. Piece your backing with a ½" (12mm) seam allowance and press seams open to distribute the bulk.

THREAD I like to use pure cotton thread for my piecing and I use a neutral grey/beige shade which blends with pretty much everything. For machine quilting I like a cotton or cotton polyester mix, although rayon, metallic thread and silk are all possible.

FUSIBLE WEB A fine web of glue adhered to a paper backing used for fusible appliqué. Various weights are available depending on the results you want.

FUSIBLE AND SEW-IN INTERFACING A non-woven 'fabric' that is bonded or stitched to lighter-weight fabrics in order to make them heavier or more stable. Can also be used as a foundation in place of paper for foundation piecing.

QUILT WADDING (BATTING) There is far more choice in quilt waddings now than there was when I started quilting. In addition to pure cotton or polyester, you will now find silk, bamboo and wool as well as blends of some of these fibres. My general preference is for a pure cotton or a cotton and polyester blend (80/20 or 70/30), which has slightly more loft (thickness) and shows off machine or hand quilting better than the very thin cotton waddings. Wool is a great choice in temperate climates and bamboo or recycled polyester is a good choice and an 'eco-friendly' alternative.

100 QUILTS

ONE-PATCH QUILTS

Think of a quilt and the chances are you'll imagine one made of hexagons. Hand stitched into rosettes, this is the quintessential image of a patchwork quilt and a great example of a one-patch quilt – one that uses one simple repeating shape. One-patch quilts really prove that 'it ain't what you do, it's the way that you do it', as they are among the simplest of quilts to construct but can still be stunning – it's all about the design and the fabric that you use.

ONE IS FUN!

Log cabins, half square triangle quilts, postage stamp scrap quilts, Irish chains... all of these quilts use one simple shape, but their appeal has lasted for generations and continues to inspire quilters the world over. One-patch quilts are just so versatile! Designs like Tumbler (see page 50), which uses a deceptively easy to piece trapezoid, have a look that is straight out of Grandma's attic, but change the fabrics to bright, modern solids or a monochromatic scheme and you get a totally different look. Most of the quilts in this chapter use just one shape, sometimes in a consistent size, sometimes in different sizes, to create a stunning quilt. Just occasionally I've slipped an extra shape or two in there, just to mix things up, and with some fun and innovative piecing methods you will find plenty to keep you inspired and excited!

KNIT ONE, PURL ONE

I love 'crossover' quilts – those inspired by or that look like another craft or art form. I've always loved knitting and this quilt reminds me of the many rows of stocking stitch I have knitted over the years!

SUGGESTED LAYOUT

For my virtual quilt I have set twenty-seven blocks in a nine by three arrangement. The finished quilt is 54" x 63" (137.2 x 160cm), but this quilt is easy to size up or down – just alter the number of rows or use larger or smaller flying geese units.

To determine the cut size for QSTs, take the finished size (e.g. 6"/15.2cm) and add a seam allowance of 1¼" (3.2cm) to get the cut size of square. Cross cut on both diagonals to yield four triangles. To determine the cut size for HSTs, take the finished size (e.g. 3"/7.6cm) and add ⅞" (2.2cm) to get the cut size of square. Cross cut on one diagonal to yield two triangles.

For one block you will need

Finished block size: 6" x 21" (15.2 x 53.3cm)

Eight assorted fabrics in pink and gold prints. From each fabric you will need:

- One 7¼" (18.4cm) square cross-cut on both diagonals to yield four quarter square triangles (QSTs) (three will be spare – use them for another block)
- One 3⅞" (9.8cm) square cross-cut on one diagonal to yield two half square triangles (HSTs)

Assembling the block

1. Arrange your large QST and your smaller HST units to resemble the diagram (right). Follow the HSTs with a matching QST, add two different HSTs and then repeat.
2. Sew the HST and QST units together to make a flying geese unit. Make a total of seven units. Sew the units together.

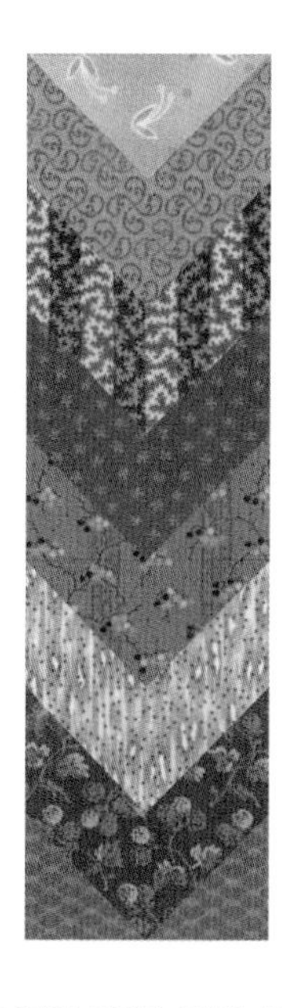

HONEY TO THE BEE

Hexagon quilts have always been a staple in the world of patchwork, but they come in and out of favour... sometimes we have the time for hand stitching and sometimes we just don't. This quilt features my first foray into the world of fabric designing and reflects my love of sewing - and of bees! My quilt is completely machine sewn and doesn't use a single tricky Y seam - easy with half hexagons!

SUGGESTED LAYOUT

For my virtual quilt I have used 144 half hexagons to make a quilt that measures approximately 54" x 52" (137.2 x 132cm). To create the illusion of full hexagons, cut your shapes in pairs of the same fabrics. For my virtual quilt, I have used 144 half hexagons in nine vertical columns of sixteen, with alternate columns starting with a single half hexagon in a different colour.

You will need

Assorted print and solid fabrics in various yellow, grey and blue greys

Assembling the quilt

1. Download and print (see page 220 for link) or photocopy the Honey to the Bee template on page 220. Following the instructions on page 15, cut out your chosen number of half hexagons in pairs of the same fabrics.
2. Lay your half hexagons out in vertical columns, making sure that as you add the next column you 'complete' the hexagons in the column to the left and start new ones in the column to the right. When you are happy with the layout, sew the half hexagons into long columns. Press the seams open.
3. Join the columns together, matching the seam intersections carefully.
4. Once you've quilted your top, either bind the uneven edges or trim them straight, then bind.

I label my blocks and rows by pinning sticky notes to the fabric - then I can take a whole stack of blocks to my machine to sew them, confident that I can't get them in a muddle!

WOVEN #1

Even the simplest of quilts can be elevated with interesting fabric placement. This ultra-easy quilt, made using nothing but squares, creates the illusion of woven strips through the careful positioning of fabrics. A design wall is useful here (see page 27)!

For one block you will need

Finished block size: 12" (30.5cm) square

- 4½" (11.4cm) squares in assorted lime green prints
- 4½" (11.4cm) squares in assorted purple prints
- 4½" (11.4cm) squares in pale grey solid

Assembling the quilt

1. Decide how large you want your finished quilt to be, then lay out the squares to plan the colour placement. Use the picture (right) to help you lay out your squares. The greens and purples should sit in groups of three to create the woven effect.
2. Sew groups of nine squares together into a simple nine-patch, to make the 12" (30.5cm) blocks, pressing the seams in opposite directions as you go.
3. Lay your blocks out and check their orientation!
4. Sew the blocks together.

Use quilting to emphasize the 'woven' effect: straight lines, quilted ½" (12mm) apart in each 'band' of three similar coloured squares, will help to join them up. Use green thread on green fabric and purple on the purple. You could leave the grey background unquilted to really create dimension.

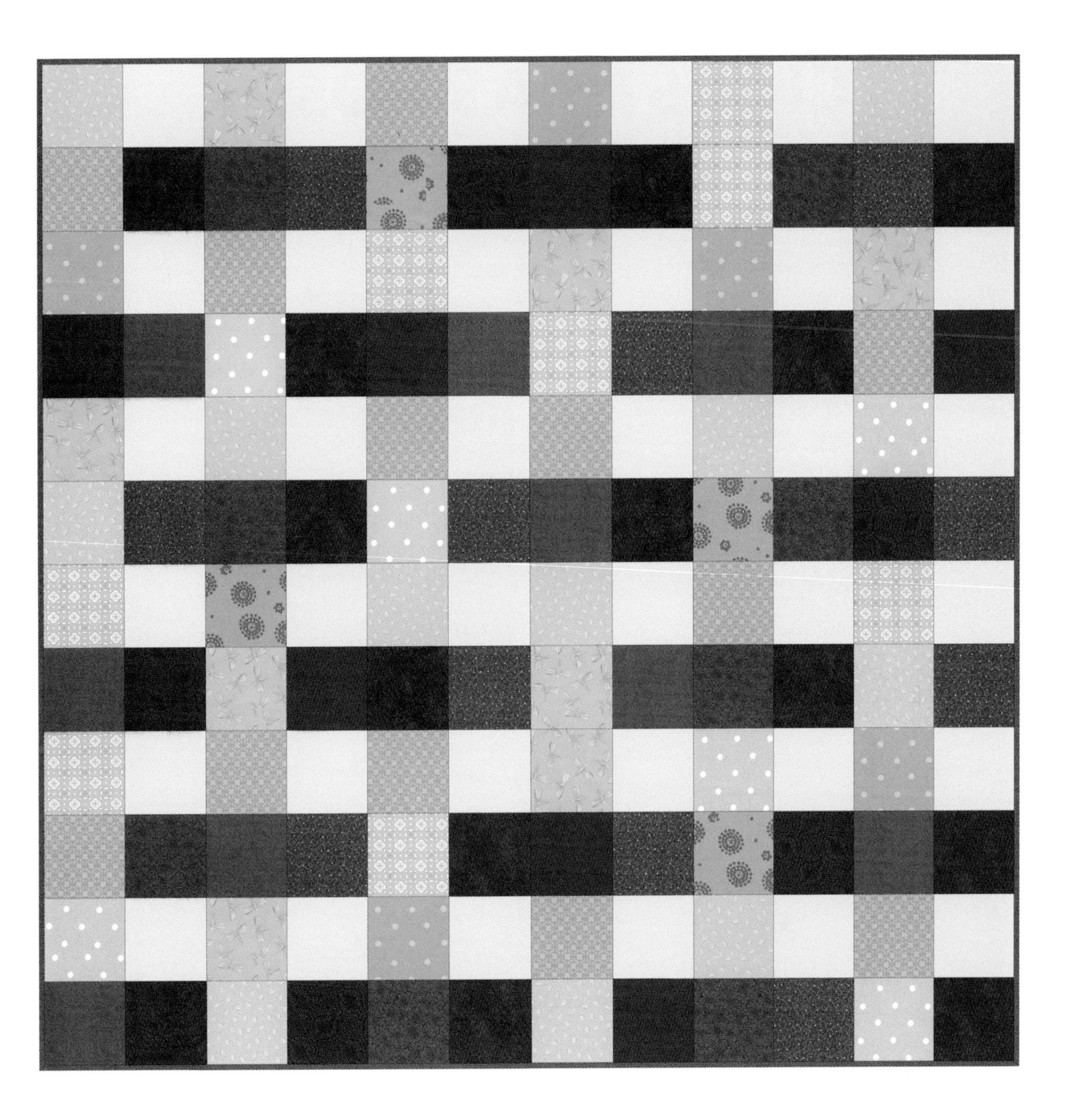

SUGGESTED LAYOUT

My virtual quilt is 48" x 48" (122 x 122cm), great for a throw or large baby quilt. For a larger quilt, add more blocks or use larger squares.

CHRISTMAS ROSE

This pattern works perfectly with those pre-cut stacks of 10" (25.4cm) squares I find so irresistible. You could also cut your own from your stash. It is super-easy to piece and super-quick too which is a good thing when you're busy getting ready for the holidays!

For one block you will need

Finished block size: 9" (22.9cm) square

- One 6" (15.2cm) square of cream fabric, cut accurately into four 3" (7.6cm) squares.
- One 10" (25.4cm) square of print fabric, cut accurately into four 5" (12.7cm) squares

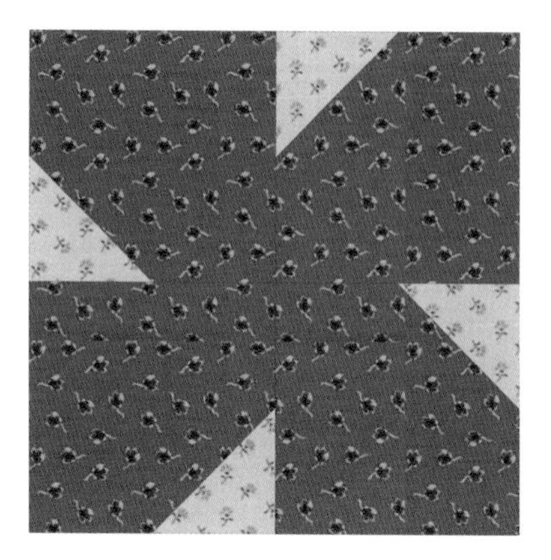

Assembling the block

1. Mark the diagonal lightly in pencil on the back of each cream square. Layer one marked 3" (7.6cm) cream square on top of one 5" (12.7cm) print square, right sides together. Matching the raw edges on one corner, pin in place. The diagonal pencil line should cut across the corner of the larger square. Sew along the marked diagonal line, then flip the cream square back and press. Trim away the fabrics underneath, leaving a ¼" (6mm) seam allowance.
2. Repeat with the remaining three 5" (12.7cm) and 3" (7.6cm) squares.
3. Arrange the pieced units into a 'pinwheel' or flower shape and sew together.

When cutting pre-cut squares apart, I like to butt two rulers together to make sure I am cutting really accurately: measure 5" (12.7cm) from one side with one ruler, 5" (12.7cm) from the the other side with the second, then remove one of the rulers and make the cut.

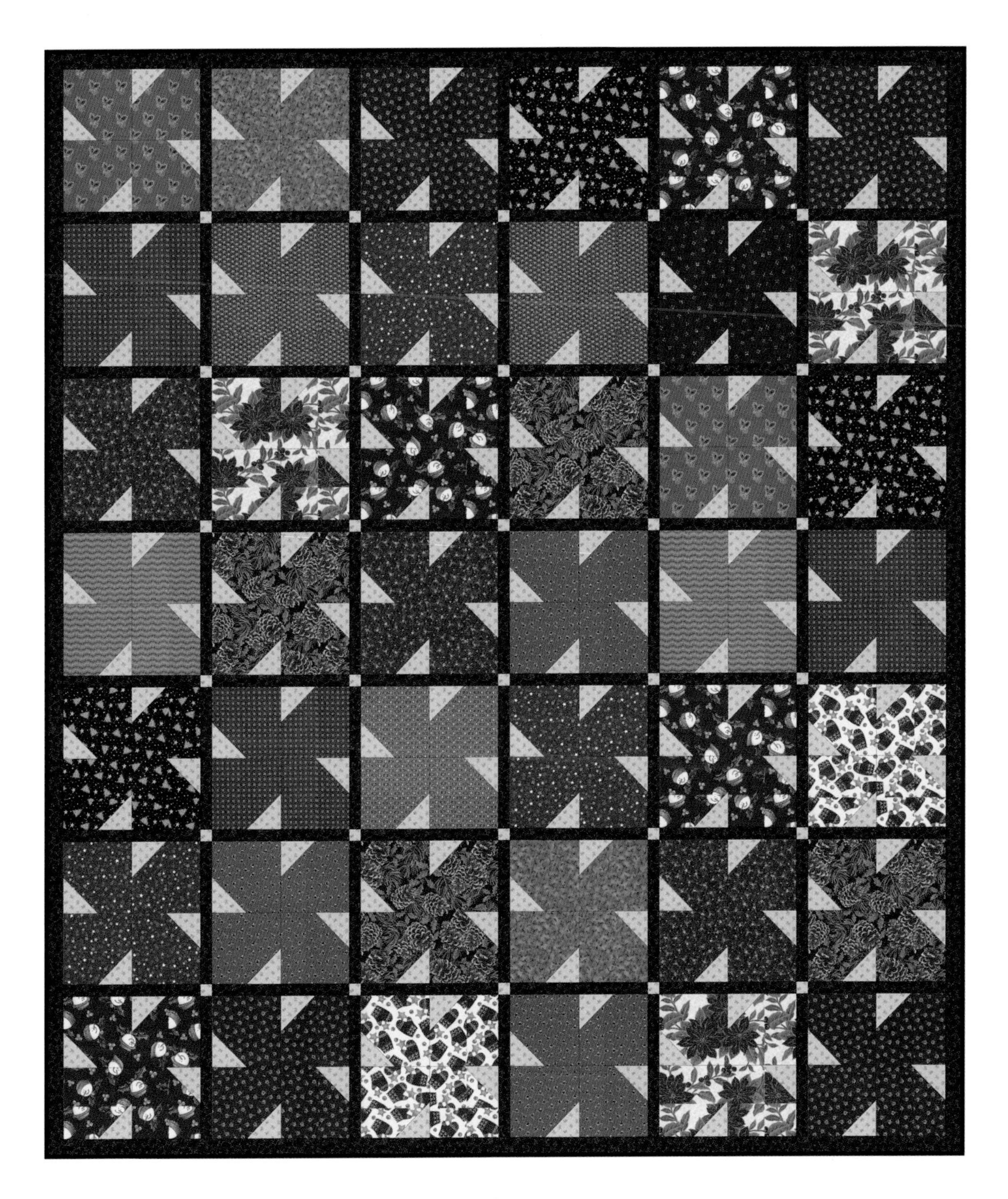

SUGGESTED LAYOUT

For my virtual quilt I have used a full stack of forty-two 10" (25.4cm) squares to make forty-two Christmas Rose blocks. I've added ¾" (19mm) finished sashing around the blocks and a 1" (2.5cm) finished border to nicely frame the quilt, which measures approximately 60" x 70" (152.4 x 177.8cm) – the perfect size to dress up a bed for the holidays!

5 HOUNDSTOOTH

The houndstooth check is synonymous with 1960s style, but it still looks very modern and chic! It has a wonderful interconnectedness, which makes the pattern seem more complex than it actually is, made simply from squares. To achieve the 'connected' weave, careful planning is needed, so crack out the design wall (see page 27) or clear the floor!

For one block you will need

Finished block size: 8" (20.3cm) square

- Three different black fabrics overprinted with white
- Three different white fabrics overprinted with black

Assembling the block

1. Take one black fabric and one white fabric and cut a 4½" (11.4cm) square from each (two in total).
2. Taking the same two prints again, cut two 2½" (6.4cm) squares from each (four in total).
3. Taking the remaining four fabrics, cut one 2½" (6.4cm) square from each (four in total).
4. Arrange the fabrics following the diagram (above). Sew two four-patch units using the smaller squares, then sew the four-patch units to the larger squares.

Give monochromatic quilts extra punch by adding a thin flange border in a bright colour.

SUGGESTED LAYOUT

For my virtual quilt I've arranged sixteen Houndstooth blocks in a four by four arrangement. Careful placement of the fabrics is everything. Most of the fabrics have one 4½" (11.4cm) square and four 2½" (6.4cm) squares, but they are spread across two rows of blocks. Lay your patches on a design wall or floor first to get the layout right. I've added one cheeky red 'tooth' to highlight the pattern and mirrored this in a ¼" (6mm) flange border (see page 30). The final 1" (2.5cm) finished border brings this quilt up to 34" (86.4cm) square – great for a very smart baby quilt!

6 TUMBLER

My tumbler quilt looks like it just came out of Grandma's attic, thanks to the choice of reproduction and vintage fabrics and the timeless elegance of the tumbler pattern. If you prefer, you can bring it bang up to date with modern geometric fabrics and solids for a very different quilt! I've used a simple dark/light pattern, but secondary designs are possible if you group lights and darks together.

SUGGESTED LAYOUT

For my quilt I cut a total of 207 dark tumblers and 207 light tumblers to make a quilt that is 72" (182.8cm) x 66" (167.6cm).

You will need

Assorted dark and light fabrics

Assembling the quilt

1. Download and print (see page 220 for link) or photocopy the Tumbler template on page 220. Following the instructions on page 14, cut out an equal number of shapes in light and dark fabrics.
2. Arrange the fabric tumblers in rows, alternating light and dark.
3. Flip two adjacent patches together and join them, right sides together, by sewing down one side. Press back and continue to add patches, creating long strips of joined tumblers.
4. Join the rows together, making sure that the seam intersections match.
5. Leave the edge 'wavy' or trim it straight before binding.

This quilt really relies on good contrast between the lights and the darks. If you're unsure where your chosen fabrics lie, try photographing them and looking at the image in black and white. Once the colour is 'gone', you'll be able to determine the relative lightness and darkness of each fabric more easily.

RAINBOW RAILS

The rail fence block is a fast and fun block to piece and creates some very dynamic quilts. Have fun playing around with the setting of your blocks or follow my directions below for a 'streak o' lightning'!

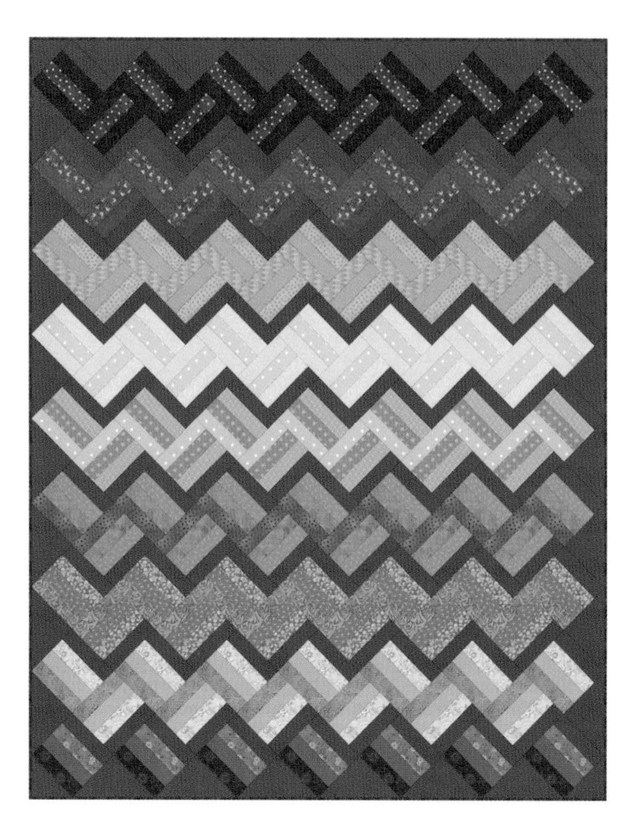

SUGGESTED LAYOUT

My virtual quilt uses thirteen Rainbow Rails blocks in each of nine different colour families. Now I know I'm taking liberties here – and a rainbow has seven colours – but I've always believed that when it comes to colour, more is more! You'll also need to cut seven 9¾" (24.8cm) squares, each cross-cut on both diagonals, to create twenty-eight setting triangles, and two 5⅛" (13cm) squares, each cut on one diagonal to yield four corner triangles. The quilt finishes at approximately 59" x 76" (149.9 x 193cm) – great for a twin bed.

Mix your genres! There is no reason why this quilt shouldn't include holiday prints, florals, batiks and homespuns... if the colour is right it deserves a place!

For one block you will need

Finished block size: 6" (15.2cm) square

- Three 2" x 7" (5.1 x 17.8) strips of assorted prints from one colour family
- One 2" x 7" (5.1 x 17.8) strip of dark charcoal grey solid

Assembling the block

1. Arrange the three coloured strips in a pleasing order, long edges together, and sew them together, side by side.
2. Sew the charcoal solid strip to one side. Press the seams one way.
3. Trim the ends of the block to create a 6½" (16.5cm) square.

CHEQUERBOARD

Choose your prettiest scraps - 2½" (6.4cm) strips, charm squares or pre-cut 10" (25.4cm) squares - to make this gorgeous quilt and combine them with a plethora of white and pale cream shirtings for a classic postage stamp quilt you'll love forever.

SUGGESTED LAYOUT

For my virtual quilt I have set forty-two blocks in a six by seven arrangement. I've added a 2" (5.1cm) finished border in light cream shirting, and a pieced border consisting of eighty-six four-patch units: sew two print 2½" (6.4cm) squares with two light cream shirting 2½" (6.4cm) squares. There is a final 2" (5.1cm) finished border made with 2½" (6.4cm) strips of light cream shirting. The finished quilt is 88" x 100" (223.5 x 254cm).

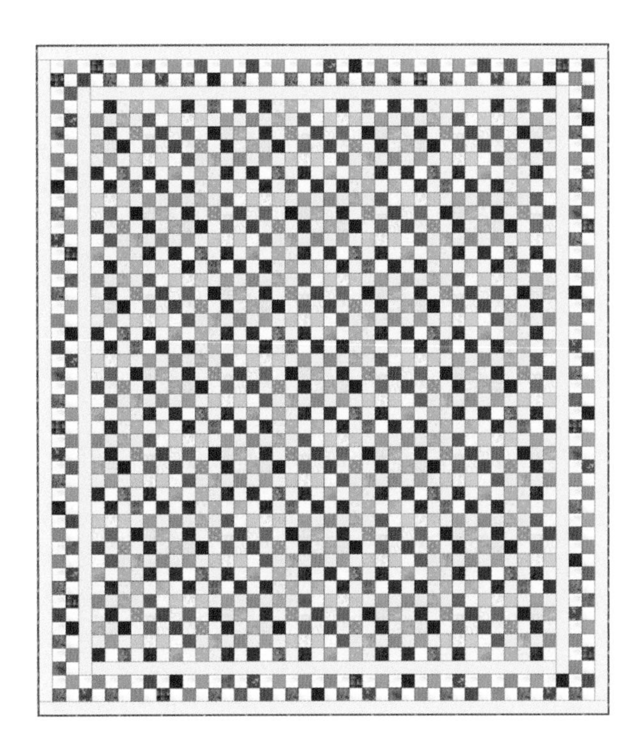

To speed up the construction cut 2½" (6.4cm) strips of six fabric - three cream and three print. Sew them together to make a strip-pieced unit then cross-cut into 2½" (6.4cm) wide segments. Make a bunch of these, switch them around, then sew together to make the blocks.

For one block you will need

Finished block size: 12" (30.5cm) square

- Eighteen 2½" (6.4cm) squares in pretty, bright pastels
- Eighteen 2½" (6.4cm) squares in white and light cream shirting print

Assembling the block

1. Arrange the squares in six rows of six squares, making sure you start with a light cream shirting square in the top left corner.
2. Sew the squares into rows, pressing the seams towards the coloured squares.
3. Sew the rows together.

9 ALL KINDS OF PEOPLE

It really does take all kinds of people to make this world of ours and I wanted to celebrate that fact in a quilt. Most of the hearts in this quilt are in rainbow shades, but the last one uses fabrics in every skin tone I could find. On their own they're just squares, but together they make a heart!

For one block you will need

Finished block size: 10" (25.4cm) square

- Two 2⅞" (7.3cm) squares, each in the same colour family
- Two 2⅞" (7.3cm) squares, each in a variety of light neutral background shades
- Seventeen 2½" (6.4cm) squares, in either one colour family or a variety of skin tones
- Four 2½" (6.4cm) squares, each in the same light neutral shade

Assembling the block

1. Pair one coloured and one neutral 2⅞" (7.3cm) squares, right sides together, and mark the diagonal lightly in pencil on one of them. Pin together.
2. Sew ¼" (6mm) either side of this line, then cut apart on the drawn line. Make two of these units, resulting in four half square triangle (HST) units.
3. Arrange the HST units with the remaining squares to form the heart. Use the diagram above to help you.
4. Sew the units into rows, then sew the rows together.

Use a fresh machine needle every 6–8 hours of sewing time. A fresh needle will produce neat, straight, consistent stitches.

SUGGESTED LAYOUT

For my quilt, I've used thirteen All Kinds of People blocks set on point with 2" (5.1cm) finished sashing and cornerstones. The setting triangles are cut from two 15½" (39.4cm) squares, each cross-cut on both diagonals to yield eight triangles, and the corner triangles are cut from two 8" (20.3cm) squares, each cut once on the diagonal to yield four triangles. The finished quilt is approximately 51" x 51" (130 x 130cm).

TWISTED RIBBONS

I love it when a super-simple block can be transformed into something complex looking and intriguing. Who would believe that this quilt is made from the humble half square triangle?

For two blocks you will need

Finished block size: 12" x 8" (30.5 x 20.3cm)

- Six 4⅞" (12.4cm) squares in cream/grey mini polka
- Six 4⅞" (12.4cm) squares in assorted bright prints

Assembling the block

1. Mark the diagonal on the back of each cream/grey square in pencil.
2. Pair one cream/grey square with a bright print, right sides together, and pin.
3. Sew ¼" (6mm) either side of the marked line. Cut apart on the line.
4. Repeat with the remaining squares. This will yield twelve half square triangle (HST) units. You need six for one block, but it's important to have lots of variety. Save the other HSTs for another block.
5. Arrange six assorted HST units in two rows of three, using the block diagram (above) to help you orientate your units.
6. Sew the units into rows of three, then join the rows.

Charm squares are ideal for this project. They are 5" (12.7cm) square, but rather than trimming ⅛" (3mm) off two sides just sew a fractionally wider seam allowance when you make the HST units – a thread or two should do it!

SUGGESTED LAYOUT

My virtual quilt uses twenty-eight Twisted Ribbon blocks in four columns of seven blocks. Each column is separated by a 1" (2.5cm) finished sashing strip. I've also added a 1" (2.5cm) finished border around the quilt to frame the blocks. The finished quilt is 53" x 58" (134.6 x 147.3cm).

STACKED BRICKS

Sometimes the simplest designs bring the most joy... I love the way this quilt comes together in rows rather than individual blocks, and the large scale is perfect for showing off a favourite colour palette or fabric collection.

SUGGESTED LAYOUT

My quilt is made up of eighteen rows; the even-numbered rows have eight bricks, while the od numbers have seven bricks plus a 4½" (11.4cm) square at each end to 'offset' the rows. My quilt finishes at 64" x 72" (162.6 x 182.8cm).

You will need

Finished block size: 8" (20.3cm) square

- 4½" x 8½" (11.4 x 21.6cm) rectangles of fabric, some patterned and coloured, some solid white

Assembling the quilt

1. Rather than making a block, set your rectangles out in rows.
2. Using the photograph to guide you, set your rectangles in rows. I've staggered the placement of solid white rectangles to create the effect of diagonal white lines running through the quilt.
3. Sew the rows together and press the seams one way.
4. Join the rows and press the seams one way.

Photograph your layout before you start to sew the patches together. Photograph each row alongside the row above and below it. Use these photographs as a reference next to you as you sew and you'll never get in a muddle!

12 QUICK AND EASY CHRISTMAS

Or any time of year for that matter! When you want a really fast seasonal quilt or one for gifting, this pattern is hard to beat and is a wonderful showcase for your favourite holiday prints.

SUGGESTED LAYOUT

My quick virtual holiday quilt uses sixteen blocks, in a four by four setting, with alternate blocks rotated through 90 degrees. I added 1½" (3.8cm) finished sashing and cornerstones and a 1½" (3.8cm) finished outer border. The quilt is 50½" (approximately 128cm) square.

If your strips aren't long enough, join two or more together to make the 11" (28cm) required. Use pieces of the same fabric, similar prints or colours or go wild and mix the whole thing up... make it your way!

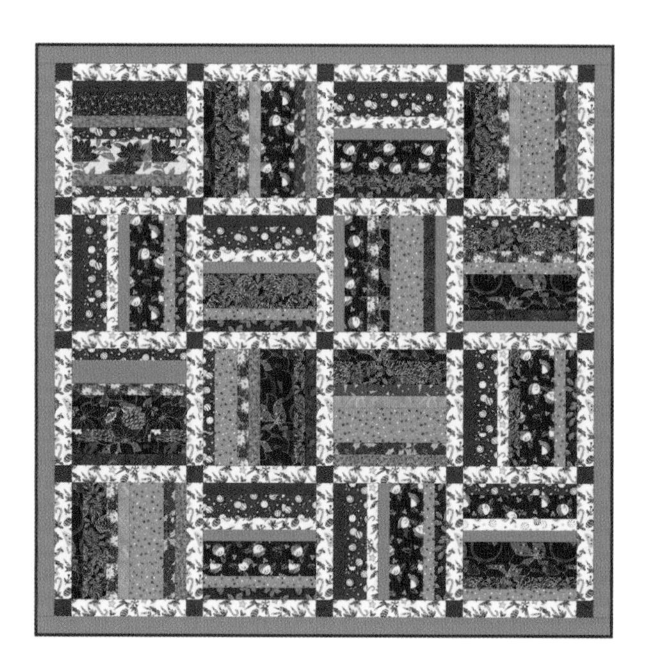

For one block you will need

Finished block size: 10" (25.4cm) square

- An assortment of print strips, ranging in width from 1½" (3.8cm) up to 3½" (8.9cm) and all 11" (28cm) long or more

Assembling the block

1. Join enough strips to make a 10½" (26.7cm) wide panel. The block shown right uses one 2½" (6.4cm) strip, one 3½" (8.9cm) strip and six 1½" (3.8cm) strips, but use whatever you have to hand.
2. Trim the block to 10½" (26.7cm) square.

13 MODERN CHAIN

Chain quilts are without doubt my favourite kind of pieced quilt. Here I've given the classic single Irish chain a modern makeover with bold fabrics and a reversal of the usual positive/negative, really making a feature of the negative (background) space to highlight those prints!

SUGGESTED LAYOUT

For my virtual quilt I've added large squares in between the nine-patch blocks, picking out fabrics from the nine-patch blocks. Use the same fabrics or a similar colour for continuity. I've alternated thirteen nine-patch blocks with twelve plain blocks for a 68 x 68" (173 x 173cm) quilt.

When cutting the large 'plain' blocks, try to centre the fabric design as much as possible. A large 15½" (39.4cm) square ruler is perfect for doing this.

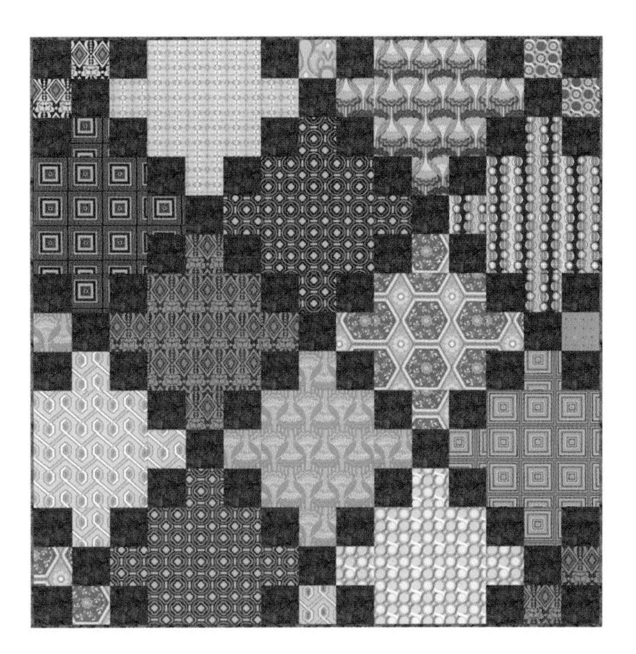

For one block you will need

Finished block size: 13½" (34.3cm) square

- Five 5" (12.7cm) squares in dark purple batik
- Four 5" (12.7cm) squares in different large-scale bright prints (charm squares are perfect)
- Five 5" (12.7cm) squares in dark purple batik

Assembling the block

Sew the nine squares together into a nine-patch, setting the dark purple squares in a 'chain' through the centre, as shown.

DISAPPEARING NINE-PATCH

Sew simple squares together, slice them up, then switch them around for this quilter's favourite!

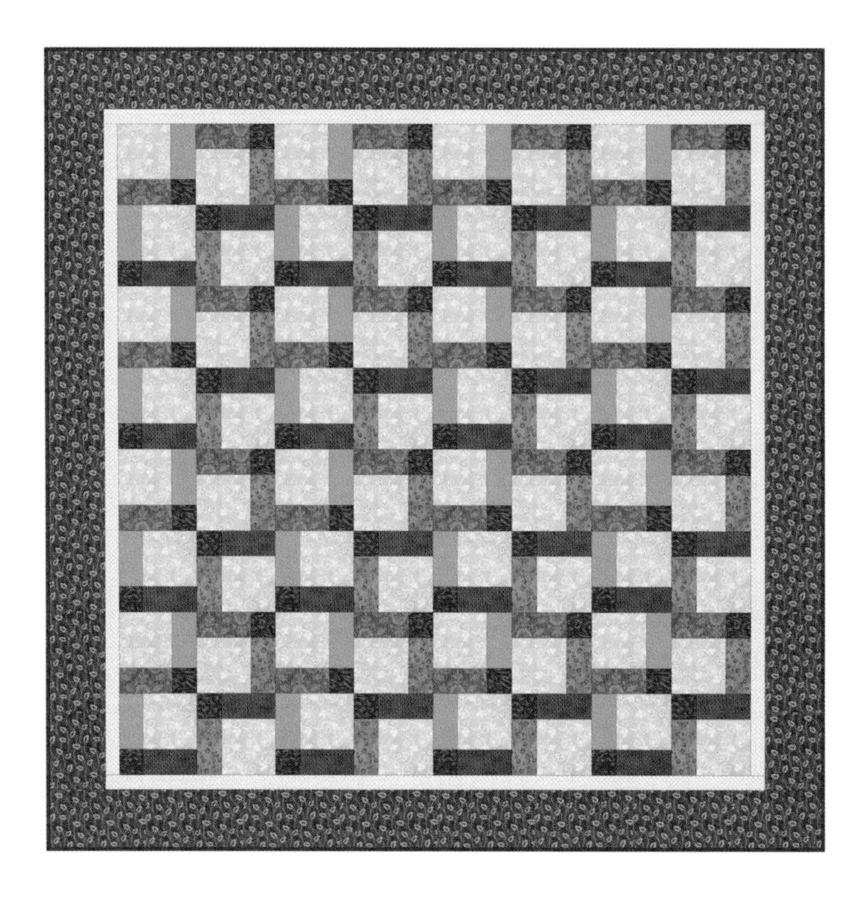

SUGGESTED LAYOUT

For my virtual quilt I made a total of sixteen blocks, set in four rows of four, with a 1" (2.5cm) and a 4" (10.2cm) finished border. The quilt finishes at 56 x 56" (142.2 x 142.3cm).

Any size square will work for this pattern – just make sure that you start with nine squares all the same size. Sew them together and then measure your block. Divide the block (raw edge to raw edge) by two to find the measurement to cut at.

For one block you will need

Finished block size: 11½" (29.2cm) square

- Four 4½" (11.4cm) squares in assorted golds/dark tans
- Four 4½" (11.4cm) squares in assorted cream prints
- One 4½" (11.4cm) square in blue/grey print

Assembling the block

1. Sew the nine squares together into a nine-patch: the blue/grey square is at the centre, the cream squares in each of the corners and the gold squares form a cross around the centre square.
2. Press the block, then carefully cut it into four quarters, each 6¼" x 6¼" (15.8 x 15.8cm).
3. Turn two diagonally opposite quarters 180 degrees, as shown below, then sew the units back together.

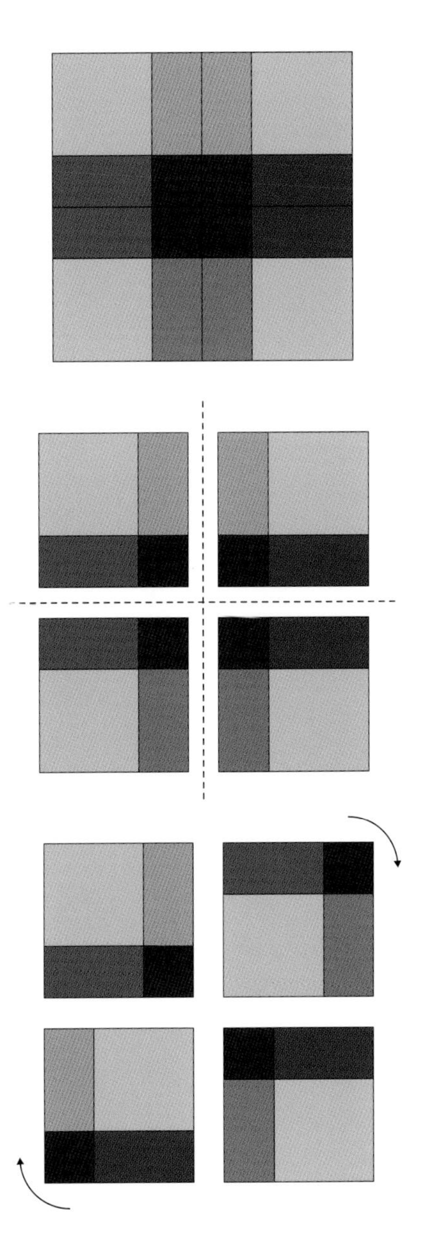

15 SYCAMORE

I've always been a fan of 'chain' quilts. Any block with a diagonal or a cross in it gets my vote, so in this quilt I have used a quilters' favourite – the hourglass unit – to create a different kind of 'chain'. Appliquéd or quilted falling leaves would look wonderful in the plain blocks!

For one block you will need

Finished block size: 9" (22.9cm) square

- At least five 4¼" (10.8cm) squares in assorted green, brown and golden yellow solids, each cross-cut on both diagonals to create quarter square triangles (QSTs)
- Four 3½" (8.9cm) squares in dark brown print

Assembling the block

1. Mix the QSTs up into groups of four. The more fabrics you use, the better. If you have leftover triangles you can use them in another block.
2. Sew the QSTs together to create five hourglass units.
3. Alternate your five hourglass units with the four dark brown print squares, as shown above.
4. Sew your patches into rows, then sew the rows together.

If you pre-wash your fabrics, it's a good idea to give them a spritz with spray starch or sizing and then iron them before cutting your patches. Whether you pre-wash fabric or not, always iron it before cutting to remove any wrinkles.

SUGGESTED LAYOUT

My virtual quilt uses thirteen Sycamore blocks and twelve plain blocks cut at 9½" x 9½" (24.1 x 24.1cm) from dark brown print fabric. Sew your blocks into five rows of five, then sew the rows together. I've added a 3" (7.6cm) finished border pieced from a further sixty-four QST hourglass units to make a quilt that is 51 x 51" (129.5 x 129.5cm).

16 HOPE AND GLORY

I've made this quilt in traditional red, white and blue, but there's no reason why you shouldn't pick your favourite colour palette and make something that matches your décor – shades of cream and cappuccino would look subtle and beautiful!

You will need

Finished quilt size: 48" x 76" (122 x 193cm)

- Red print and solid fabrics – cut eighty-four 4½" (11.4cm) squares. Also cut thirteen 4⅞" (12.4cm) squares for the half square triangle (HST) units
- Blue print and solid fabrics – cut fifty-two 4½" (11.4cm) squares. Also cut eleven 4⅞" (12.4cm) squares for the HST units
- White print and solid fabrics – cut forty-four 4½" (11.4cm) squares. Also cut twenty-four 4⅞" (12.4cm) squares for the HST units – on the back of each mark the diagonal lightly in pencil

Assembling the quilt

1. Pair up the marked white 4⅞" (12.4cm) squares with the corresponding blue and red squares. Make HST units following the instructions on page 19. You will end up with twenty-two blue-and-white units and twenty-six red-and-white units.
2. Lay out your HST units with the squares in a 12 x 19 arrangement, using the diagram above as a guide.
3. Sew the units and squares into rows. Press the seams in alternate directions.
4. Sew the rows together.

If you're struggling to find enough scraps of the right colours, organize an 'exchange' with quilting friends – you may well have just what they are looking for, too!

Louise Bourgeois
IN SEARCH OF Rex Whistler
THE ROMANCE OF ARCHITECTURE
TOM HAMMICK
in the Twentieth Century
DAVID BOWIE IS INSIDE

17 FRACTURED

Using exactly the same method you would use to join binding strips, these 'diagonal seams' create a very complex-looking block, but the construction method makes it fast and simple to achieve!

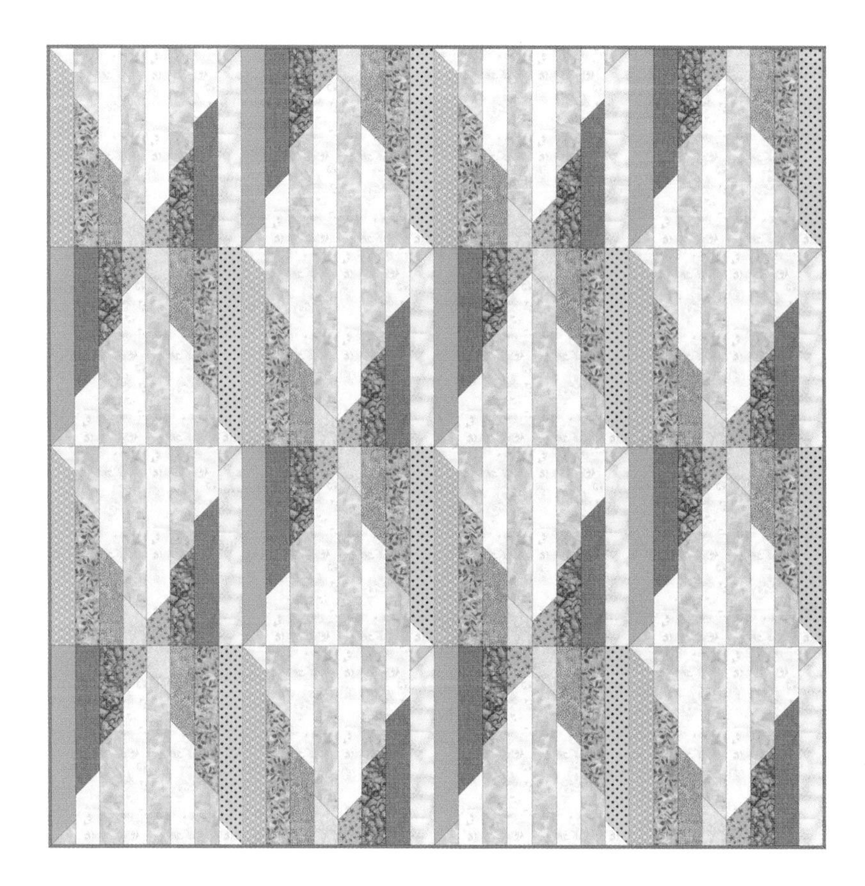

SUGGESTED LAYOUT

For my virtual quilt I made sixteen identical fractured blocks and arranged them in a four by four set, turning every alternate block through 180 degrees. The quilt finishes at 64 x 64" (162.6 x 162.6cm).

Once you have made one block in its entirety, complete the remaining blocks in halves. Make all the purple halves first, then all of the turquoise halves before sewing them together. When you can repeat the same steps over and over again, you will get into a rhythm and your construction time will be reduced.

For one block you will need

Finished block size: 16" (40.7cm) square

- Four 2½" (6.4cm) wide strips of assorted light purple fabrics at 4½" (11.4cm), 8½" (21.6cm), 12½" (31.7cm) and 16½" (42cm) long
- Four 2½" (6.4cm) wide strips of assorted light turquoise fabrics at 4½" (11.4cm), 8½" (21.6cm), 12½" (31.7cm) and 16½" (42cm) long
- Eight 2½" (6.4cm) wide light grey batik strips - two at 2½" (6.4cm), two at 6½" (16.5cm), two at 10½" (26.7cm) and two at 14½" (36.8cm)

Assembling the block

1. Lay a 2½" (6.4cm) grey square right sides together with a 16½" (42cm) purple strip. Sew from corner to corner of the grey square (mark this line or 'eyeball' it), flip the corner back and press. Trim away the underneath fabric.
2. Lay a 6½" (16.5cm) grey strip on top of a 12½" (31.7cm) strip of purple fabric, at right angles, forming an L shape. Sew a diagonal seam, flip the grey strip back and press. Ensure that the diagonal seam runs in the same direction as the first strip. Trim away the background fabric.
3. Repeat this process with a 10½" (26.7cm) strip of grey and an 8½" (21.6cm) strip of purple and a 14½" (36.8cm) strip of grey and a 4½" (11.4cm) strip of purple.
4. Repeat the entire process with the turquoise and grey strips, but stitch the diagonal seam in the opposite direction.
5. Arrange the strips to make the block and sew the strips together.

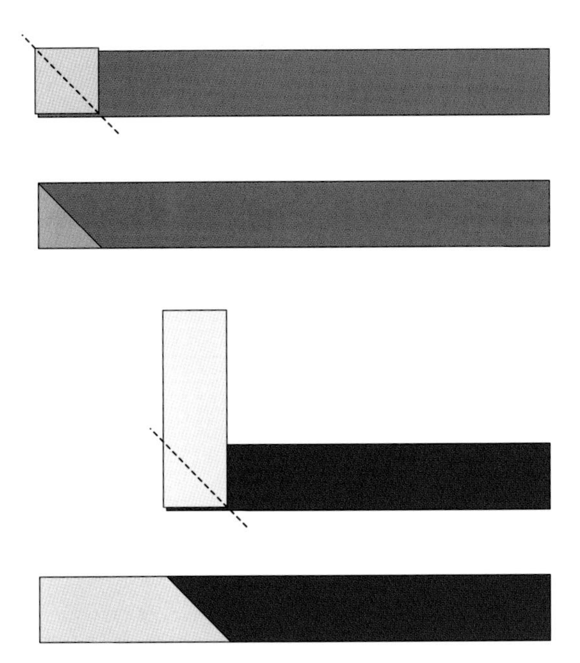

18 BOX OF CRAYONS

Log cabin blocks are some of the most perennially popular quilt patterns in the world, and with good reason. Simple to make, equally traditional and bang up to date, and with a variety of possible settings, there is always something new to discover in this particular cabin! Here the logs remind me of pencils or crayons in a box – how grey the world would be if we stopped colouring it in!

For one block you will need

Finished block size: 12" (30.5cm) square

- One 2½" (6.4cm) square of bright solid
- Assorted 1½" (3.8cm) wide strips of bright solids in five different colours
- Assorted 1½" (3.8cm) wide strips of different light, medium and the occasional dark grey solids

Assembling the block

1. Sew a 2½" (6.4cm) strip of light grey to the top edge of the bright centre 2½" (6.4cm) square. Press all the seams towards the strip you are adding. Sew a 3½" (8.9cm) strip of the same grey to the right-hand side of the centre square. Press.
2. Sew a 3½" (8.9cm) strip of bright (I used light green) to the bottom edge and press.
3. Sew a 4½" (11.4cm) strip of the same bright to the left-hand side and press.
4. Continue adding rounds as follows.
   Round 2: grey 4½" (11.4cm) and 5½" (14cm), bright 5½" (14cm), 6½" (16.5cm) – I used brown.
   Round 3: grey 6½" (16.5cm) and 7½" (19cm), bright 7½" (19cm) and 8½" (21.6cm) – I used blue.
   Round 4: grey 8½" (21.6cm) and 9½" (24.1cm), bright 9½" (24.1cm) and 10½" (26.7cm) – I used medium green.
   Round 5: grey 10½" (26.7cm) and 11½" (29.2cm), bright 11½" (29.2cm) and 12½" (31.7cm) – I used dark green.
5. Press your block.

Set up a clothes airer next to your sewing machine and drape your log cabin strips over it so that they are close to hand and do not get muddled.

SUGGESTED LAYOUT

My virtual quilt uses nine log cabin blocks, and I have turned some of the blocks so that the dark halves line up, creating strong diagonals. I added a 2" (5.1cm) finished border, making a 40 x 40" (101.6 x 101.6cm) quilt.

STRAWBERRY PATCH

My mum loves strawberries so much that she once got up at 3 a.m. to raid the refrigerator and eat the punnet she had bought before anyone else got a look in - she felt so guilty the next day she rushed out and bought more! If strawberries are your guilty pleasure (and surely there are worse things to feast on!), you'll love my strawberry patch block.

SUGGESTED LAYOUT

I've made a fun and fruity cushion using just one block (see page 121), but this design would make a great runner or picnic blanket quilt too.

For one block you will need

Finished block size: 10" x 14" (25.4 x 35.6cm)

- Five 2⅞" (7.3cm) squares in assorted light blue prints
- Two 2⅞" (7.3cm) squares in assorted green fabrics
- Three 2⅞" (7.3cm) squares in assorted red prints
- Seventeen 2½" (6.4cm) squares in assorted red prints
- Four 2½" (6.4cm) squares in assorted green prints
- Four 2½" (6.4cm) squares in assorted light blue prints
- Five 2⅞" (7.3cm) squares in assorted light blue prints

Assembling the block

1. Mark the back of each light blue print 2⅞" (7.3cm) square on the diagonal lightly in pencil.
2. Pair the light blue marked squares with green and with red squares and make four blue/green HST units and six blue/red HST units (see page 19).
3. Arrange the HST units and the blue, green and red squares to make the strawberry patch block, following the diagram.
4. Sew the units and squares into rows. Press the seams in alternate directions.
5. Join the rows together and press the seams one way.

To make a quilt specifically to use for picnics and for laying on the grass, it's worth adding a waterproof membrane (available online) between the wadding (batting) and the backing fabric.

YELLOW BRICK ROAD

Simple rectangles of cool grey and vibrant yellow make a dynamic block with plenty of movement when it's combined with others. Create your very own yellow brick road all the way to your journey's end!

SUGGESTED LAYOUT

For my virtual quilt I have set sixteen blocks in a four by four arrangement, alternating the direction of the yellow brick road to create a diagonal path. I've added a ¼" (6mm) finished folded flange border and a 2" (5.1cm) finished border. The quilt finishes at 52" (132cm) square.

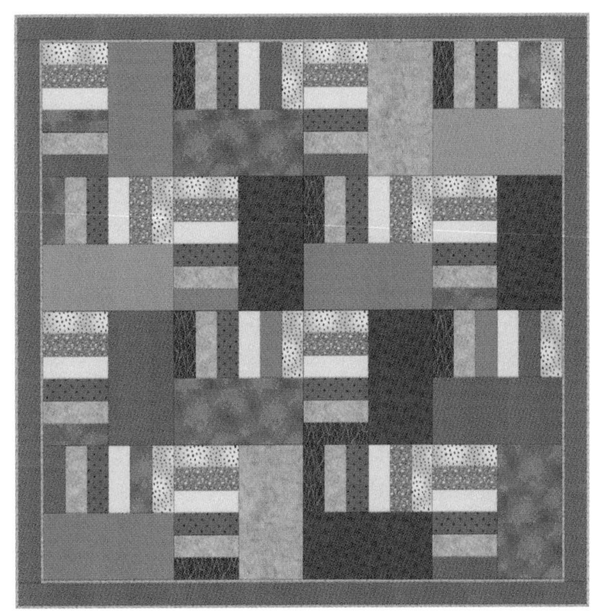

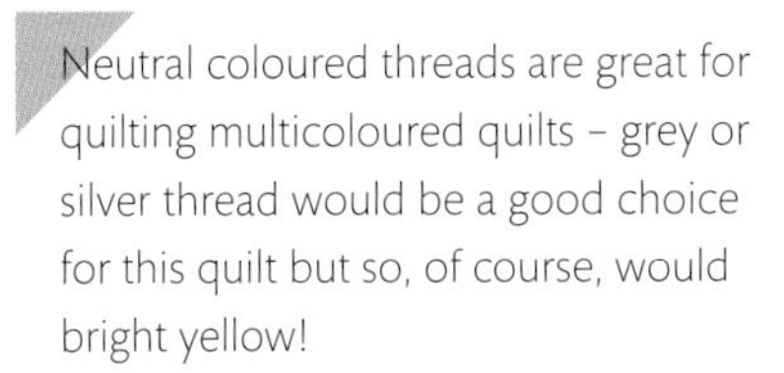

Neutral coloured threads are great for quilting multicoloured quilts – grey or silver thread would be a good choice for this quilt but so, of course, would bright yellow!

For one block you will need

Finished block size: 12" (30.5cm) square

- Three 2½" x 6½" (6.4 x 16.5cm) rectangles in bright yellow prints
- Three 2½" x 6½" (6.4 x 16.5cm) rectangles in assorted blue prints
- One 6½" x 12½" (16.5 x 31.7cm) rectangle in blue print

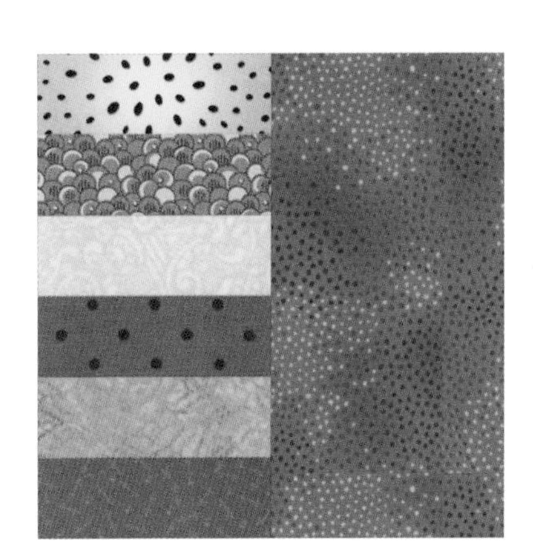

Assembling the block

1. Sew the small yellow and blue rectangles together, alternating the colours.
2. Press the seams towards the blue rectangles.
3. With a yellow rectangle at the top, sew the large blue rectangle to the right-hand edge. Press the seams towards the blue fabric.

STRIPS AND SQUARES

Walk into any quilt shop and you'll see pre-cut bundles of 2½" (6.4cm) strips and 5" (12.7cm) and 10" (25.4cm) squares. We love pre-cuts and I think that's for several reasons. As quilters, most of us fantasize about having 'just a little' of every fabric in the quilt shop... come on, it's not just me, is it? We also love the cute bundles, they are just so appealing – and of course we get to jump straight into the piecing, often with no pre-cutting required!

TWICE AS NICE!

For me, the biggest appeal of strips and squares is their sheer versatility. Indeed, they deserve a chapter all of their own! Many of the quilts in this book are pre-cut friendly, particularly when combined with some extra scraps or yardage, but you can also delve into your stash and cut strips and squares quickly and easily. Some of the strips and squares are bigger or smaller than the ones you can buy pre-cut, so this gives you even more options for using your leftovers, bundles of fat quarters or fabrics that have simply been waiting for the right project. Rest assured that these quilts are easy to piece, yield stunning results and contain some tips and tricks that will have you asking, 'Are those really only made from strips and squares?'

SAVE YOUR KISSES

What better way to show someone you care than a quilt covered in kisses? The kiss blocks in this quilt can be made with 2½" (6.4cm) strips from a roll – just find a wonderful co-ordinate like the big polka dots I used for the outer border and you're sure of a winner!

SUGGESTED LAYOUT

My virtual quilt uses thirty-four Save Your Kisses blocks. I set thirty of them in a five by six arrangement for the quilt centre. I've added 1" (2.5cm) finished sashing in blue solid in between the blocks and 1" (2.5cm) finished cornerstones in white at the intersections. The remaining four blocks are used as the quilt corners and there is an 8" (20.3cm) finished border in a large red-and-white polka dot. The final outer border is 1" (2.5cm) finished in blue solid. The whole quilt measures 64" x 73" (162.6 x 185.4cm).

In quilting, the 'finished' size is always ½" (12mm) smaller than the cut size. So for 1" (2.5cm) finished sashing, cut your strips at 1½" (3.8cm) and for a 4" (10.2cm) finished border, cut your strips at 4½" (11.4cm). Use ¼" (6mm) seams throughout!

For one block you will need

Finished block size: 8" (20.3cm) square

- One 8½" (21.6cm) square in cream , cross-cut on both diagonals to yield four triangles
- One 2½" (6.4cm) x approximately 26" (66cm) strip of coloured print fabric

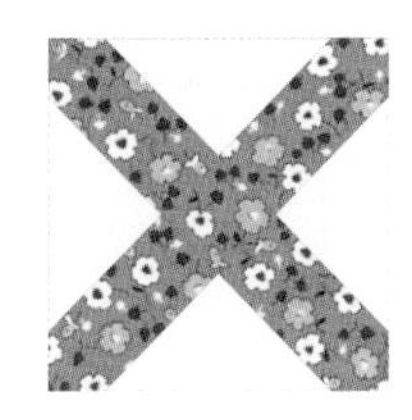

Assembling the block

1. Download and print (see page 220 for link) or photocopy one each of Save Your Kisses foundations A and B (page 221).
2. Following the instructions for paper foundation piecing (see page 21), piece the units in numerical order, trimming the seam allowances as you go.
3. Stitch foundation A to foundation B, then trim the block to 8½" (21.6cm) square.

DESERT BLOOMS

Even in the desert, flowers grow, so grab a bunch of your favourite bright fabrics, mix in a little greenery and the deep cheddars and gold of the desert and you'll have this lovely wallhanging made in no time. Easy and accurate 'stitch and flip' sewing makes for very accurate shapes without ever cutting a single triangle!

SUGGESTED LAYOUT

My virtual wallhanging consists of four identical blocks, sewn in a two by two arrangement, making a 32" (81.2cm) finished quilt centre. Next I've added a 1" (2.5cm) finished border in purple, a 4" (10.2cm) finished border in green and a 1" (2.5cm) finished border in purple to make a finished wallhanging that measures 44 x 44" (111.8 x 111.8cm).

Use a mechanical pencil to mark diagonals on fabric – the lead is always a consistent width and gives a more accurate line to sew on.

For one block you will need

Finished block size: 16" (40.7cm) square

- White/cream solid: four 2½" (6.4cm) squares and four 4½" (11.4cm) squares
- Medium purple: eight 2½" (6.4cm) squares and four 2½" x 4½" (6.4 x 11.4cm) rectangles
- Medium plum: twelve 2½" (6.4cm) squares
- Dark purple: four 2½" (6.4cm) squares
- Assorted gold and cheddar prints: fourteen 2½" (6.4cm) squares, six 2½" x 4½" (6.4 x 11.4cm) rectangles, plus one 4½" (11.4cm) square for the block centre
- Light green: two 2½" (6.4cm) squares and two 2½" x 4½" (6.4 x 11.4cm) rectangles

Assembling the block

1. Arrange one white, two medium purple and one medium plum 2½" (6.4cm) squares together to make a four-patch and join together. Make four units.
2. Set aside your dark purple 2½" (6.4cm) squares for the corners. On all of the remaining 2½" (6.4cm) squares, mark the diagonal lightly in pencil on the wrong side.
3. Using the 'stitch and flip' method (see page 20), add two plum and two gold/cheddar corners to the four white 4½" (11.4cm) squares, making sure that the plum corners are on two adjacent corners and the gold corners are on the other two adjacent corners. These make the 'square in a square' units.
4. Using the stitch and flip method again, make two flying geese using the medium purple rectangles and four of the remaining gold/cheddar 2½" (6.4cm) squares. Make two more flying geese using the last two medium purple rectangles and add a gold and a green corner to each.
5. Arrange your prepared units as shown in the diagram.
6. Start by sewing the corner units together. For the top left corner, sew a green 2½" x 4½" (6.4 x 11.4cm) rectangle to the left-hand side of a four-patch. Make sure your four-patch is orientated the correct way.
7. Next sew one of the reserved dark purple 2½" (6.4cm) squares to the side of the other green rectangle. Sew this pieced rectangle to the top of the four-patch unit. Piece the other corners in the same way, but use the gold/cheddar rectangles.
8. Sew a flying geese unit to the top (plum corners) edge of each of the square in a square units.
9. Finally sew the units together to make three rows, using the gold/cheddar square for the centre piece, then sew the rows together.

23 CONTAINED CHAOS

When your stash and scraps are threatening a takeover, you have to show them who's boss and impose some order on that chaos! A simple shape and strong frames help to make sense of the jumble of print fabrics contained within.

For one block you will need

Finished block size: 20" (50.8cm) square

- Three 1½" x 42" (3.8 x 106.7cm) strips in chocolate brown solid for the frames
- Seventy-three 2½" (6.4cm) squares in assorted patterns

Assembling the block

1. From the brown solid, cut two rectangles 2½" (6.4cm) long and sew them to opposite sides of one 2½" (6.4cm) print square. Press.
2. Cut two 4½" (11.4cm) strips from the brown solid and sew them to the remaining two sides of the print square. Press.
3. Join two 2½" (6.4cm) print squares together. Make two of these units. Sew these units to either side of the framed block centre. Sew four more 2½" (6.4cm) print squares together, in a row; make two of these units. Sew these units to the remaining two sides of the block centre. Press.
4. Add a solid brown frame around the block centre as before: two pieces cut at 8½" (21.6cm) and two pieces cut at 10½" (26.7cm).
5. Join five print squares together in a row and sew to one side of the block. Repeat on the other side. Sew seven print squares together and add to the top and bottom of the block.
6. Frame the block again with two pieces of brown solid cut at 14½" (36.8cm) and two pieces cut at 16½" (42cm).
7. Sew eight print squares together in a row and sew to one side of the block. Repeat on the other side. Sew ten print squares to each of the remaining two sides in the same way.

'Neutrals' need not only be white, cream, tan or black. Navy is great, purple and red look amazing and any brown shade is worth a look. Mock up a block before you start piecing and try out different frame colours.

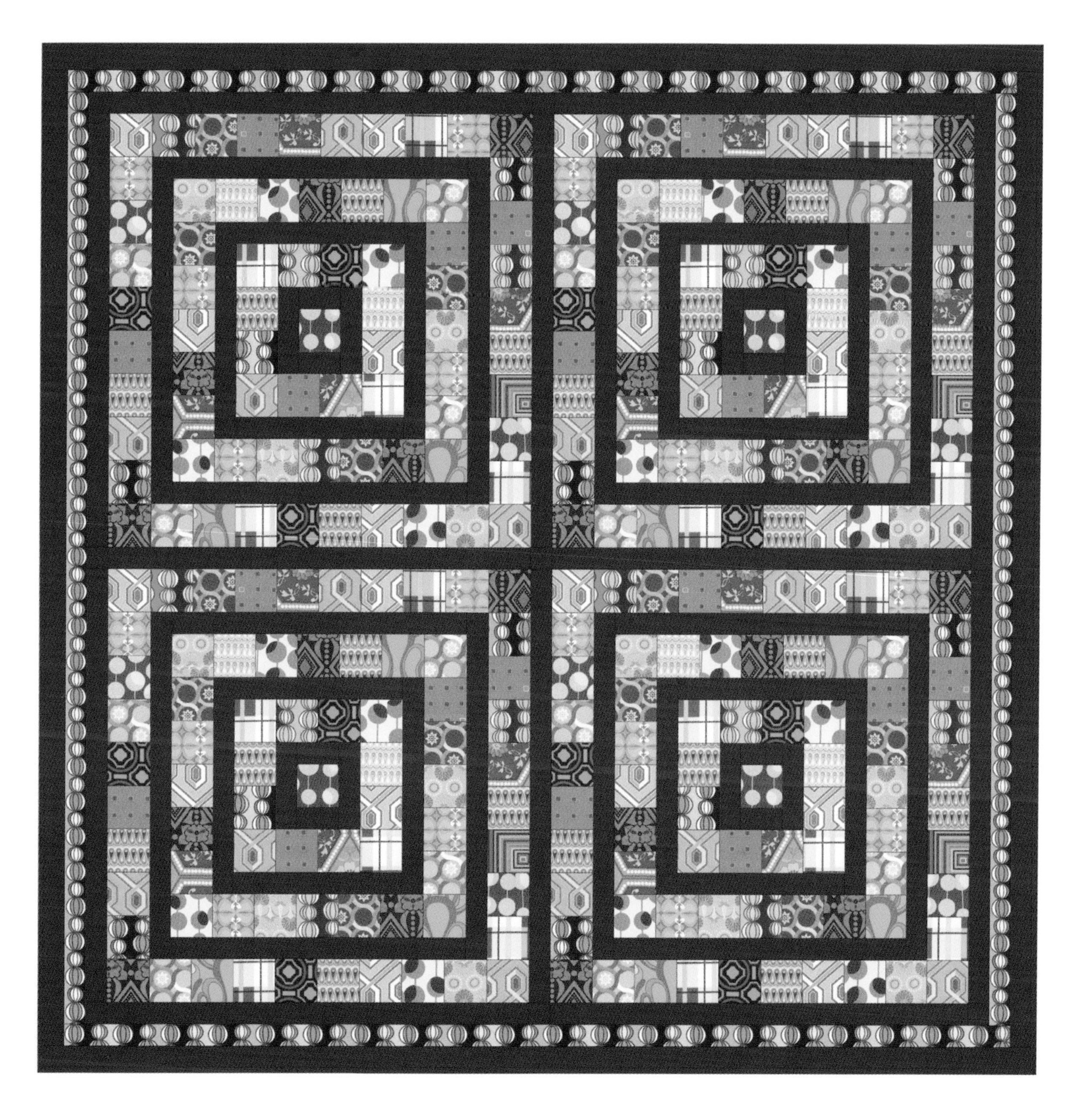

SUGGESTED LAYOUT

For my quilt I made four Contained Chaos blocks. I joined them together with 1" (2.5cm) finished sashing, added a 1" (2.5cm) finished border, again in the brown solid, then added a 1" (2.5cm) finished print border and a final 1" (2.5cm) finished outer border in brown solid. The quilt measures 47" (119.4cm) square and will almost certainly put some kind of dent into your stash. If not, make a bigger quilt!

24 LAQUERWORK

I've travelled to China many times and one of my greatest inspirations is the architecture and the old carved screens in the temples. This block is surprising in that it only really makes sense when you put four blocks together and add sashing. I believe patchwork is always more fun when the whole is worth more than the sum of its parts! I've given this quilt a fresh modern look by combining 'on-trend' dark chocolate with duck egg blue and restful ivory.

For one block you will need

Finished block size: 12" (30.5cm) square

- 1½" (3.8cm) x approximately 25" (63.5cm) strip in duck egg blue print
- 1½" (3.8cm) x approximately 25" (63.5cm) strip in dark chocolate brown mini polka dot fabric
- Background fabric in light ivory print – a fat quarter is plenty

When cutting long strips of fabric (such as for the border on this quilt) try wherever possible to cut the strips on the lengthwise grain (parallel with the selvedge). This will give you the most stable strips, which are less likely to stretch and distort.

SUGGESTED LAYOUT

For my virtual quilt I have made thirteen Laquerwork blocks and set them on point with 1" (2.5cm) finished sashing, made from the same chocolate brown polka dot print. The setting triangles are made from two squares cut at 18¼" (46.3cm), then cross-cut on both diagonals to yield eight setting triangles. The corner triangles are cut from two 9⅜" (23.8cm) squares, each cut on one diagonal to yield a total of four corner triangles. Sew the blocks and triangles in diagonal rows, then join the rows. I've added a 1" (2.5cm) finished border and the quilt measures approximately 57 x 57" (145 x 145cm).

LAQUERWORK

Assembling the block

1. Start by cutting your pieces. From the duck egg blue strip cut the following: two 1½" (3.8cm) squares, two 2½" (6.4cm) strips, two 4½" (11.4cm) strips and two 5½" (14cm) strips. From the chocolate polka dot print cut exactly the same pieces.
2. From the ivory fat quarter cut one strip 2½" x 12½" (6.4 x 31.7cm), two strips each 2½" x 5½" (6.4 x 14cm), four strips each 2½" x 4½" (6.4 x 11.4cm) and four 2½" (6.4cm) squares. Also cut twelve 1½" (3.8cm) squares.
3. Sew one duck egg blue and one ivory 1½" (3.8cm) square together and press. With the ivory square at the top, add a 1½" x 2½" (3.8 x 6.4cm) rectangle of duck egg blue fabric to the right-hand side. Press.
4. Draw a line on the diagonal on the wrong side of one of the 1½" (3.8cm) ivory squares. Lay this on the lower corner (where the duck egg blue fabrics meet) of the unit made in step 3. Sew on the line and flip back. Press, then trim away the underneath fabrics (stitch and flip method, see page 20).
5. Repeat steps 3 and 4 using the 2½" (6.4cm) square and the 2½" x 4½" (6.4 x 11.4cm) rectangle of ivory fabric and then the duck egg blue strips in 4½" (11.4cm) and 5½" (14cm) lengths. 'Corner' the square once more with a marked 1½" (3.8cm) square of ivory fabric.
6. Make three more units in the same way -one more in duck egg blue and two in chocolate polka dot print.
7. Arrange your units with the remaining ivory strips forming a cross in the centre.
8. Sew two units to a 2½" x 5½" (6.4 x 14cm) strip of ivory and press. Make two of these units, then join them either side of the 2½" x 12½" (6.4 x 31.7cm) strip of ivory fabric.

EVERY SCRAP

I adore scrap quilts and one of my favourite ways to 'tame' my scraps is to cut them into 2½" (6.4cm) strips. This block uses those 2½" (6.4cm) strips in a 'can't fail' method that's sure to please!

SUGGESTED LAYOUT

My virtual quilt uses thirteen full blocks, set on point. From blue solid, I cut two 18¼" (46.3cm) squares, each cut on both diagonals to make the eight setting triangles, and two 9⅜" (23.8cm) squares, each cut on one diagonal to make the four corner triangles.

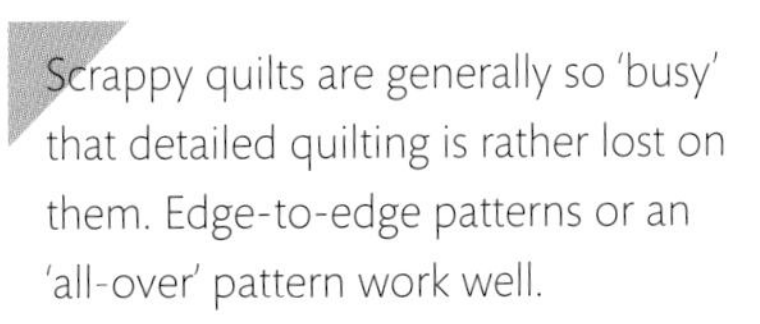

Scrappy quilts are generally so 'busy' that detailed quilting is rather lost on them. Edge-to-edge patterns or an 'all-over' pattern work well.

For one block you will need

Finished block size: 12" (30.5cm) square

- Assorted light, medium and dark 2½" (6.4cm) strips of various lengths

Assembling the block

1. Cut your 2½" (6.4cm) strips into various lengths, from 2½" (6.4cm) to 7½" (19cm).
2. Sew several pieces together, end to end, to create a strip that is at least 12½" (31.7cm) long. Repeat to make a total of six pieced strips.
3. Arrange the pieced strips as shown, offsetting the seams as much as you can. Be prepared to add an extra square or rectangle to the odd strip just to make sure that your seams always offset.
4. When you're happy with the arrangement, sew the strips together.
5. Trim your block to 12½" x 12½" (31.7 x 31.7cm).

26 ROTATION

Simple strip-pieced units are sewn around a centre square with an easy partial seam construction for a quilt that looks much harder to make than it actually is!

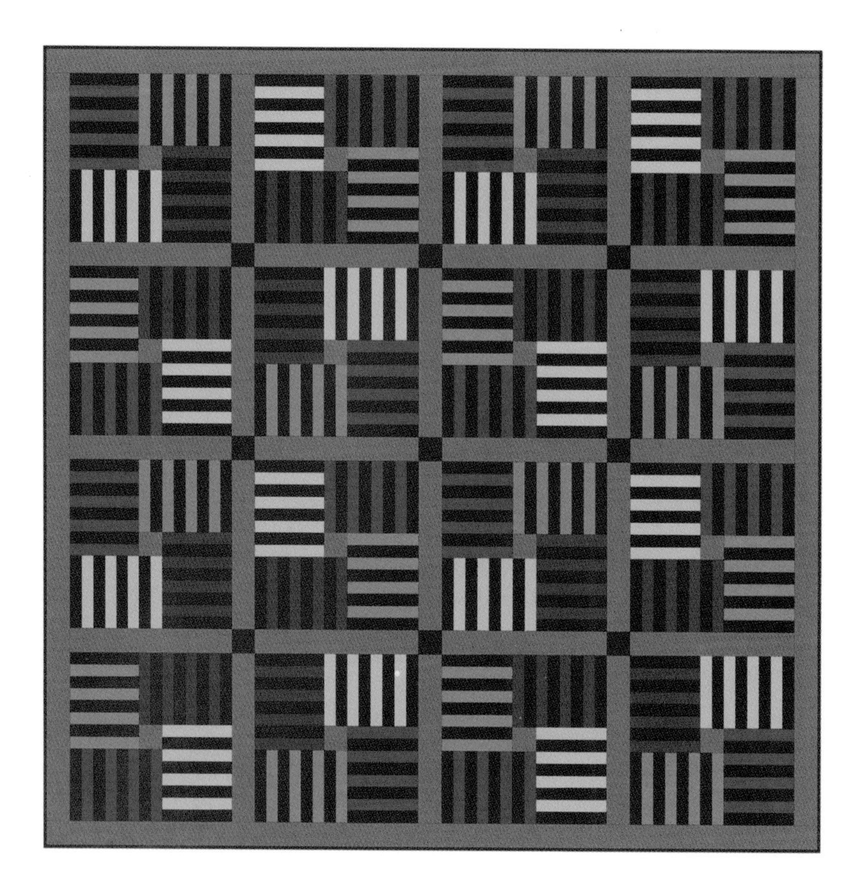

SUGGESTED LAYOUT

My virtual quilt uses sixteen Rotation blocks joined together in a four by four arrangement, separated by 2" (5.1cm) finished sashing and 2" (5.1cm) finished cornerstones. There's a 2" (5.1cm) finished border to complete this 66" x 66" (167.6 x 167.6cm) square quilt.

For easy accuracy, cut your strips for the strip-pieced units a little longer than 6½" (16.5cm) – you'll need a little more of each fabric to do this. Piece your strips together and then cut the strip-pieced unit to 6½" x 8½" (16.5 x 21.6cm).

For one block you will need

Finished block size: 14" (35.6cm) square

- Four different assorted medium and light brown solids – one 1½" x 26" (3.8 x 66cm) strip of each
- One dark brown solid strip – 1½" x 104" (3.8 x 264.1cm) in total (doesn't need to be in a continuous length)
- One 2½" (6.4cm) square of medium tan for the block centre

Assembling the block

1. Cut each of the four assorted medium and light brown solids into four 1½" x 6½" (3.8 x 16.5cm) strips.
2. Cut the dark brown solid fabric into sixteen 1½" x 6½" (3.8 x 16.5cm) strips.
3. Sew each of the four medium and light brown strips of each colour with four of the dark brown strips to create four striped panels, as shown, each 6½" x 8½" (16.5 x 21.6cm). Press.
4. Arrange the four striped panels around the centre square and sew around it using a partial seam as shown. For the first side, sew only the first 1" (2.5cm) – seam 1.
5. Now working in an anti-clockwise direction, sew the remaining full seams around the centre square (seams 2, 3 and 4).
6. Finally sew seam 5, completing seam 1 by sewing across the remaining centre square and off the end of the strip-pieced unit.

RAINBOW HEART

I designed and made this quilt to honour diversity and the beauty of our rainbow-coloured world. It's easy to piece from simple rectangles, but keep in mind that there are eighteen seams one way and only two the other way. Seams need to be sewn an accurate ¼" (6mm) throughout if your block is to turn out square! Don't be alarmed by the number of steps – it's a very simple block. Just take it one step at a time!

For one block you will need:

Finished block size: 38" (95.5cm) square

- 2½" (6.4cm) strips of 19 different fabrics, ranging from red through the rainbow to deep violet (or pick a favourite colour and shade from light at the outer edge to dark in the centre and back out to light)
- 2½" (6.4cm) black strips, trimmed to length as you go

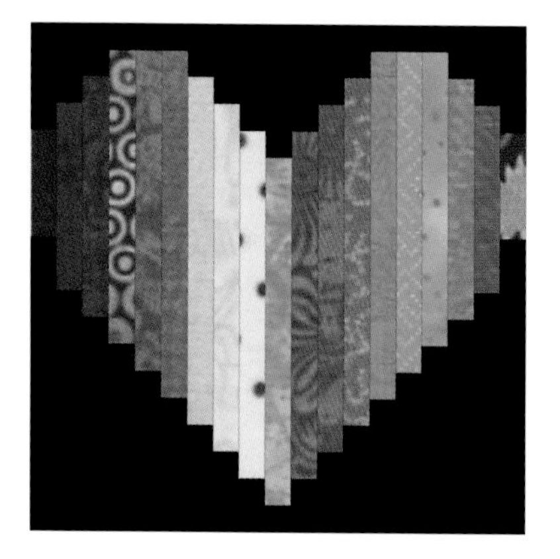

Use the same colour for the centre cornerstone, binding and quilting thread for a nicely harmonized look to your quilt. Pick your favourite rainbow colour for this!

27 RAINBOW HEART

Assembling the block

All sequences go: black, rainbow colour, black. Work in vertical rows from left to right. Cut your pieces to size and arrange the strips as follows.

1. Row 1: 8½" (21.6cm), 8½" (21.6cm), 22½" (57.2cm).
2. Row 2: 6½" (16.5cm), 14½" (36.8cm), 18½" (47cm).
3. Row 3: 4½" (11.4cm), 18½" (47cm), 16½" (42cm).
4. Row 4: 2½" (6.4cm), 22½" (57.2cm), 14½" (36.8cm).
5. Row 5: 2½" (6.4cm), 24½" (62.2cm), 12½" (31.7cm).
6. Row 6: 2½" (6.4cm), 28½" (72.4cm), 10½" (26.7cm).
7. Row 7: 4½" (11.4cm), 26½" (67.3cm), 8½" (21.6cm).
8. Row 8: 6½" (16.5cm), 26½" (67.3cm), 6½" (16.5cm).
9. Row 9: 8½" (21.6cm), 26½" (67.3cm), 4½" (11.4cm).
10. Row 10: 10½" (26.7cm), 26½" (67.3cm), 2½" (6.4cm).

The remainder of the block is the flip side of the first nine rows, however, make sure you change the colours as you go to continue the rainbow!

11. Row 11: as row 9.
12. Row 12: as row 8.
13. Row 13: as row 7.
14. Row 14: as row 6.
15. Row 15: as row 5.
16. Row 16: as row 4.
17. Row 17: as row 3.
18. Row 18: as row 2.
19. Row 19: as row 1.
20. Sew the three rectangles of each row together.
21. Sew the rows together.
22. Press the seams one way.

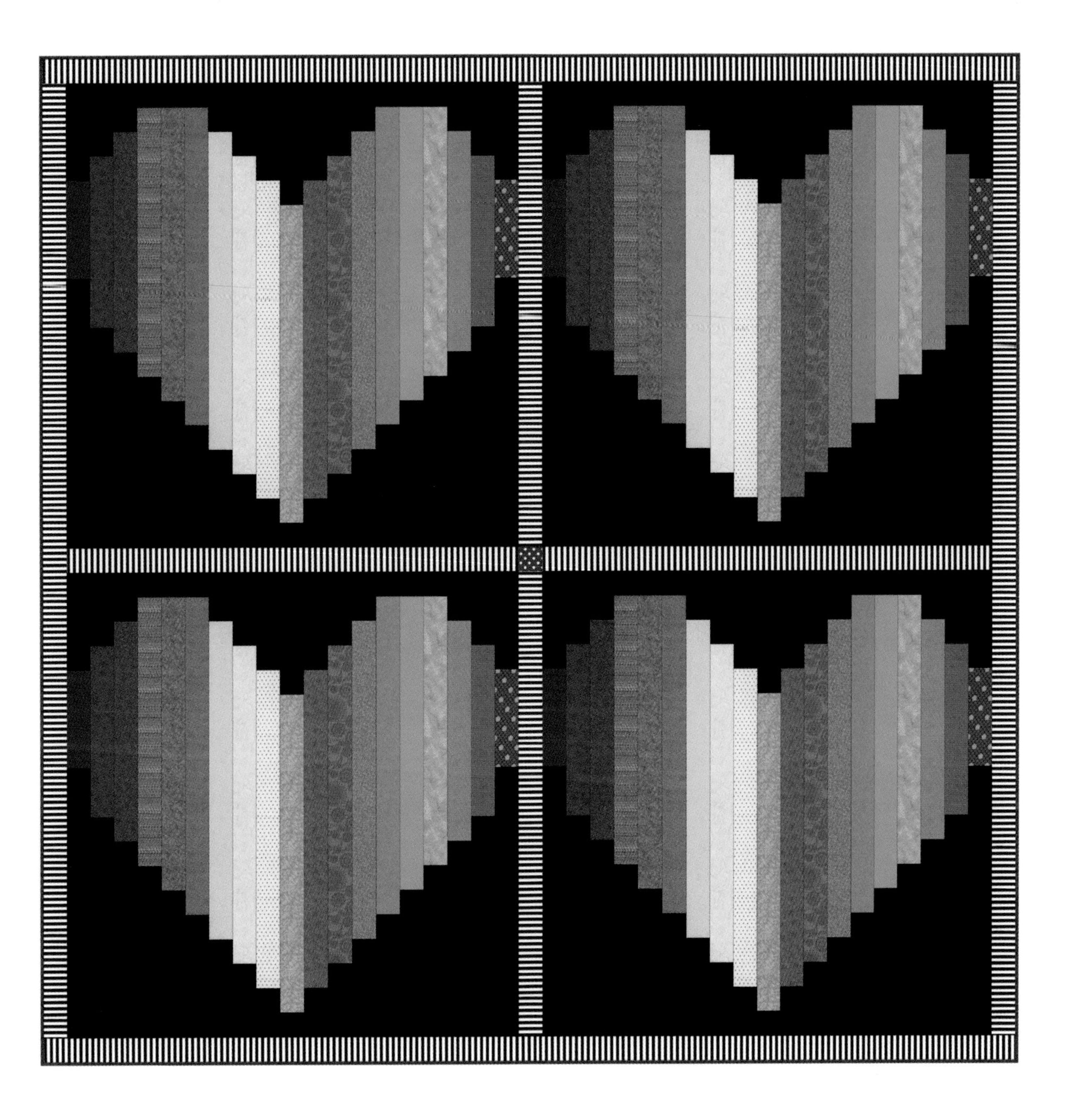

SUGGESTED LAYOUT

For my virtual quilt, I have set four blocks together in a two by two arrangement with 2" (5.1cm) finished black-and-white striped sashing and border. There's a 2" (5.1cm) finished square in the centre, too. The quilt finishes at 82" x 82" (208.3 x 208.3cm).

OLD GLORY (FAUX LOG CABIN)

Faux log cabin blocks are super fast, super easy and give just as many setting options as the more traditional log cabin block. I've made a quilt to celebrate my love of Americana, but you could easily use this block in so many more different ways.

SUGGESTED LAYOUT

My virtual quilt uses thirty-six faux log cabin blocks, with alternate blocks rotated 90 degrees, plus twelve assorted navy blue blocks each cut at 10½" (26.7cm) square and appliquéd with a tan star (see template on page 221). The finished quilt is 80" x 60" (203.2 x 152.4cm).

For old world charm and a little naivety, enlarge or reduce the star template (see page 221) to create different-sized stars, as I have. Allow your scissors to wobble slightly as you cut to make each one just a little bit different to all the others.

For one block you will need

Finished block size: 10" (25.4cm) square

- Five assorted red print strips, each 2½" (6.4cm) wide, then cut at 2½" (6.4cm), 4½" (11.4cm), 6½" (16.5cm), 8½" (21.6cm) and 10½" (26.7cm)
- Four assorted tan print strips each 2½" (6.4cm) wide, then cut at 2½" (6.4cm), 4½" (11.4cm), 6½" (16.5cm) and 8½" (21.6cm)

Assembling the block

1. Arrange the strips as shown.
2. Sew the units into pieced strips. Press the seams one way.
3. Join the strips together.

FLOATING TILES

Most of us have fallen in love with a beautiful large-scale fabric, bought it and then had a crisis of conscience... what to do with it? How can you cut something so pretty into tiny pieces? Don't! Feature your favourite large-scale prints in this easy optical illusion quilt instead!

SUGGESTED LAYOUT

For my virtual quilt, I have set sixteen Floating Tiles blocks in a four by four arrangement, separated by 1" (2.5cm) finished sashing using the same light tan print as I used in the blocks. A 1" (2.5cm) finished border makes the whole centre of the quilt 'float' and then I've added a final 3" (7.6cm) finished border using one of the feature prints. The whole quilt measures 51" x 51" (129.5 x 129.5cm).

Other solid shades can be used to create the 'shadow' – medium to dark grey works well with a white print for the 'highlight' instead of light tan. Use a 'shadow' and 'highlight' that complement your choice of feature prints.

For one block you will need

Finished block size: 10" (25.4cm) square

- One 9½" (24.1cm) square of large-scale feature print
- Two 1½" (3.8cm) strips of medium brown solid, one cut at 8½" (21.6cm) and one cut at 9½" (24.1cm)
- Two 1½" (3.8cm) squares of light tan print

Assembling the block

1. Sew a light tan print square to one end of each of the medium brown solid strips. Press.
2. Sew the 9½" (24.1cm) pieced strip to the bottom of your feature fabric, ensuring that the light tan square is on the right. Press.
3. Sew the 10½" (26.7cm) pieced strip to the left-hand side of the feature print, ensuring that the light tan square is at the top.

30 JEWEL BOX

A strikingly modern quilt made of simple strips and squares. Select jewel-bright tones and surround them in platinum or 24-carat gold – the choice is yours!

For one block you will need

Finished block size: 8" x 16" (20.3 x 40.7cm)

- Sapphire blue solid: one 3½" x 10½" (8.9 x 26.7cm) rectangle
- Platinum solid: two 1½" x 2½" (3.8 x 6.4cm) rectangles and two 1½" x 12½" (3.8 x 31.7cm) rectangles
- Emerald solid: two 2½" x 12½" (6.4 x 31.7cm) rectangles and two 2½" x 8½" (6.4 x 21.6cm) rectangles
- Light grey/blue: two 2½" (6.4cm) squares, diagonals marked on the wrong side of each square, lightly in pencil
- Medium grey/blue: two 2½" (6.4cm) squares of each, diagonals marked on the wrong side of each square lightly in pencil

Assembling the block

1. Sew the short platinum rectangles to the short edges of the sapphire blue rectangle, press.
2. Sew the long platinum rectangles to the remaining two sides of the sapphire blue rectangle, press.
3. Sew the long emerald green rectangles to the long sides of the block centre, press, then sew the short emerald green rectangles to the remaining two sides, press.
4. Using the stitch and flip method (see page 20), sew the light grey/blue squares to the upper right and lower left corners, sewing along the line you marked and trimming the background away. Repeat on the remaining two corners with the medium grey/blue squares.

Sew a thread's width inside the marked line when using the 'stitch and flip' method – this will allow for the top fabric to be pressed back and is more accurate than sewing right on the line.

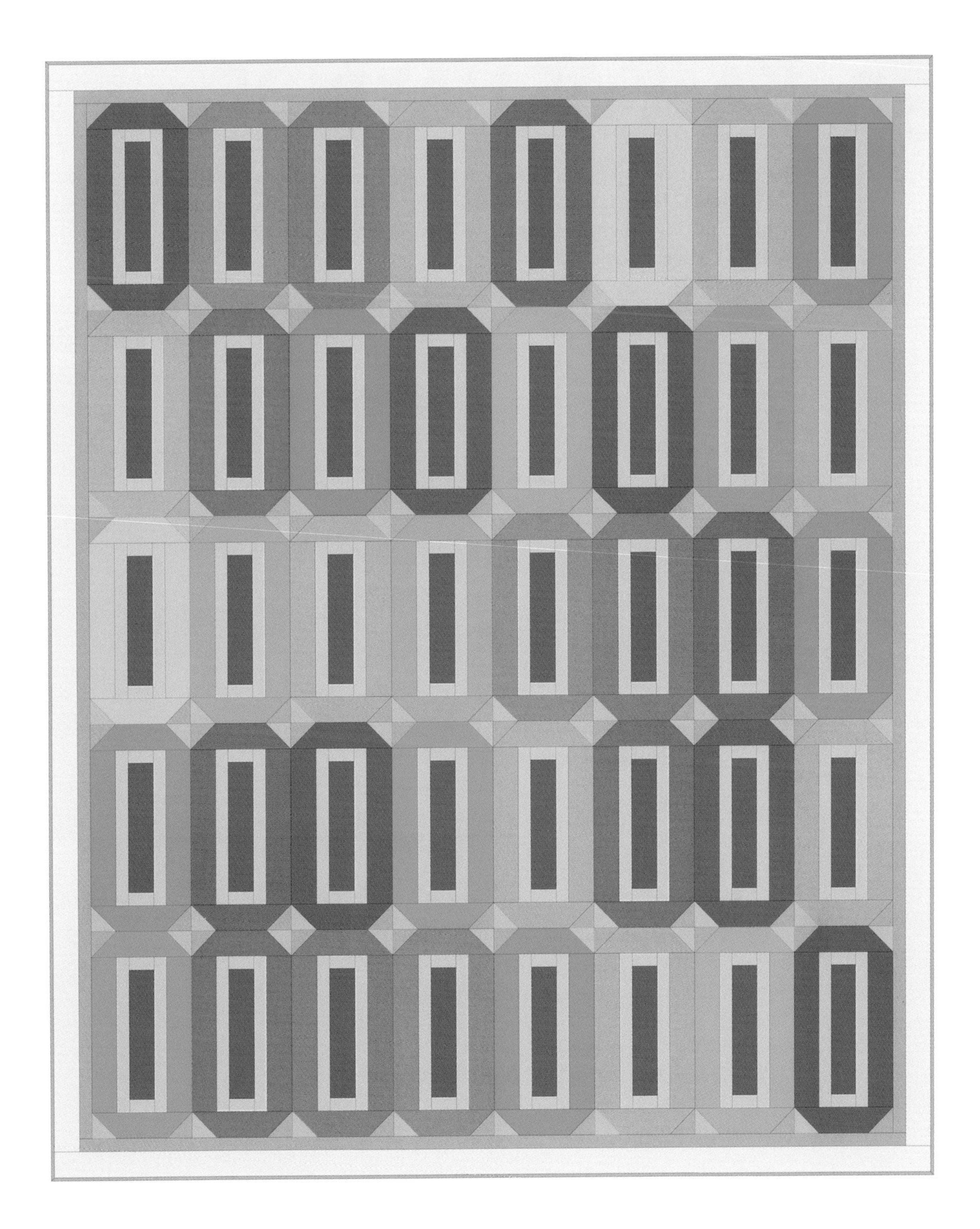

SUGGESTED LAYOUT

For my virtual quilt, I have made forty Jewel Box blocks in different colours and set them in an eight by five arrangement. With 1" (2.5cm) and 2" (5.1cm) finished borders, the quilt measures 70" x 86" (177.8 x 218.4cm).

31 KANSAS HAYRIDE

Dark and snuggly quilts are always the best when you need a little comfort and this chequered rail fence block is the perfect place to show off your favourite 'Kansas Troubles' prints. I just love their designs for Moda – but any collection of high-contrast fabrics would work well in this pattern.

SUGGESTED LAYOUT

For my virtual quilt, I have set twenty-five blocks in a five by five arrangement, turning every other block through 90 degrees. The finished quilt is 60" x 60" (152.4 x 152.4cm).

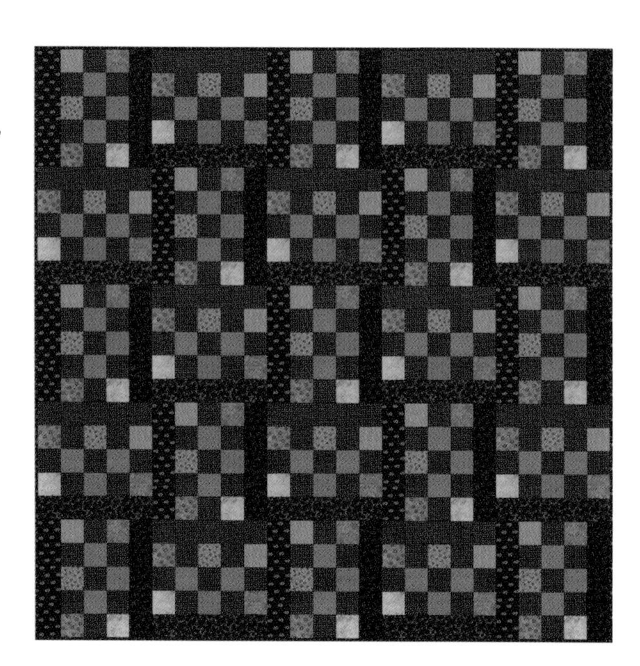

Strip piece the chequerboard sections for a faster quilt (see page 17). This quilt would look lovely with an appliqué border – use the swags and flowers from my Pineapple Log Cabin quilt (page 160) to add extra va va voom!

For one block you will need

Finished block size: 12" (30.5cm) square

- Eight 2½" (6.4cm) squares in assorted gold and cheddar prints
- Seven 2½" (6.4cm) squares in black print fabric
- Two 2½" x 10½" (6.4 x 26.7cm) strips in black/gold print

Assembling the block

1. Arrange the 2½" (6.4cm) squares into three columns of five squares, alternating the colours. Columns 1 and 3 start with a gold square, column 2 starts with a black square.
2. Sew the columns of squares into strips, then sew the strips together.
3. Sew the 2½" x 10½" (6.4 x 26.7cm) black print strips either side of the chequerboard centre.

PUSS IN THE CORNER

Rather too simply referred to sometimes as the 'uneven nine-patch', I much prefer the rather more fanciful name of 'puss in the corner' for this block. Although it's often relegated to the role of 'alternate block' and paired with something showier and more attention seeking, I rather like a quilt made with just this block. The large centre squares are a great place to show off quilting, appliqué, embroidery or just a favourite piece of (cat-themed?!) fabric.

SUGGESTED LAYOUT

For my virtual quilt, I have set sixteen blocks in a four by four arrangement. This would be a great project for using a 2½" (6.4cm) pre-cut strip roll. I've added finished 2" (5.1cm) sashings and cornerstones and a final 2" (5.1cm) finished border. The quilt measures 46" x 46" (116.8 x 116.8cm).

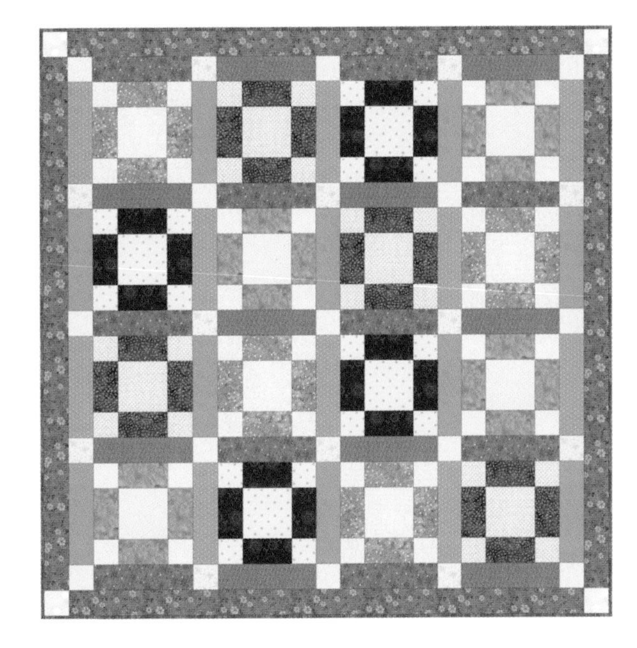

If you want to feature machine embroidery in the centre squares, stabilize and hoop 8" (20.3cm) squares of fabric, embroider your design, then centre and trim to 4½" x 4½" (11.4 x 11.4cm). If you have vintage embroideries that you'd like to feature, it's a good idea to stabilize these too with light fusible interfacing before you cut them to size.

For one block you will need

Finished block size: 8" (20.3cm) square

- Four 2½" x 6½" (6.4 x 16.5cm) rectangles in coloured batik
- Four 2½" (6.4cm) squares in light cream batik
- One 4½" (11.4cm) square in light cream batik

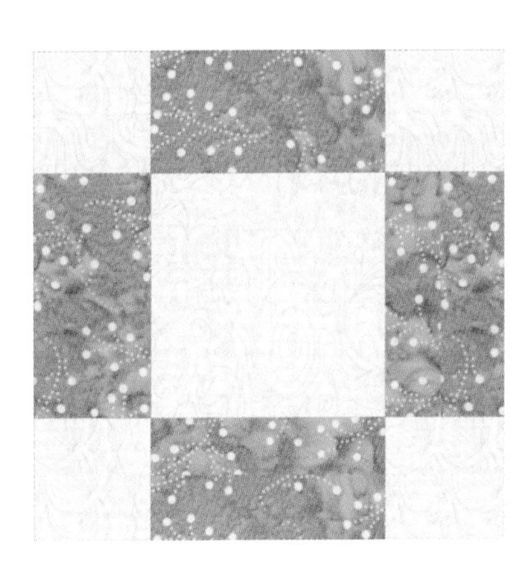

Assembling the block

1. Arrange the patches as shown.
2. Sew the patches into rows, pressing the seams towards the coloured batik.
3. Join the rows together, matching the seam intersections carefully.

33 GIFTED

Beautifully wrapped gifts, trimmed with ribbon and maybe a bow - the anticipation of unwrapping is always the most fun! These 'gifts' could be made using a pack of pre-cut 10" (25.4cm) squares for a super-quick quilt - perfect for 'gifting'!

For one block you will need

Finished block size: 10" (25.4cm) square

- One 10" (25.4cm) square in print fabric
- One 1½" x 21" (3.8 x 53.3cm) strip in co-ordinating or contrasting solid

Assembling the block

1. From the 10" (25.4cm) square cut one 3½" (8.9cm) strip. Sub-cut this into a 3½" (8.9cm) square and a 6½" (16.5cm) rectangle
2. From the remainder of the 10" (25.4cm) square cut a 6½" (16.5cm) square and a 3½" x 6½" (8.9 x 16.5cm) rectangle... no waste! Ta dah!
3. Cut the 1½" (3.8cm) solid strip into three pieces: one 3½" (8.9cm), one 6½" (16.5cm) and one 10½" (26.7cm).
4. Arrange the pieces as shown.
5. Sew the 3½" (8.9cm) print square, 1½" x 3½" (3.8 x 8.9cm) solid strip and 3½" x 6½" (8.9 x 16.5cm) print rectangle together. Sew the 6½" x 3½" (16.5 x 8.9cm) print rectangle, the 1½" x 6½" (3.8 x 16.5cm) solid strip and the 6½" (16.5cm) print square together. Join these units to either side of the 1½" x 10½" (3.8 x 26.7cm) solid strip.

Check your pre-cuts carefully! Measure them from side to side to determine the actual size and trim down if necessary.

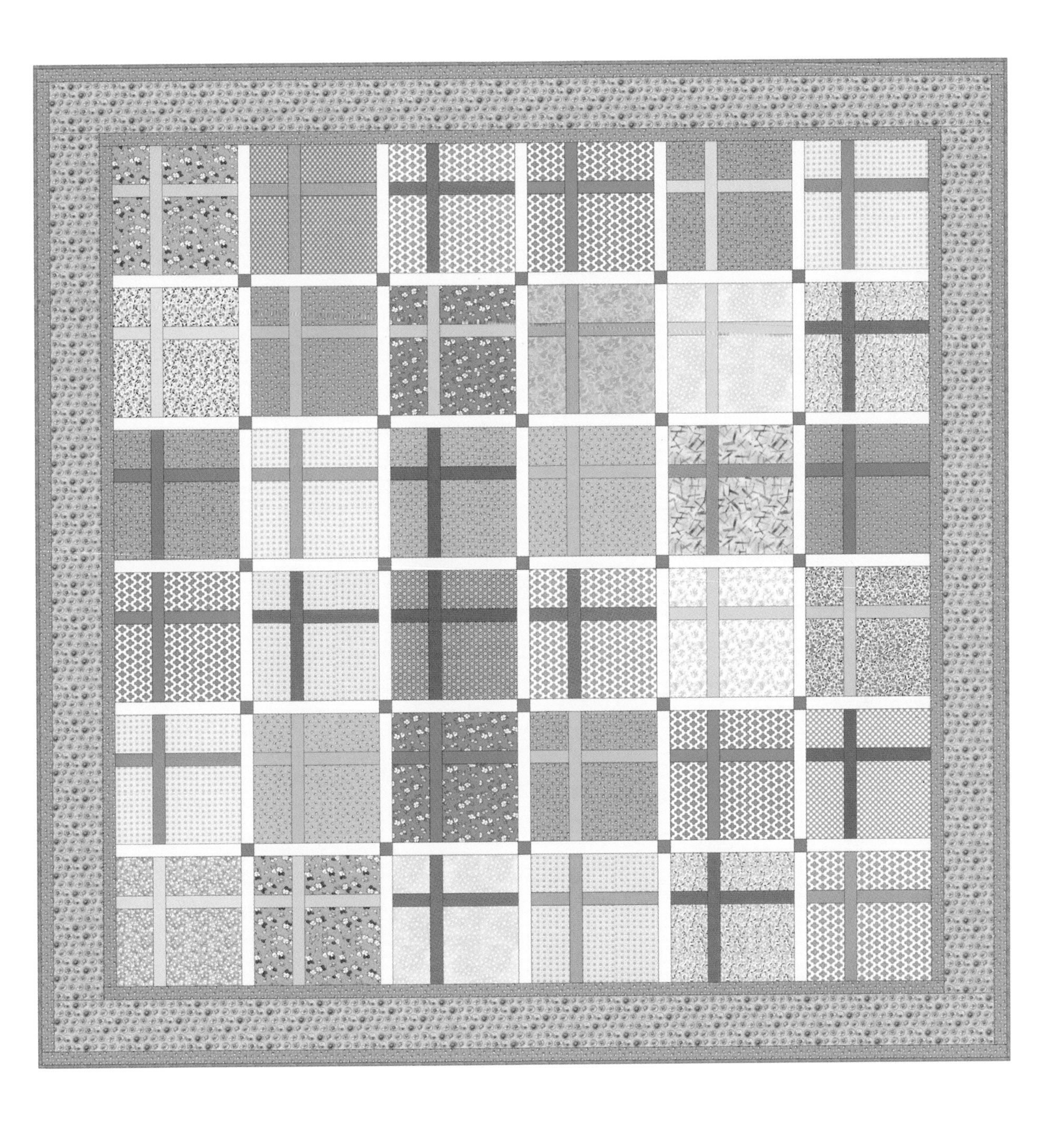

SUGGESTED LAYOUT

For my virtual quilt I have set thirty-six blocks in a six by six arrangement, separated by 1" (2.5cm) finished sashing and cornerstones, a 1" (2.5cm) finished border, a 4" (10.2cm) finished border and a final 1" (2.5cm) finished border. The whole quilt measures 77" x 77" (195.6 x 195.6cm).

SPRINGTIME IN OSLO

This cute baby quilt is simplicity itself and is made just from three pieces of fabric: two strips and a square. This block is designed to use pre-cut charm squares and 2½" (6.4cm) strips so you can get straight to the sewing! Also pictured right (on the bed), Kites (page 112).

SUGGESTED LAYOUT

My quilt alternates A and B blocks. The A blocks are described below. The B blocks are made in exactly the same way, but the fabrics are reversed: use a 5" (12.7cm) charm square of print fabric and 2½" (6.4cm) strips of white fabric. Set twenty-five A blocks with twenty-four B blocks in a seven by seven arrangement. I've added a 4" (10.2cm) finished border by sewing odd lengths of 2½" (6.4cm) pre-cut strips together until they are long enough to cut borders from. I've added two of these informal borders. The quilt finishes at 53½" x 53½" (135.9 x 135.9cm).

For one A block you will need

Finished block size: 6½" (16.5cm) square

- One 5" (12.7cm) charm square in white
- Two 2½" (6.4cm) strips in pattern, each 13" (33cm) long

Assembling the block

1. Cut the 2½" (6.4cm) strips into two pieces, one 5" (12.7cm) in length and the other 7" (17.8cm). (You will have pieces left over for another block.)
2. Sew one of the short strips to the bottom edge of the 5" (12.7cm) charm square. Press the seam towards the strip.
3. Sew the 7" (17.8cm) strip of patterned fabric to the left-hand side of the block. Press the seam towards the strip you just added.

Remember to label every quilt you make. Include your name, the date you started and finished your quilt and other pertinent information, such as who the quilt was made for or the designer. Use a fabric marking pen or machine embroider the label and handstitch it to the back of your quilt.

MANHATTAN

Quentin Crisp has always been something of a hero to me... I remember him saying that when people say America they mean New York – and by New York they mean Manhattan. When I think of Manhattan, I think of the skyline at night and all those twinkling lights in a sea of blue and grey and shadow...

SUGGESTED LAYOUT

For my virtual quilt, I made twenty-five Manhattan blocks and set them in a five by five arrangement, turning alternate blocks through 90 degrees in each row. I added a ¼" (6mm) folded flange border in bright yellow and a final 2" (5.1cm) finished border in bright blue. The quilt is 34" x 34" (86.4 x 86.4cm) and would make a very special modern baby quilt.

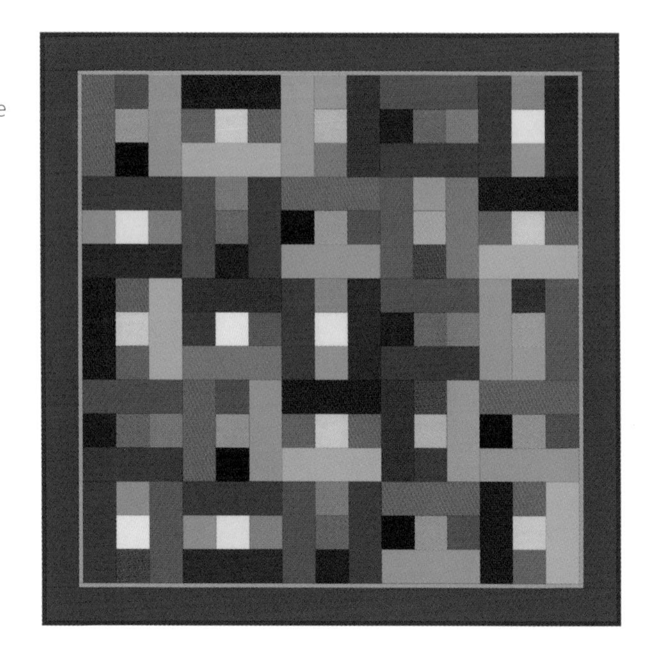

Use a #75 needle for your piecing. My favourites are Schmetz Microtex needles. Use a nice fine thread in them.

For one block you will need

Finished block size: 6" (15.2cm) square

- One 2½" (6.4cm) square in bright yellow solid
- Two 2½" (6.4cm) squares in assorted bright and medium dark blue solids
- Two 2½" x 6½" (6.4 x 16.5cm) rectangles, each in a different medium grey/blue/turquoise

Assembling the block

1. Sew a 2½" (6.4cm) blue square either side of the centre yellow square. Press the seams away from the centre.
2. Sew a 2½" x 6½" (6.4 x 16.5cm) blue/grey/turquoise rectangle either side of the centre unit. Press the seams towards the rectangles.

36 COBBLES

I live in North Yorkshire in the UK, and one of the most famous places in the whole county is the city of York. I love to visit 'The Shambles', an ancient cobbled street much loved by visitors and locals alike. The cobbled street inspired this very easy quilt.

SUGGESTED LAYOUT

For my virtual quilt, I have made a total of sixteen blocks. Eight of the blocks start and finish with a red rectangle (as in the instructions below) and eight of them start and finish with a gold rectangle. Sew the blocks into four rows of four. I've added borders 1 and 3 at 2" (5.1cm) finished and border 2 at 6" (15.2cm) finished, making a 56" x 68" (142.2 x 172.7cm) quilt.

To vary the number of 'fabrics' in a quilt without buying extras, take a look at the 'wrong' side of your fabrics. Some of the reverse sides will be softer and more subtle versions of the fabric and are perfect to use 'wrong way up' for extra variety.

For one block you will need

Finished block size: 9" x 12" (22.9 x 30.5cm)

- Two 3½" x 6½" (8.9cm) rectangles in assorted red prints
- Two 3½" x 6½" (8.9cm) rectangles in assorted gold prints
- Four 3½" (8.9cm) squares in assorted cream prints

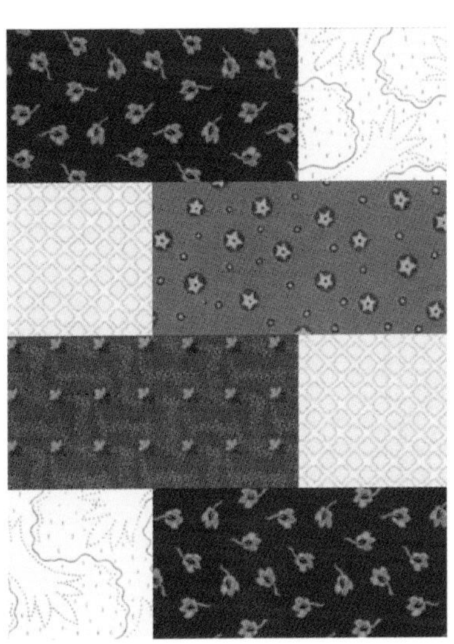

Assembling the block

1. Sew a red or gold rectangle to a cream square as shown. Press the seams towards the rectangle. Make four.
2. Arrange the pieced units, alternating the end with the square, and placing the red rectangles at the top and bottom of the stack and the gold rectangles in the second and third rows. Sew the block together.
3. Press the seams one way.

RUSSELL SQUARE

I'm always looking for fresh quilting inspiration so I ventured once more into the London Underground (after the success of the 'Covent Garden' quilt in my last book) where I found a wonderful quilting pattern on the walls of Russell Square tube station platform.

For one block you will need

Finished block size: 10" (25.4cm) square

- Dark grey mottled print: five 2½" x 4½" (6.4 x 11.4cm) rectangles plus one 2½" (6.4cm) square
- Assorted light turquoise prints: three 2½" x 4½" (6.4 x 11.4cm) rectangles plus two 2½" (6.4cm) squares
- Assorted light purple prints: two 2½" x 4½" (6.4 x 11.4cm) rectangles plus two 2½" (6.4cm) squares

Assembling the block

1. Arrange your rectangles and squares in vertical columns, as shown.
2. Sew the units into columns. Press the seams towards the dark grey fabric patches.
3. Sew the columns together, then press the seams one way.

This would make a great wall quilt for a teenager's bedroom. Add a hanging sleeve by following the instructions on page 33.

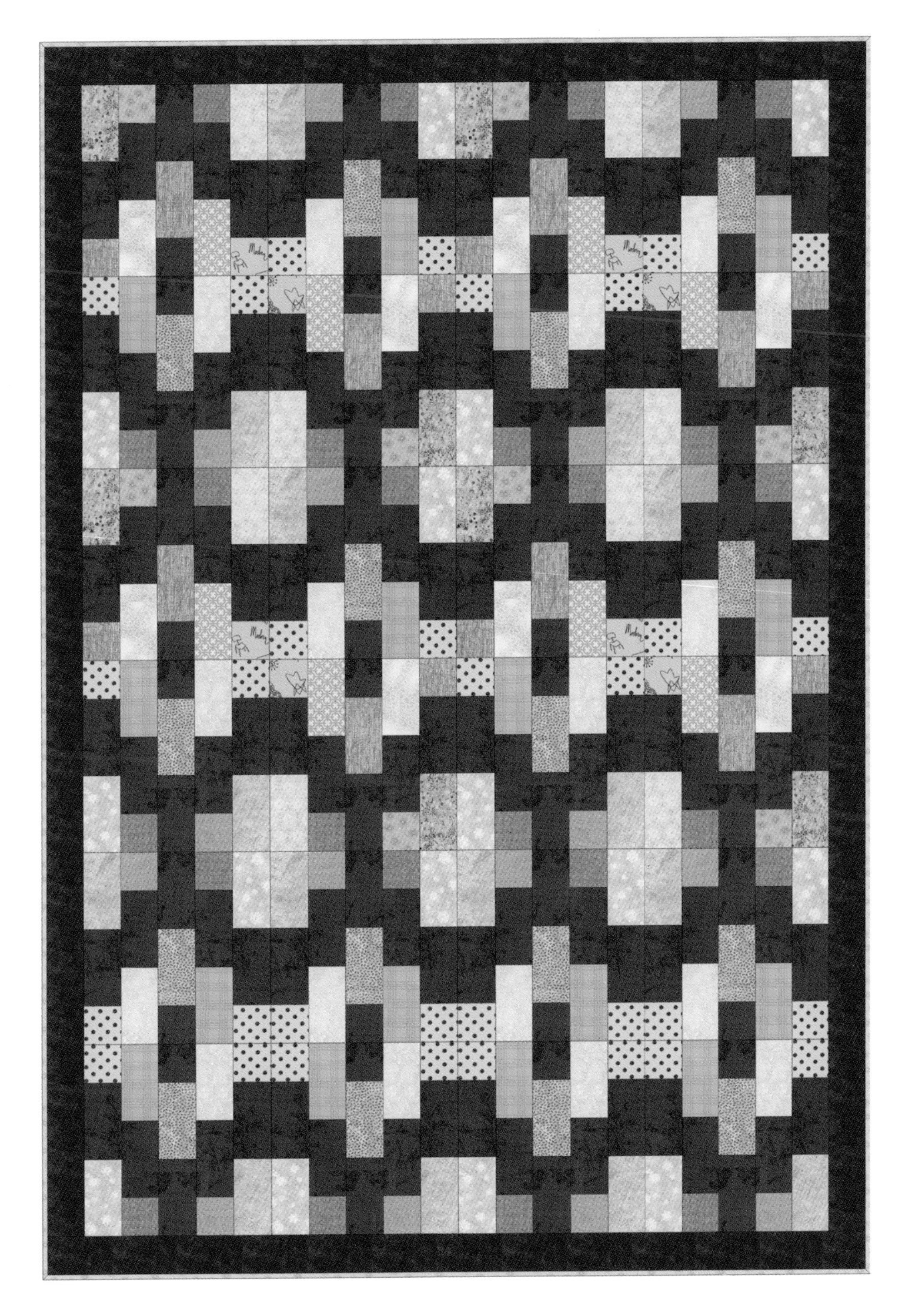

SUGGESTED LAYOUT

For my virtual quilt I've arranged twenty-four Russell Square blocks in a four by six arrangement. I've added a 2" (5.1cm) finished border all around in dark grey mottled fabric to frame the quilt. The finished quilt is 44" x 64" (111.8 x 162.6cm).

NICELY FRAMED

Perfect for those fabrics that are just too gorgeous to cut up! In this design, 12½" (31.7cm) squares of your favourite fabrics can take centre stage, surrounded by simple pieced sashings that really frame the prints to perfection.

For one block you will need

Finished block size: 20" (50.8cm) square

- One 12½" (31.7cm) square in bold feature print
- Two 4½" (11.4cm) squares in light green print or solid
- One 2½" x 55" (6.4 x 139.7cm) strip in light green print or solid
- Two 4½" (11.4cm) squares in medium purple print or solid
- One 2½" x 55" (6.4 x 139.7cm) strip in medium purple print or solid

Assembling the block

1. Sew the green and purple 2½" (6.4cm) strips together down one long side, to make a strip-pieced unit 4½" x 55" (11.4 x 139.7cm). (This can be in two sections if you cannot find fabrics that are 55"/139.7cm in length.)
2. Press the seam allowance towards the darker fabric.
3. Subcut the strip-pieced unit into twelve units, each 4½" x 4½" (11.4 x 11.4cm).
4. Arrange three of the units on each side of the feature square and place a 4½" (11.4cm) plain square at each corner. Note the order of colours in the diagram.
5. Sew the units and the squares together into rows, then sew the rows together.

As an alternative, make this quilt with a pack of pre-cut 10" (25.4cm) squares for the centres. Trim the squares to 9½" x 9½" (24.1 x 24.1cm) and use strips that are 2" (5.1cm) cut. Cut your strip-pieced units into 3½" (8.9cm) segments for 15" (38.1cm) finished blocks.

SUGGESTED LAYOUT

My quilt uses thirteen Nicely Framed blocks set on point with 1½" (3.8cm) finished sashing and cornerstones. For the setting triangles, cut two 29⅝" (75.2cm) squares and then cross-cut them on both diagonals to yield eight triangles. You'll also need to cut two 15⅛" (38.4cm) squares and cross-cut them on one diagonal to yield four triangles for the corners. The quilt finishes at approximately 91" x 91" (231 x 231cm).

I SPY THROUGH THE ATTIC WINDOW

'I spy' quilts are fun on every level - gathering the conversational prints gives up a chance to indulge the big kid in all of us, making them is super and the joy of playing with younger generations keeps us all young at heart.

For one block you will need

Finished block size: 10" (25.4cm) square

- One 6½" (16.5cm) square in conversational print
- One 5" x 11" (12.7 x 28cm) strip in light green tone-on-tone print
- One 5" x 11" (12.7 x 28cm) strip in medium green tone-on-tone print

Assembling the block

1. Use the template provided (see page 222) to cut the two outer pieces of the 'I-spy' window frame. Make sure that the light side of the frame uses the template as it is and the dark side of the frame uses the template in reverse.
2. Sew the medium green strip to the bottom edge of the conversational print square, stopping ¼" (6mm) in from the left-hand side and backstitching. Sew the light green strip to the left-hand side of the conversational print square, again stopping ¼" (6mm) from the lower edge.
3. Fold the block in half on the diagonal, matching up the light and medium green strips. Pin at the point you stopped sewing and backstitched on both strips, which should match up perfectly. Sew the last part of the seam from that point out towards the slanted edge of the strips.
4. Press the seam open.

If you can only find 5" (12.7cm) charm squares for your conversational prints, add a strip of solid fabric all around each patch and trim back to a 6½" (16.5cm) square.

SUGGESTED LAYOUT

For my virtual quilt I have set sixteen blocks in a four by four arrangement. I've added a 1" (2.5cm) finished border in a black-and-white stripe. The quilt finishes at 42" x 42" (106.7 x 106.7cm).

40 WOVEN #2

A lattice framework is the perfect complement to a favourite large-scale floral, or use the same frames to surround a collection of conversational or novelty prints. What a great alternative to a child's 'I spy' quilt!

For one block you will need

Finished block size: 8" (20.3cm) square

- Four 3½" (8.9cm) squares in large-scale floral print
- Two assorted dark brown prints, each cut into one 1½" x 4½" (3.8 x 11.4cm) rectangle and one 1½" x 3½" (3.8 x 8.9cm) rectangle
- Two assorted golden yellow prints, each cut into one 1½" x 4½" (3.8 x 11.4cm) rectangle and one 1½" x 3½" (3.8 x 8.9cm) rectangle

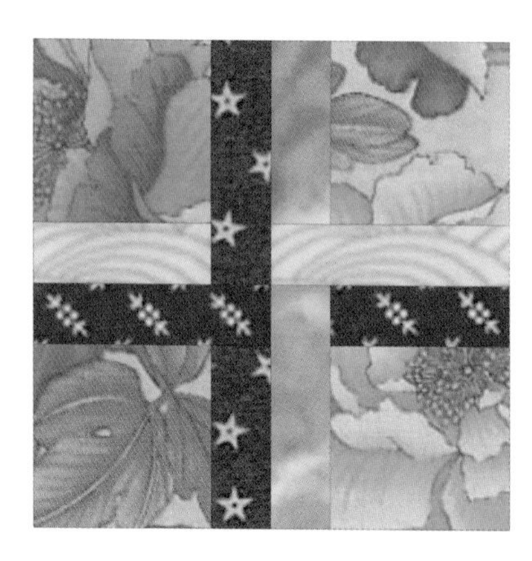

Assembling the block

1. Arrange your golden yellow and dark brown strips around the four floral print squares to create the woven effect, as shown.
2. Separate your block into four units: sew the shorter rectangle to the floral square first, press back, then add the longer rectangle to the adjacent side. Sew all four units.
3. Join the units together.

Flange borders are a great way to add a 'pop' of colour around a block or in a border without affecting the size of the quilt. Follow the instructions on page 30 to learn how to make and sew a flange border.

SUGGESTED LAYOUT

My quilt uses sixteen Woven #2 blocks joined in a four by four arrangement. I've added a ¼" (6mm) finished flange border in golden yellow, a 1" (2.5cm) finished border in dark brown and a final 4" (10.2cm) finished border using the same large-scale floral as the blocks. My quilt finishes at 42" x 42" (106.7 x 106.7cm).

TRIANGLES

Triangles are, for me, the most exciting of patchwork shapes, since they introduce a diagonal to our piecing – and with diagonals comes the possibility of endless movement and direction. The quilts in this chapter showcase that wonderful trinity of sides in projects that really celebrate the shape in all its glory.

THREE STEPS TO HEAVEN...

Quilting heaven, that is! Yes, there are triangles in many of the other quilts in this book, but here they take centre stage and work their magic in an array of beautiful projects, some easy, others a challenge. Whether it's the never-so-humble half square triangle, its rather more exotic cousin, the half rectangle triangle, the 'couldn't quilt without' flying geese and ever-so-popular quarter square triangle, the equilateral triangle or that queen of the optical effect, the triangle in a square... I love these three-sided beauties with a passion.

Triangle piecing has probably attracted the most attention over the last few years, with increasingly wild and imaginative ways to create and use them. Whether you make them large and trim them back, foundation paper piece, add 'stitch and flip' corners or use a template, the key to success is accuracy – so use whichever method gives you the best results, regardless of my instructions.

MIGRATION

I love the changing seasons and this quilt sums up Autumn or Fall for me - warm rich browns, golds and plums as the leaves change colour, the fruits ripen and the geese fly South for the Winter. It would look equally stunning in your favourite palette.

SUGGESTED LAYOUT

My virtual quilt uses thirty-six blocks in a six by six arrangement to make a quilt that is 72" x 72" (182.8 x 182.8cm).

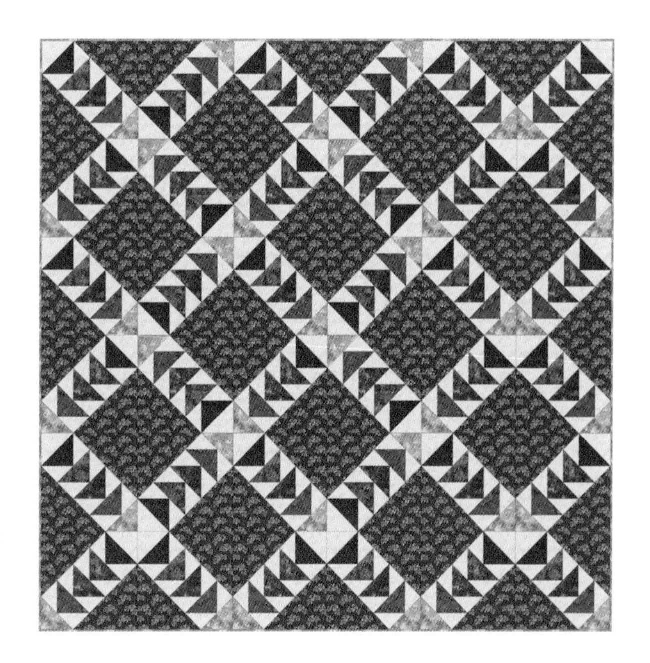

If your pattern calls for triangles with bias edges (as this pattern does), it's a good idea to starch your fabrics before you cut them. A light spray of starch, followed by pressing, will stiffen the fabric slightly, helping to control any stretch in the fabric. A second light spray followed by pressing will give a firmer finish and is preferable to one really heavy spray.

For two blocks you will need

Finished block size: 12" (30.5cm) square

- Five batiks in rich shades of purple, brown, gold, orange and yellow (5"/12.7cm charm squares are ideal), cut into 4⅞" (12.4cm) squares and then cross-cut on one diagonal to yield half square triangles (HSTs)
- Four 3¼" (8.3cm) squares of light tan batik, cross-cut on both diagonals to yield eight quarter square triangles (QSTs)
- One 4⅞" (12.4cm) square of light tan batik, cross-cut on one diagonal to yield two half square triangles (HSTs)
- Two 8⅞" (22.5cm) square of brown leaf print fabric, cross-cut on one diagonal to yield two half square triangles (HSTs)

Assembling the block

1. Sew the small light tan batik HSTs to the assorted purple, brown, gold and orange triangles to make four flying geese units.
2. Sew these together in a row and add the gold HST at one end and the light tan large HST at the other, as shown.
3. Sew the brown leaf print triangles to either side of the flying geese unit.

42 KITES

You might see stars when you first look at this quilt, but look at those stars and you should see four kites coming together. See page 99 for photograph of a finished quilt.

For one block you will need

Finished block size: 9" (22.9cm) square

- 5" (12.7cm) squares in four assorted blue print fabrics
- 5" (12.7cm) squares in four assorted cream or tan prints

Assembling the block

1. Download and print (see page 220 for link) or copy the kite and side templates A and B on page 222.
2. Cut the shapes out carefully from fabric. Cut four kite shapes from blue fabrics, and eight side triangles from cream or tan fabrics. Note that the side triangles are not the same: there is a left- and a right-facing triangle in each unit. (You will need to flip the template.)
3. Sew two of the side triangles to the sides of one of the kite piece. Press the first side back before you add the second. Make four units.
4. Join the four units together, as shown.

These Kite units are very versatile and can be set in all kinds of fun ways. When you have made a batch of units, have fun trying out different patterns before you sew them together. You might just come up with a brand new design!

SUGGESTED LAYOUT

For my virtual quilt, I have made thirty Kite blocks and set them together with 4½" (11.4cm) finished sashing and four-patch cornerstones. The cornerstones are made from 2¾" (7cm) squares – two blue and two cream, sewn together to make a 4½" (11.4cm) finished four-patch. The whole quilt measures 72" x 85½" (182.8 x 217.2cm).

43 JEWEL OF THE NILE

The 'jewel box' block is an easy, classic block that combines triangles and squares to great effect. Those diagonal 'chains' of squares can be turned this way and that to create all kinds of beautiful settings.

For one block you will need

Finished block size: 8" (20.3cm) square

- Four 2½" (6.4cm) squares in assorted jewel-coloured batiks
- Four 2½" (6.4cm) squares in assorted ivory prints
- Two 4⅞" (12.4cm) squares in assorted ivory print squares
- Two 4⅞" (12.4cm) squares in assorted jewel-coloured batiks

Assembling the block

1. Join two jewel-coloured 2½" (6.4cm) squares with two ivory 2½" (6.4cm) squares to make a four-patch. Make two units.
2. Mark the diagonal lightly in pencil on the back of the ivory print 4⅞" (12.4cm) squares. Layer each one, right sides together, with a 4⅞" (12.4cm) jewel-coloured square. Sew ¼" (6mm) either side of the drawn line and cut apart along the line to yield four half square triangle units (HSTs). You will need two for this block.
3. Arrange the four-patch units and the HSTs, as shown. Sew the units together.

Always make one block in its entirety and make sure you are happy with the colours, your accuracy and the methods used, before you commit to making the whole quilt.

SUGGESTED LAYOUT

For my virtual quilt, I set eighty blocks in an eight by ten formation and added borders 1 and 3 at 1" (2.3cm) finished and border 2 at 4" (10.2cm) finished. The quilt measures 76" x 92" (193 x 233.7cm), a great size for a double bed or a large single.

PINE BLOSSOM

No need for tricky templates when you can use the stitch and flip method to add triangle tips to simple strips. This makes a great four-block quilt and would make a stunning wall quilt, or a bed quilt if you enlarged the blocks.

SUGGESTED LAYOUT

My quilt uses four Pine Blossom blocks, joined together with 2" (5.1cm) finished dark green sashing and another quarter square triangle (QST) unit in the centre. I've added a 1" (2.5cm) finished border, a 2" (5.1cm) finished border with QST units at the corners, another 1" (2.5cm) finished border and a final 2" (5.1cm) finished border, again with QST units at the corners. The quilt finishes at 38" (95.5cm) square.

Use units in your pieced borders that are the same size as your blocks for a 'natural fit' border that is easy to figure and looks 'right'.

For one block you will need

Finished block size: 12" (30.5cm) square

- Three 3¼" (8.3cm) squares in orange batik
- Three 3¼" (8.3cm) squares in golden yellow batik
- Nine 2½" (6.4cm) squares in white solid
- Two 2½" (6.4cm) strips in green batik, each 10½" (26.6cm) long
- Two 2½" (6.4cm) strips in medium purple batik, each 8½" (21.5cm) long
- Two 2½" (6.4cm) strips in medium light purple batik, each 6½" (16.5cm) long
- Two 2½" (6.4cm) strips in light purple batik, each 4½" (11.4cm) long
- One 2½" x 4½" (6.4 x 11.4cm) rectangle in white solid

Assembling the block

1. Use the three orange and three golden yellow batik squares to make a total of six quarter square triangle (QST) units. You will need five for this block.
2. Mark the diagonal lightly in pencil on the back of eight of the white 2½" (6.4cm) squares.
3. Using the stitch and flip method (see page 20) add white 'corners' to each of the green and purple batik strips. Note that the corner on one of each colour of strip should slant to the left and the other should slant to the right.
4. Starting with the upper right portion of the block, sew a QST unit to the remaining 2½" (6.4cm) white square. Press, then sew the 2½" x 4½" (6.4 x 11.4cm) white rectangle to the right-hand, as shown.
5. Join one of the light purple strips to one side, as shown. Sew a QST unit to the bottom of the other light purple strip and sew this to the adjacent side.
6. Continue in this manner until all the pieced strips and QST units have been added.

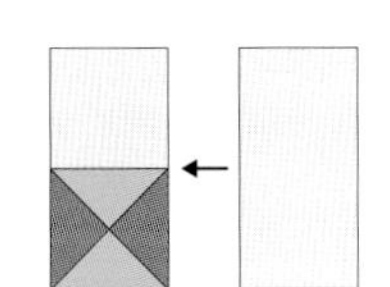

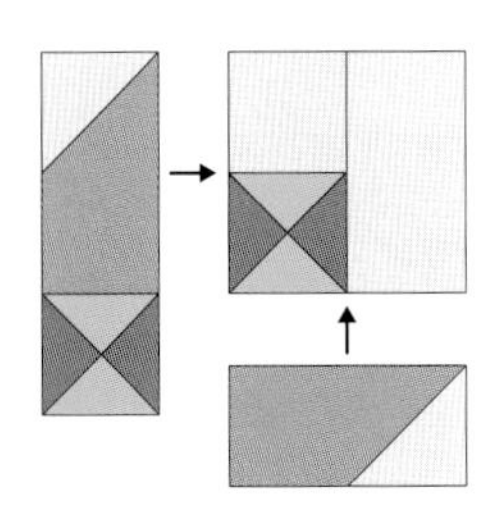

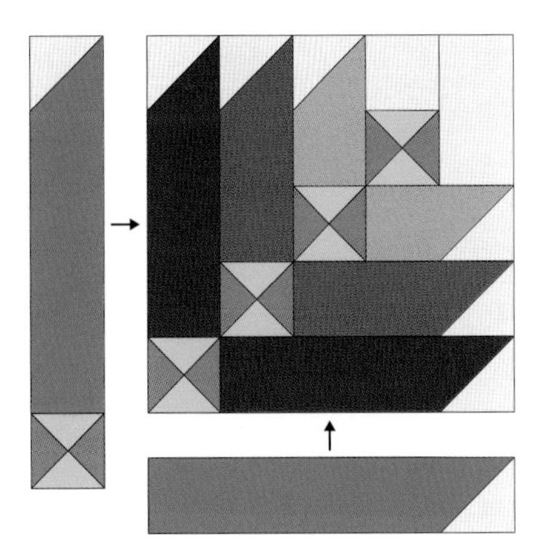

45 STACKED

I love the look of bricks laid on an angle - it's such an elegant way to use a simple shape to create a more complex and stylish-looking result. Neutral fabrics usually hide away in the background, but this quilt celebrates their simple, calm beauty.

For one block you will need

Finished block size: 18" (45.7cm) square

- Four 10¼" (26cm) squares in assorted navy prints
- Four 10¼" (26cm) squares in assorted cream prints
- Eight 9⅞" (25cm) squares in assorted cream prints

Note: The quantities above give enough for four blocks, so you could use a quarter of the requirements, but then you won't get the same variety!

Assembling the block

1. Cut all of the navy and cream 10¼" (26cm) squares on both diagonals to yield four quarter square triangles (QSTs) each. Keep one from each square for each block.
2. Cut the 9⅞" (25cm) squares in half on one diagonal to yield a total of sixteen half square triangles (HSTs). Keep four for this block.
3. Sew a navy and a cream QST together and press the seam towards the darker fabric. Sew a cream HST to the other side, as shown. Press the seam towards the HST. Make four units like this.
4. Use the block diagram to arrange the pieced units into a four-patch. Join the patches into rows, then join the rows together.

There are lots of ways to make a quilt smaller, but reducing the number of blocks sometimes loses the pattern we've fallen in love with. Instead, reduce the size of the blocks. For example, in this quilt use 5¾" (14.6cm) and 5⅜" (13.7cm) squares to piece the units. The blocks will be 9" (22.9cm) instead of 18" (45.7cm). Reduce the size of the sashing to 3" (7.6cm) and the finished quilt will be 45" x 54" (114.3 x 137.2cm) but will, to all intents and purposes, look the same as my larger quilt.

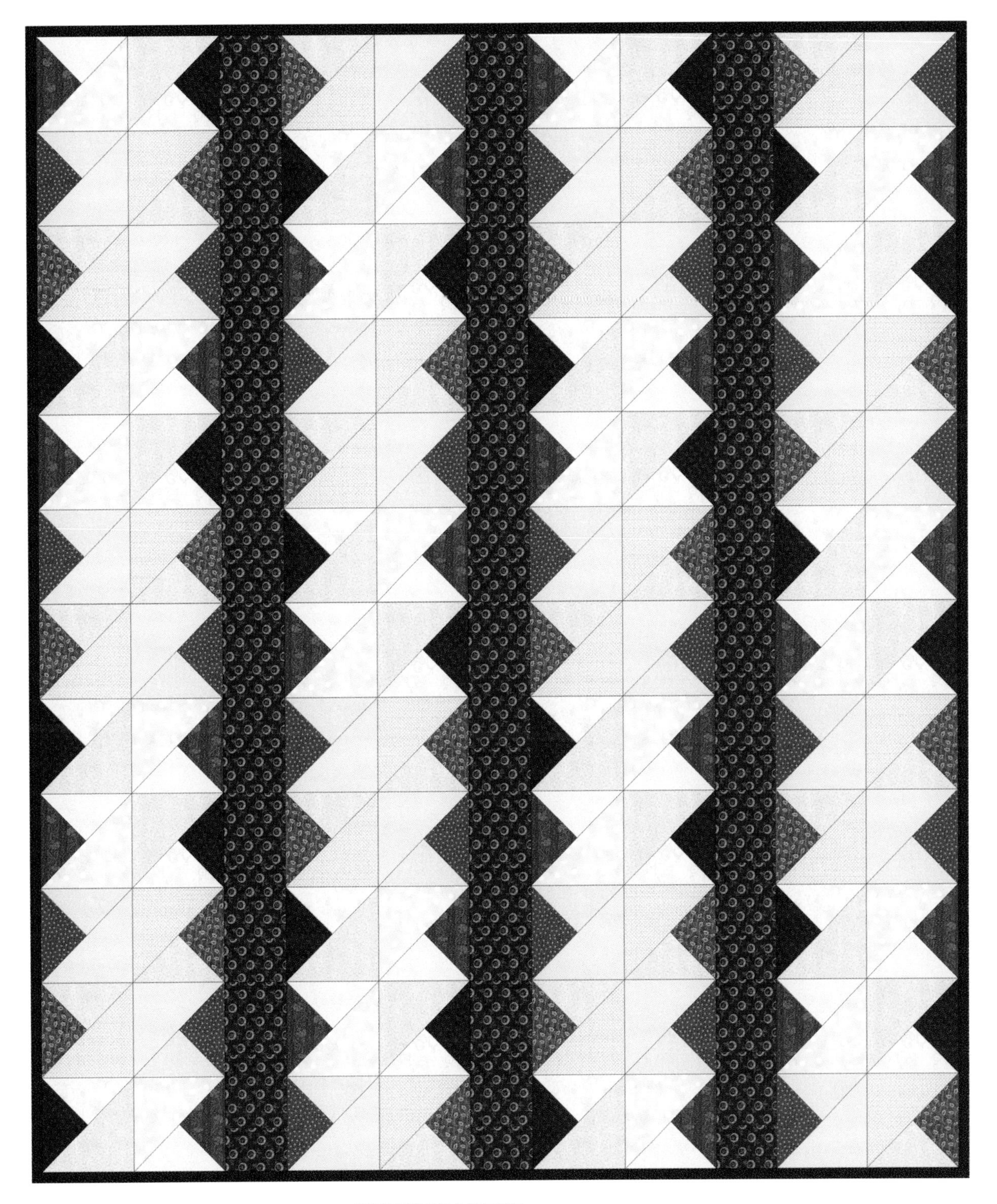

SUGGESTED LAYOUT

My virtual quilt uses twenty-four Stacked blocks set in a four by six arrangement separated by 6" (15.2cm) finished vertical sashing in a navy print – this has the effect of 'floating' the stacks of cream bricks. The quilt finishes at 90" x 108" (228 x 274.3cm) – the perfect queen size.

46 PINEAPPLE PARADE

When I was a child the only pineapple I ever saw was in chunks spooned out of a tin, so it came as something of a revelation when I finally saw the actual fruit! It's a thing of beauty and worthy of rendering in fabric for a fun cushion. Also pictured, Strawberry Patch, (page 72).

SUGGESTED LAYOUT

This block makes a perfect cushion and is a great partner for the Strawberry Patch. You could also make a fun table runner for parties by placing five or six blocks side by side and adding a border.

For one block you will need

Finished block size: 10" x 18" (25.4 x 45.7cm)

- Assorted yellow prints: twenty-two 2½"(6¼cm) squares, four 3¼" (8.3cm) squares, two 2⅞" (7.3cm) squares
- Assorted green prints: four 2½" (6.4cm) squares, three 2⅞" (7.3cm) squares, two 3¼" (8.3cm) squares
- Blue batik: three 2½" (6.4cm) squares, five 2⅞" (7.3cm) squares

Assembling the block

1. Pair the two yellow and two blue batik 2⅞" (7.3cm) squares together and make four half square triangle (HST) units following the instructions on page 19.
2. Pair the three green print 2⅞" (7.3cm) squares with the remaining 2⅞" (7.3cm) blue batik squares and make six HST units
3. Make four QST units using the 3¼" (8.3cm) yellow squares and then do the same with the two green 3¼" (8.3cm) squares.
4. Arrange your units with the unused squares to make the pineapple, as shown.
5. Sew the units into rows then sew the rows together.

47 OLD-FASHIONED FRAMES

A lovely reminder of quilts past and very possibly a quilt for the future! This simple piecing combined with plain frames is the perfect showcase for your favourite prints and a great way for newer quilters to practise simple piecing in a spectacular quilt.

SUGGESTED LAYOUT

For my virtual quilt, I first framed the centre Star block with a 1" (2.5cm) finished border in gold print. I then added a HST frame, made up of thirty-two HST units made using sixteen red and sixteen cream 2 ⅞" (7.3cm) squares. I added a second 1" (2.5cm) finished border in gold, before the four-patch checkerboard frame.of twenty-four four-patch units, each one made from two red and two cream 2½" (6.4cm) squares. Then I added a third 1" (2.5cm) finished border in gold. For the final pieced border, I used twenty-four Churn Dash blocks. There is a final 1" (2.5cm) finished frame in golden tan. The quilt measures 44" x 44" (111.8 x 111.8cm).

For one Star block (centre) you will need

Finished block size: 12" (30.5cm) square

- One gold/tan 5¼" (13.3cm) square, cross-cut on both diagonals to yield four quarter square triangles (QSTs)
- One cream 5¼" (13.3cm) square, cross-cut on both diagonals to yield four quarter square triangles (QSTs)
- Two red 5¼" (13.3cm) squares, cross-cut on both diagonals to yield eight quarter square triangles (QSTs)
- Four cream 4½" (11.4cm) squares
- One red 4½" (11.4cm) square

Assembling the Star block

1. Make the hourglass units first by sewing one gold, one cream and two red QSTs together, following the diagram for colour placement. Make four.
2. Arrange the QST units and the remaining 4½" (11.4cm) squares together to form the block and sew together in rows. Sew the rows together.

Test your seam allowances throughout this project. Make just one or two of each unit and check its finished measurement before you make the others to ensure that everything will fit together well at the end.

For one Churn Dash block (outer border) you will need

Finished block size: 6" (15.2cm) square

- Two 2⅞" (7.3cm) squares in red
- Two 2⅞" (7.3cm) squares in cream
- Four 1½" x 2½" (3.8 x 6.4cm) rectangles in red
- Four 1½" x 2½" (3.8 x 6.4cm) rectangles in cream
- One 2½" (6.4cm) square in cream

Assembling the Churn Dash block

1. Make four HST units from the red and cream 2⅞" (7.3cm) squares (see page 19).
2. Sew the red and cream rectangles together down one long edge in pairs.
3. Arrange the units around the 2½" (6.4cm) cream square, as shown. Sew the units into rows, then sew the rows together.

48 ICE CRYSTALS

This is one of those quilts that looks very complex, but is actually made of very simple units. Take your time, cut and piece accurately and you'll end up with a wonderful wintery quilt to banish the blues.

SUGGESTED LAYOUT

For my quilt I have made five of block 1 and four of block 2 and sewn them together in a three by three arrangement. I've added borders at 1" (2.5cm) and 4" (10.2cm) finished. The final quilt measures 58" x 58" (147.3 x 147.3cm).

When matching points, pin either side of the point, rather than pushing a pin right through the point. Forcing a pin through the point will distort your fabric whereas a pin either side will hold it in place and give better results.

48 ICE CRYSTALS

For one block 1 you will need

Finished block size: 16" (40.7cm) square

For the outer corner units:

- Four 3⅜" (8.6cm) squares in light blue medium-scale print for the 'square on point' units at the block corners
- Two 2⅞" (7.3cm) squares of medium tan print, each cross-cut on one diagonal to yield a total of four half square triangles (HSTs) for the 'square on point' units
- Two 2⅞" (7.3cm) squares in light tan print, each cross-cut on one diagonal to yield a total of four HSTs for the 'square on point' units
- Four 2⅞" (7.3cm) squares in light cream print, each cross-cut on one diagonal to yield a total of eight HSTs for the 'square on point' units
- Eight 2½" (6.4cm) squares in medium blue print
- Eight 2½" (6.4cm) squares in light tan print
- Four 2½" (6.4cm) squares in medium tan print

For the middle units:

- Four 2⅞" (7.3cm) squares in medium blue, each cross-cut on one diagonal to yield a total of eight HSTs
- Two 5¼" (13.3cm) squares in medium light blue print, each cross-cut on both diagonals to yield a total of eight quarter square triangles (QSTs)
- One 5¼" (13.3cm) square in light cream print, cross-cut on both diagonals to yield a total of four QSTs
- Four 3⅜" (8.6cm) squares in medium tan print

For the block centre:

One 4½" (11.4cm) square in large-scale blue floral print

Assembling block 1

1. Sew the 'square on point' units first. These are made of a centre light blue medium-scale print, one medium tan, one light tan and two light cream HSTs. Make a total of four units.
2. Arrange two blue, two light tan and one medium tan 2½" (6.4cm) square around the square on point unit to match the diagram below. Note that you will make two units with the squares on the top and left sides of the 'square on point' and two units with the squares on the left and bottom.
3. Sew the middle units. Sew medium blue HSTs to two adjacent edges of the light tan square on point, then add a light blue QST to one of the upper edges. Sew a light blue and a light cream QST together and then add this to the remaining side of the square on point. Make a total of four units.
4. Arrange the units as shown, around the centre 4½" (11.4cm) square. Sew the block together.

For one block 2 you will need

Finished block size: 16" (40.7cm) square

For the corner units:

- Four 2½" (6.4cm) squares in medium blue print
- Eight 2½" (6.4cm) squares in medium tan
- Twelve 2½" (6.4cm) squares in dark blue
- Eight 2½" (6.4cm) squares in dark tan

For the middle units:

- Four 3" x 6" (7.6 x 15.2cm) rectangles in light cream each cross-cut on one diagonal to yield eight half rectangle triangles
- Four 5" (12.7cm) squares in dark blue

Use these fabrics to paper piece a total of four triangles in a square units using the method on page 21. Use template A on page 222.

For the block centre:

- Four 5" (12.7cm) squares in large scale medium blue floral fabric
- Eight 2" x 6" (5.1 x 15.2cm) rectangles in light cream fabric
- Four 3" (7.6cm) squares in dark blue fabric, each cross-cut on one diagonal to yield eight HSTs

Use these fabrics to paper piece a total of four centre units using the method on page 21. Use template B on page 222. Sew the four units together to make the block centre.

Assembling block 2

1. Arrange the paper-pieced units and the assorted squares to make the block.
2. Sew the top two rows of six squares together to make a rectangular unit. Sew this to one side of the triangles in a square unit. Sew a mirror image of these six squares for the other side and sew to the opposing side of the triangles in a square unit. Make two.
3. Sew a dark blue and a dark tan square together. Make four. Sew these units to the sides of the remaining two triangles in a square units.
4. Sew the units into rows and then join the rows. Remove the foundation papers.

49 BOUND FOR GLORY

Another beautifully patriotic quilt, this time inspired by an encaustic tiled floor I photographed many years ago in Ireland. Tiled floors (and tiles in general) are always inspiring me to quilt - their simple shapes and almost limitless possibilities lie at the heart of my quilting.

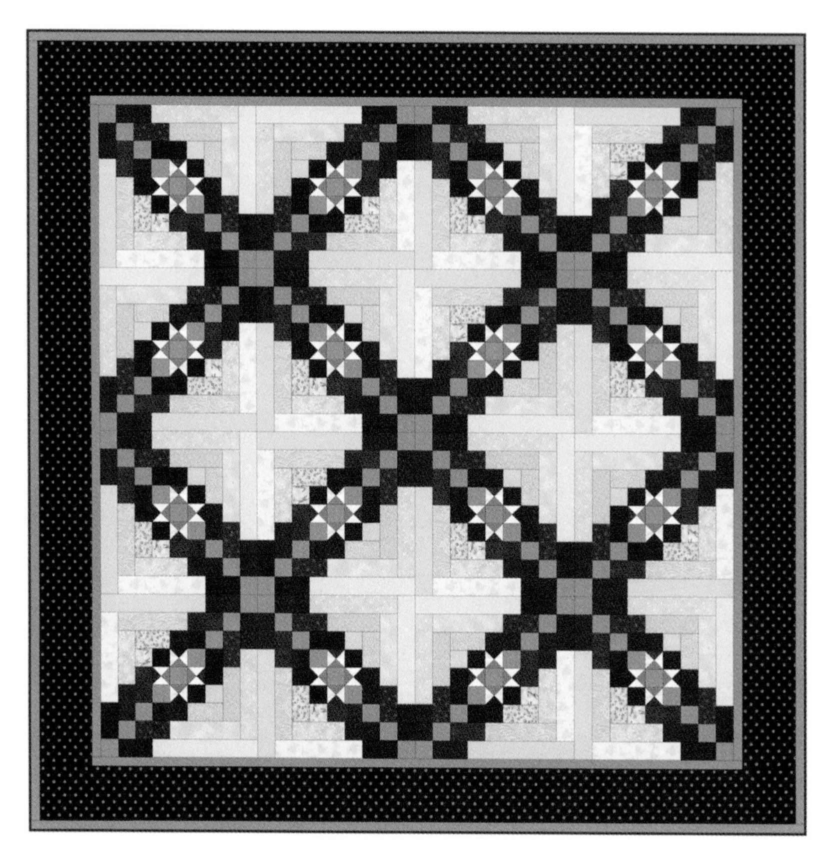

SUGGESTED LAYOUT

My virtual quilt uses sixteen Bound for Glory blocks in a four by four arrangement. I've added borders 1 and 3 which both finish at 1" (2.5cm) and the middle border, 2, finishes at 6" (15.2cm) – the whole quilt measures 88" (223.5cm) square.

Large open areas in a quilt, such as the ones where four Bound for Glory blocks meet, lend themselves to beautiful quilting. It's an opportunity to show a really lovely quilted motif. If quilting isn't your thing, you could add appliqués to this area – use motifs from other quilts in this book to add your own design elements.

For one block you will need

Finished block size: 18" (45.7cm) square

- One 3¼" (8.3cm) square in mid blue, cross-cut on both diagonals to yield four quarter square triangles (QSTs)
- One 3¼" (8.3cm) square in white mottled print, cross-cut on both diagonals to yield four QSTs
- Two 3¼" (8.3cm) squares in red print, cross-cut on both diagonals to yield eight QSTs
- Nine 2½" (6.4cm) squares in gold print
- Two 2½" (6.4cm) squares in red
- Twelve 2½" x 4½" (6.4 x 11.4cm) rectangles in assorted red prints
- Two 2½" (6.4cm) squares in cream
- Two 2½" x 4½" (6.4 x 11.4cm) rectangles in cream
- Two 2½" x 6½" (6.4 x 16.5cm) rectangles in cream
- Two 2½" x 8½" (6.4 x 21.6cm) rectangles in cream
- Two 2½" x 10½" (6.4 x 26.7cm) rectangles in cream
- Two 2½" x 12½" (6.4 x 31.7cm) rectangles in cream

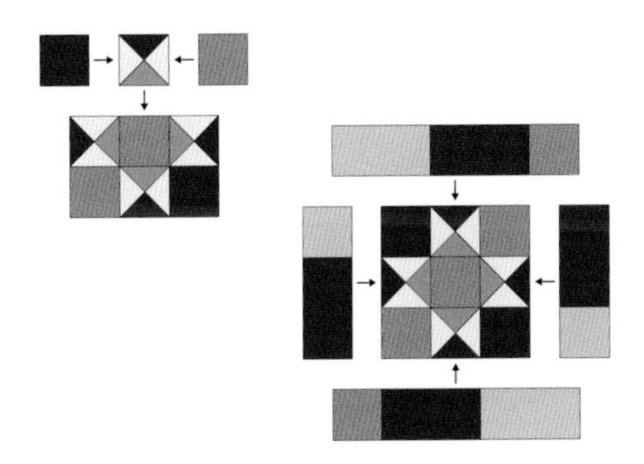

Assembling the block

1. Start by making the centre star block. Join two white, one mid blue and one red QST together to make a QST unit, following the diagram for colour placement. Make four.
2. Lay out the four QST units with three gold squares and two red squares in a 3 x 3 arrangement. Sew into rows and then join the rows. The remainder of the block is sewn in rounds.
3. Round 1: Join one 2½" x 4½" (6.4 x 11.4cm) red rectangle to a 2½" (6.4cm) cream square. Make two. Sew these to the right and left sides of the centre star block. Join a 2½" x 4½" (6.4 x 11.4cm) red rectangle to a 2½" x 4½" (6.4 x 11.4cm) cream rectangle, then sew a gold square to the red end. Make two. Sew these units to top and bottom of the star block.
4. Round 2: Join a 2½" x 4½" (6.4 x 11.4cm) red rectangle to a 2½" x 6½" (6.4 x 16.5cm) cream rectangle. Make two. Sew these units to the left and right sides of the block. Join a 2½" x 4½" (6.4 x 11.4cm) red rectangle to a 2½" x 8½" (6.4 x 21.6cm) cream rectangle. Sew a 2½" (6.4cm) gold square to the red end. Make two. Sew these units to the top and bottom of the star block.
5. Round 3: Join a 2½" x 4½" (6.4 x 11.4cm) red rectangle to a 2½" x 10½" (6.4 x 26.7cm) cream rectangle. Make two. Sew these units to the left and right sides of the block. Finally, join a 2½" x 4½" (6.4 x 11.4cm) red rectangle to a 2½" x 12½" (6.4 x 31.7cm) cream rectangle, then sew a gold square to the red end. Make two. Sew these to the top and bottom of the block.

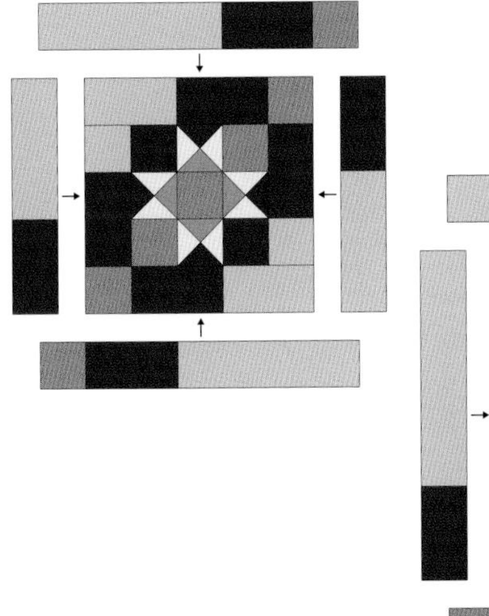

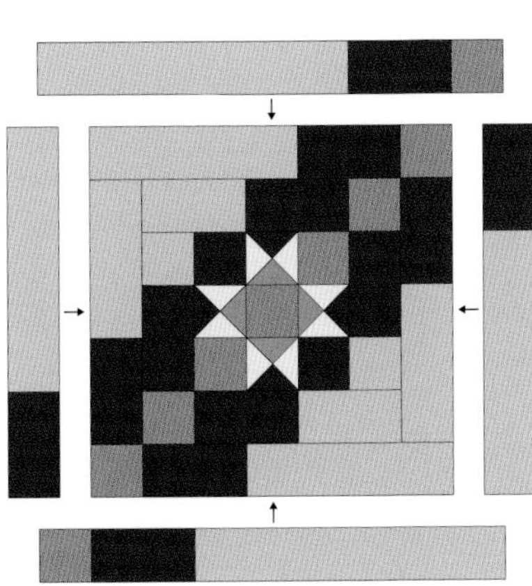

50 CROSSING BORDERS

This quilt takes a different approach to quiltmaking. Rather than working on blocks set in rows or a strippy approach, this is a frame quilt. Strips of fabric define and space out the simple pieced units of this lovely lap quilt - perfect for scraps and a great way to practise making those basic units.

You will need:

- A large variety of scraps in greens, reds, yellows and creams
- Yardage for the solid 'frames' in green stripe, jade green and yellow print

Assembling the quilt

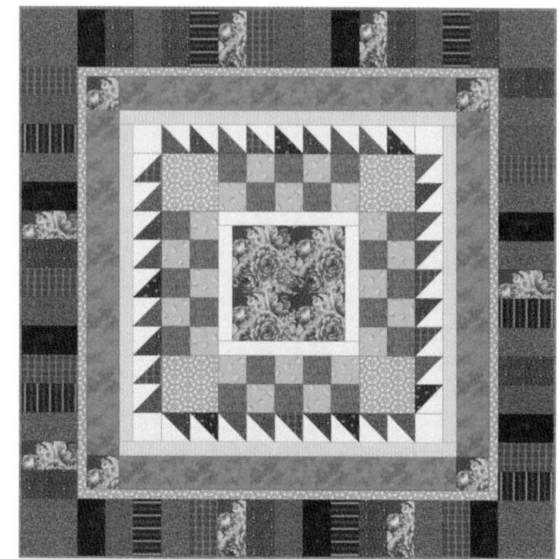

1. Cut one 12½" (31.7cm) central square of large-scale floral fabric. Add a cream frame: cut 2" (5.1cm) strips, two at 12½" (31.7cm) and two at 15½" (39.4cm). Sew the short strips to the sides of the centre square, then add the longer strips top and bottom. Your quilt should measure 15½" (39.4cm) square.
2. Make the chequerboard frame by sewing 3½" (8.9cm) squares of light green and dark green print fabrics together - you'll need twenty light and twenty dark. Sew together five light and five dark squares per side. The yellow print cornerstones are cut at 6½" (16.5cm) square and you will need four. Your quilt should now measure 27½" (69.9cm) square.
3. The half square triangle (HST) border is next. Cut out eighteen cream and eighteen red 3⅞" (9.8cm) squares and mark the diagonal lightly on the back of the cream squares. Use the HST method (see page 19) to make a total of thirty-six HST units. You will also need four cream cornerstones, each cut at 3½" (8.9cm) square. Add the HST border - your quilt should now measure 33½" (85cm) square.
4. Add a striped border. Cut 2" (5.1cm) strips - two at 33½" (85cm) and two at 36½" (92.7cm). Sew the shorter strips to the sides, and the longer strips to the top and bottom. Your quilt should now measure 36½" (92.7cm) square.
5. The next frame is made from 4" (10.2cm) wide strips - cut four pieces each 36½" (92.7cm) long. You'll also need four cornerstones cut from floral fabric, each 4" (10.2cm) square. Sew the shorter strips to the sides, then sew the cornerstones to either end of the last two strips. Sew these strips to the quilt top and bottom. Your quilt should now measure 43½" (110.5cm) square.
6. The next border is made from simple strips cut at 1½" (3.8cm) wide - two at 43½" (110.5cm) and two at 45½" (115.6cm). Sew these strips to the quilt - it should now measure 45½" (115.6cm) square.
7. The final border is made up of sixty rectangles of assorted red prints cut at 3½" x 6½" (8.9 x 16.5cm). Sew them together in four sets of fifteen. You'll also need four cornerstones, each 6½" (16.5cm) square. Sew this final border to the quilt which should now measure 57½" (146cm) square.

ABCDEF
GHIJKLM
NOPQRST
UVWXYZ
0123456789

WINDMILL

I adore simple two-colour quilts: red and white, yellow and white, navy and white - they have that ability to be all things at once. Classic yet ultra modern; simple in colour and yet complex in form. I've revved this one up by using three shades of red - light, medium and dark - to create extra definition and drama.

SUGGESTED LAYOUT

For my virtual quilt, I have made twelve Windmill blocks and sewn them together in a three by four arrangement to make a quilt centre that is 48½" x 64½" (123.2 x 163.8cm). To this I've added a 4" (10.2cm) finished border in dark red with 4" (10.2cm) finished cornerstones in light red. The whole quilt measures 56" x 72" (142.2 x 182.8cm).

For one block you will need

Finished block size: 16" (40.7cm) square

- Twelve 2⅞" (7.3cm) squares in white – cut four of them in half once on the diagonal to yield eight half square triangles (HSTs). On the wrong side of the remaining eight white squares, mark the diagonal lightly in pencil
- Eight 2⅞" (7.3cm) squares in light red
- Two 8⅞" (22.5cm) squares in medium red, each cross-cut once on the diagonal to yield four HSTs
- Two 4⅞" (12.4cm) squares in dark red, each cross-cut once on the diagonal to yield four HSTs
- Four 2½" (6.4cm) squares in light red

Assembling the block

1. Pair each marked white square with a corresponding light red square, right sides together. Sew ¼" (6mm) either side of the drawn line, then cut apart on the drawn line. Press seam allowances towards the red fabric and clip off the dog-ears to make HST units.
2. Arrange one large medium red triangle, one dark red triangle, four light red/white HST units, one light red square and two white triangles to form a quarter block, as shown. Join two HSTs together, then add a light red square at one end and a white triangle at the other. Sew two more HSTs together and sew a white triangle to the end. Sew this unit to the side of the dark red triangle, then add the other HST unit to the other side to make a large pieced triangle.
3. Sew this large pieced triangle to the medium red triangle. Make four quarter blocks in total.
4. Sew the quarter blocks together.

When making 'high-contrast' quilts like this, test your fabrics before you start to make sure they are colourfast. Wet a piece of each fabric and then rub it with a cotton bud. If the colour 'bleeds,' it's definitely worth pre-washing your fabrics and then testing again. If the fabric still bleeds, use a different fabric!

52 NINE STARS

I have fallen in love with modern quilts over the last few years - there's something so appealing to me about classic blocks given new life with bright fresh solids and a simplicity of treatment that lets the purity of our craft shine through.

For one block you will need

Finished block size: 9" (22.9cm) square

- Bright pink solid: one 3½" (8.9cm) square, and two 4¼" (10.8cm) squares cross-cut on both diagonals to yield eight quarter square triangles (QSTs)
- Medium pistachio green solid: four 3½" (8.9cm) squares, and two 4¼" (10.8cm) squares cross-cut on both diagonals to yield eight QSTs

Assembling the block

1. Sew two pink and two green QSTs together to make a QST unit. Make a total of four units.
2. Arrange the QST units and the squares as shown.
3. Sew the units and patches into rows and press the seams towards the solid patches.
4. Sew the rows together.

Try taking an 'all-inclusive' approach to colours in your quilts. The greens here are yellow greens, leafy greens, Kelly green, even blue greens. A variety of tones and 'personalities' in your fabrics will bring greater visual interest and greater pizzazz to your quilts than an over-matched approach.

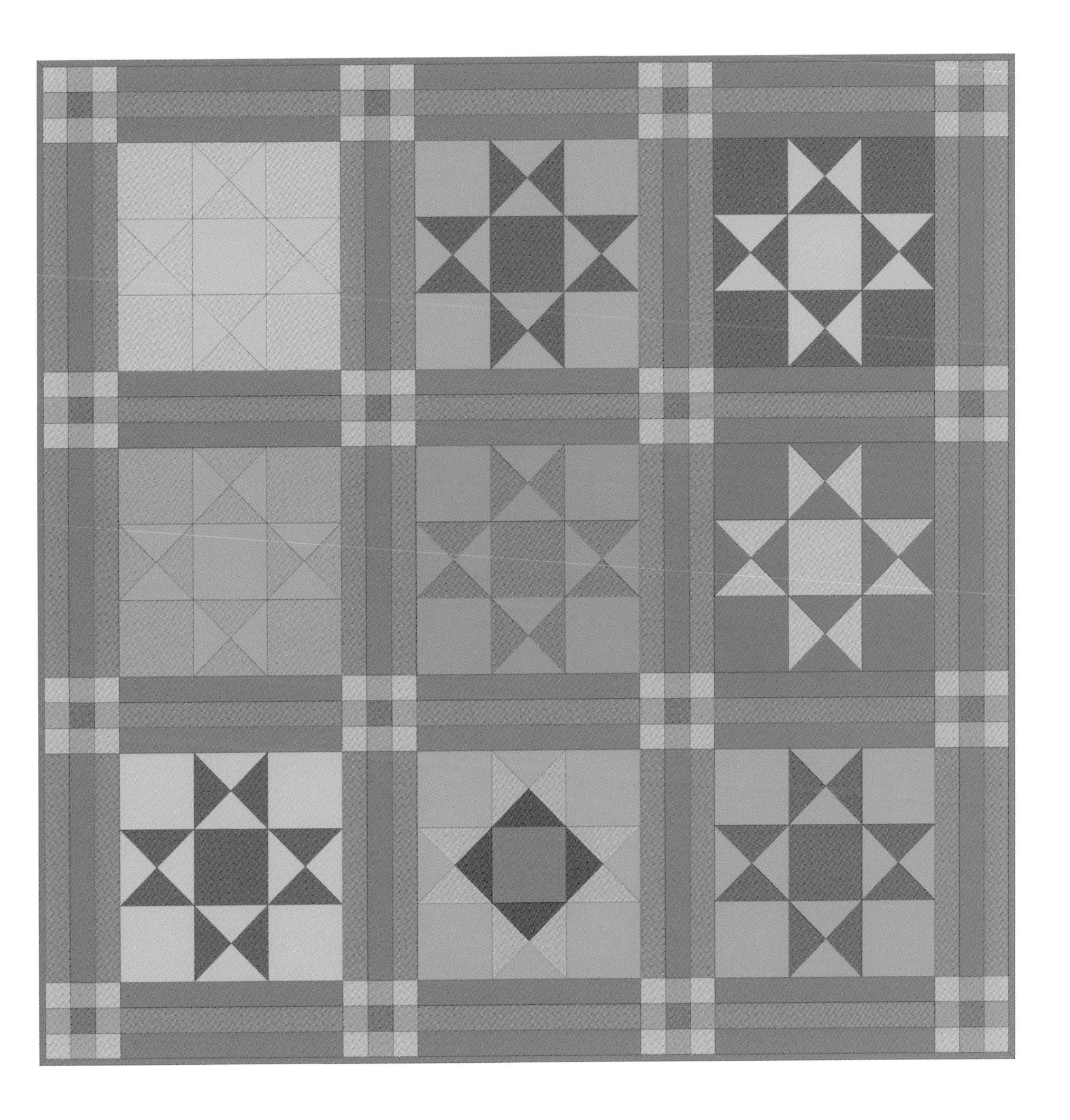

SUGGESTED LAYOUT

For my virtual quilt, I have made nine Nine Star blocks and set them together in a three by three arrangement with sashing and pieced cornerstones. The sashing is made up of three 1½" (3.8cm) strips sewn together to make a 3" (7.6cm) wide finished sashing. The cornerstones are simple nine-patch blocks made up of 1½" (3.8cm) squares sewn together to make a 3" (7.6cm) finished cornerstone block. The finished quilt is 39" x 39" (99 x 99cm).

CHRISTMAS CACTUS

Every year before the holidays my Mum would buy a Christmas cactus. We'd enjoy the spiky red blooms for a month, but we never kept one alive beyond February! My Christmas cactus quilt will bloom all year round, guaranteed!

Suggested layout

For my quilt I have made eight of block 1 and eight of block 2 and sewn them together in four rows of four, clustering the block 2s in the centre and at the corners. I've added a 2" (5.1cm) finished border and cornerstones in red, followed by a final 3" (7.6cm) finished border in green to make a 46" x 46" (116.8 x 116.8cm) wallhanging.

For block 1 you will need:

Finished block size: 9" (22.9cm) square

- Six assorted green solid 2¾" (7cm) squares
- Two 2¾" (7cm) squares in white solid
- Two patches cut using the trapezoid template on page 223 in dark green solid
- One 5⅜" (13.7cm) square in white solid, cross-cut on one diagonal to yield two large half square triangles (HSTs)
- One 3⅛" (7.9cm) square in white solid, cross-cut on one diagonal to yield two small HSTs

Assembling block 1

1. Sew three assorted green and one white 2¾" (7cm) squares together to make a four-patch. Make two.
2. Sew the small white HST to the green trapezoid shape, as shown. Sew a large white HST to the other side of the trapezoid. Make two.
3. Arrange the units to make the block, as shown.
4. Sew the units together in rows. Sew the rows together and press.

Quilting that contrasts with your piecing is a nice contrast – for example, curved quilting lines against the angular piecing of my Christmas Cactus quilt.

53 CHRISTMAS CACTUS

For block 2 you will need:

Finished block size: 9" (22.9cm) square

- Four assorted green solid 2¾" (7cm) squares
- Four white solid 2¾" (7cm) squares
- Four patches in assorted red solid, cut using the half rectangle triangle (HRT) template on page 223. Cut two HRTs and two reverse HRTs (flip the template)
- Two white HRTs and two reverse HRTs, cut using the template on page 223

Assembling block 2

1. Sew two green and two white squares together to make a four-patch unit. Make two.
2. Sew a red HRT and a matching white HRT together to make a pieced rectangle. Make two the same and sew them together as shown.
3. Sew a red reverse HRT to a matching white reverse HRT. Make two and sew them together.
4. Arrange your units to make the block and sew the units together in rows.
5. Sew the rows together and press.

54 NANNA'S HOUSE

Not a house block, so why the name? I wanted to design a quilt that would remind anyone around in the '60s or '70s of trips to see their Nanna - the wallpaper, the china, the carpets on the floors and the quilts we wrapped ourselves in to watch Saturday night TV.

For one block you will need

Finished block size: 12" (30.5cm) square

- Four 3⅞" (9.8cm) squares in pink solid, cross-cut on one diagonal to yield a total of eight half square triangles (HSTs)
- One 7¼" (18.4cm) square in yellow solid, cross-cut on both diagonals to yield four quarter square triangles (QSTs)
- One 2" x 17" (5.1 x 43.2cm) strip in pink solid
- One 2" x 17" (5.1 x 43.2cm) strip in pink/yellow print fabric
- Four 3½" (8.9cm) squares in yellow solid

Assembling the block

1. Make four flying geese units by sewing a pink solid HST to each short side of each of the yellow QSTs.
2. Sew the 2" (5.1cm) pink solid strip and the 2" (5.1cm) pink/yellow print strip together along one long edge. Press the seam towards the solid fabric. Cut this strip-pieced unit into eight sections, each 2" (5.1cm) wide.
3. Join the eight 'two-patch' segments from step 2 into a simple sixteen-patch block to make the centre of the block.
4. Arrange the sixteen-patch centre, the flying geese units and the yellow squares to form the block as shown.
5. Sew the units into rows and press the seams towards the squares. Join the rows together and press.

This would make a wonderful memory quilt if you are lucky enough to have clothes kept from your childhood (or indeed someone else's!). If you're combining cotton with cotton, proceed as normal; however, the 1970s weren't known for their natural fibres, so you may need to interface your cotton fabrics to bring them up the weight of any clothing remnants.

SUGGESTED LAYOUT

For my virtual quilt, I have joined thirteen Nanna's House blocks together on point and added a really wild '70s-style print in the setting triangles. The brown and orange centre block is particularly significant to me – brown and orange are synonymous with the 1970s! The setting triangles are made from squares cut at 18¼" (46.3cm), then cross-cut on both diagonals to yield four triangles – you need a total of eight setting triangles, so cut two squares. You'll also need two squares cut at 9⅜" (23.8cm) and cross-cut on one diagonal to yield four corner triangles. The quilt finishes at approximately 51" x 51" (130 x 130cm).

55 GOOSE IN THE POND

Crisp, fresh, classic red-and-white quilts never disappoint and this combination of half square triangles, squares and quickly strip-pieced units is sure to become a family favourite.

For one block you will need

Finished block size: 15" (38.1cm) square

- Assorted red print fabrics - six 3⅞" (9.8cm) squares plus some 1½" (3.8cm) strips
- Assorted white print fabrics - six 3⅞" (9.8cm) squares, five 3½" (8.9cm) squares, plus some 1½" (3.8cm) strips, each approximately 15" (38cm) long

Assembling the block

1. Use the red and white 3⅞" (9.8cm) squares to make a total of twelve half square triangle (HST) units, following the instructions on page 19.
2. Sew two red and one white 1½" (3.8cm) strips together, alternating the colours. Do the same with two white and one red 1½" (3.8cm) strip.
3. Cut four segments from the red/white/red strip-pieced unit, each 3½" (8.9cm) square. Also cut four segments, each 1½" (3.8cm) wide, for the nine-patch units.
4. From the white/red/white strip-pieced unit ,cut eight segments each 1½" (3.8cm) wide for the nine-patch units.
5. Combine two white/red/white 1½" (3.8cm) segments with one red/white/red 1½" (3.8cm) segment to make a nine-patch unit. Sew together. Make four.
6. Arrange your HST units, strip-pieced units, nine-patch units and white print squares to form the block, as shown.
7. Sew the units into rows, then sew the rows together.

When you're making a 'high-contrast' quilt like this, it is essential to press the seams towards the darker fabric (red) wherever possible to prevent seams from showing through the lighter patches.

SUGGESTED LAYOUT

For my virtual quilt, I have sewn sixteen Goose in the Pond blocks together in a four by four arrangement, with 1" (2.5cm) finished white sashing and 1" (2.5cm) finished red cornerstones. I've added a 5" (12.7cm) finished border to make a quilt that is 75" x 75" (190.5 x 190.5cm).

56 A WALK IN THE WOODS

Just twelve 12" (30.5cm) finished blocks are needed for this quilt, which is perfect for keeping snug on a crisp evening.

SUGGESTED LAYOUT

I have sewn twelve blocks and arranged them with six setting squares, each cut at 12½" (31.7cm); setting triangles cut from three 18¾" (46.4cm) squares, each cross-cut on both diagonals to yield twelve triangles (you'll only need ten of them); and four corner triangles cut from two 9⅜" (23.8cm) squares, each cross-cut on one diagonal to yield four triangles. I've added a ¾" (19mm) finished border in dark brown and a 6" (15.2cm) finished border. The quilt finishes at 64" x 81" (162.6 x 205.7cm).

For one block you will need

Finished block size: 12" (30.5cm) square

- Five 3⅞" (9.8cm) squares in assorted cream or tan prints, cross-cut on one diagonal to yield ten half square triangles (HSTs)
- One 3⅞" (9.8cm) square in dark green print, cross-cut on one diagonal to yield two HSTs
- Two 3⅞" (9.8cm) squares in gold print or plaid, cross-cut on one diagonal to yield four HSTs
- Four 3½" (8.9cm) squares in assorted tan or cream prints
- One 6⅞"(17.5cm) square in medium green print, cross-cut on one diagonal to yield two half square triangles (HSTs)

Assembling the block

1. Make six HST units with the cream and dark green/cream and gold triangles.
2. Arrange two gold and cream HST units and two cream squares into a four-patch. Sew together. Make two.
3. Arrange a dark green and cream HST unit with two cream HSTs and sew together. Sew this pieced triangle to one of the large medium green HSTs. Make two.
4. Arrange the four units to make the block as shown. Sew the units together in rows. Sew the rows together.

SUNSHINE IN THE FOREST

Deep woody browns, a plethora of greens and the warmth of sunshine yellows make this quilt calming and the perfect antidote to a stressful day. I always feel relaxed when I'm close to nature and if I can't have the real thing I'll always have my quilts.

SUGGESTED LAYOUT

For my virtual quilt, I have arranged nine blocks in a three by three arrangement. I've added a 3" (7.6cm) finished border to make a 51" x 51" (129.5 x 129.5cm) quilt.

I love it when the quilting reflects the theme or sentiment behind a quilt. This quilt would look wonderful quilted with leaves scattered all across the surface.

For one block you will need

Finished block size: 15" (38.1cm) square

- Assorted dark brown prints: two 4¼" (10.8cm) squares cross-cut on both diagonals to make eight quarter square triangles (QSTs), and four 3⅞" (9.8cm) squares cross-cut on one diagonal to make eight half square triangles (HSTs)
- Light cream/tan prints: four 3½" (8.9cm) squares, one 4¼" (10.8cm) square cross-cut on two diagonals to make four QSTs, two 3⅞" (9.8cm) squares cross-cut on one diagonal to make four HSTs)
- Assorted yellow prints and solids: one 4¼" (10.8cm) square cross-cut on both diagonals to make four QSTs, and six 3⅞" (9.8cm) squares cross-cut on one diagonal to make twelve HSTs
- Assorted dark green prints: one 3⅞" (9.8cm) square and four 3⅞" (9.8cm) squares, cross-cut on one diagonal to make eight HSTs

Assembling the block

1. Gather together your QSTs and arrange two brown, one cream and one yellow to make a QST unit. Sew together. Make four.
2. Sew a yellow and a cream HST together to make an HST unit. Make four.
3. Sew a dark brown HST and a yellow HST together to make an HST unit. Make eight.
4. Sew a dark green HST to another, different dark green HST to make an HST unit. Make four.
5. Arrange the QST units, the HST units and the squares together to make the block, as shown.
6. Sew the units into rows, then press the seams in opposite directions. Join the rows.

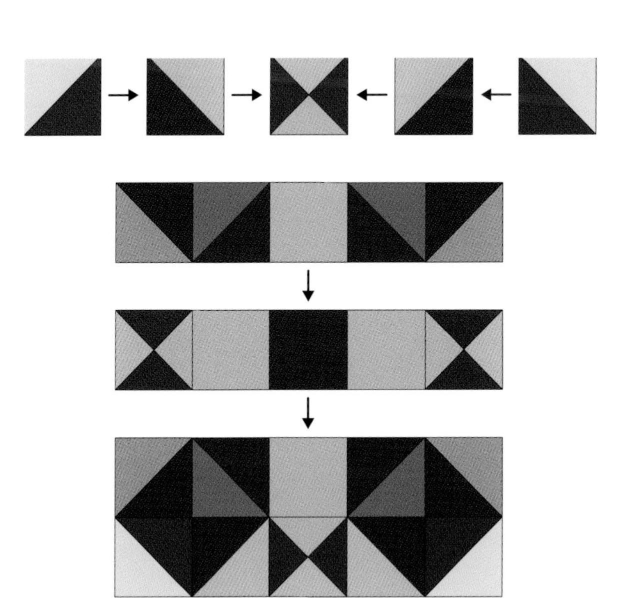

58 LADY OF THE LAKE

The Lady of the Lake block is an absolute classic and any quilt made from it is sure to become a treasured heirloom. Traditionally made with just two fabrics, often red and white, I've given this timeless beauty a quick makeover with assorted red and cream/tan prints. It is essentially still a 'two-colour' quilt, but with so much more visual interest.

For one block you will need

Finished block size: 12" (30.5cm) square

- Ten 2⅞" (7.3cm) squares in assorted cream/tan prints
- One 8⅞" (22.5cm) square of cream or tan print
- Ten 2⅞" (7.3cm) squares in assorted red prints
- One 8⅞" (22.5cm) square of larger-scale red print fabric

Assembling the block

1. On the back of each of the eleven cream/tan print squares (ten small and one large), mark one diagonal lightly in pencil.
2. Layer one cream and one red square, right sides together, and sew either side of the marked line with a ¼" (6mm) seam. Cut the square apart on the drawn line. Repeat for all squares, including the larger ones.
3. Arrange all of the small HST units around one of the large HST units (you will have made two - keep one for your next block). Note the orientation of the small HST in the diagram - small cream triangles against the large cream triangle, red triangles against the large red triangle.
4. Sew the units together as shown.

To improve the accuracy of your small HST units, cut 3" (7.6cm) squares (rather than 2 ⅞"/7.3cm). Make the HST units and then trim them down to 2½" (6.4cm) squares. Ensure that the diagonal seam runs right through from corner to corner before you trim!

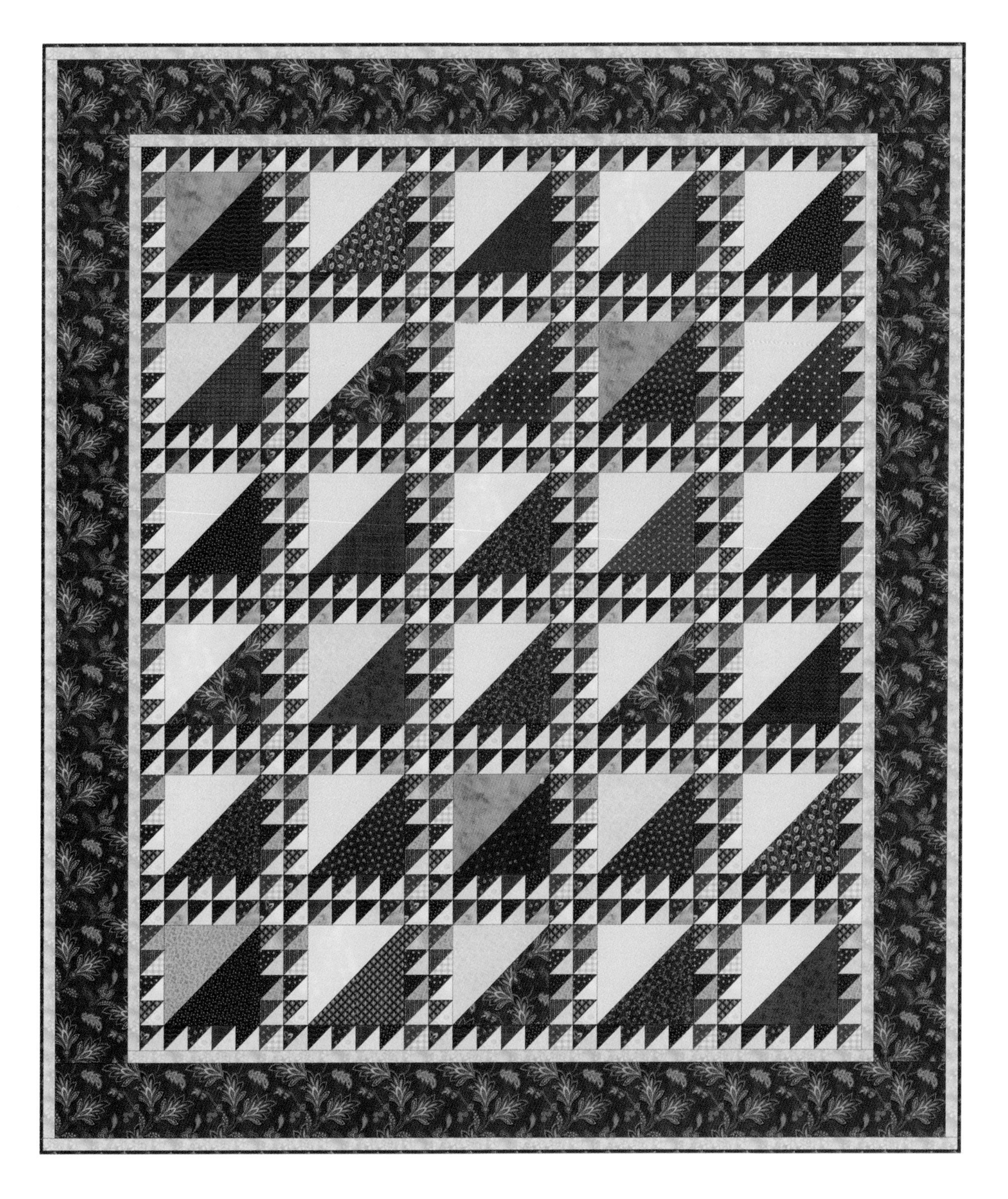

SUGGESTED LAYOUT

For my virtual quilt, I have made a total of thirty Lady of the Lake blocks and set them in a five by six arrangement. A 1" (2.5cm), 6" (15.2cm) and 1" (2.5cm) finished border treatment brings this quilt up to 76" x 88" (193 x 223.5cm).

SHARDS OF GLASS

Two blocks plus some additional units to finish the edges are all it takes to make this stunning quilt. I wanted to show how dramatic a difference a change of colour scheme can make, so this quilt is shown in two colourways - rich antique reproduction fabrics in tan and blue (opposite) and a bright version using my favourite modern quilt fabrics from designer Alison Glass, who inspired this quilt's name (see page 3)!

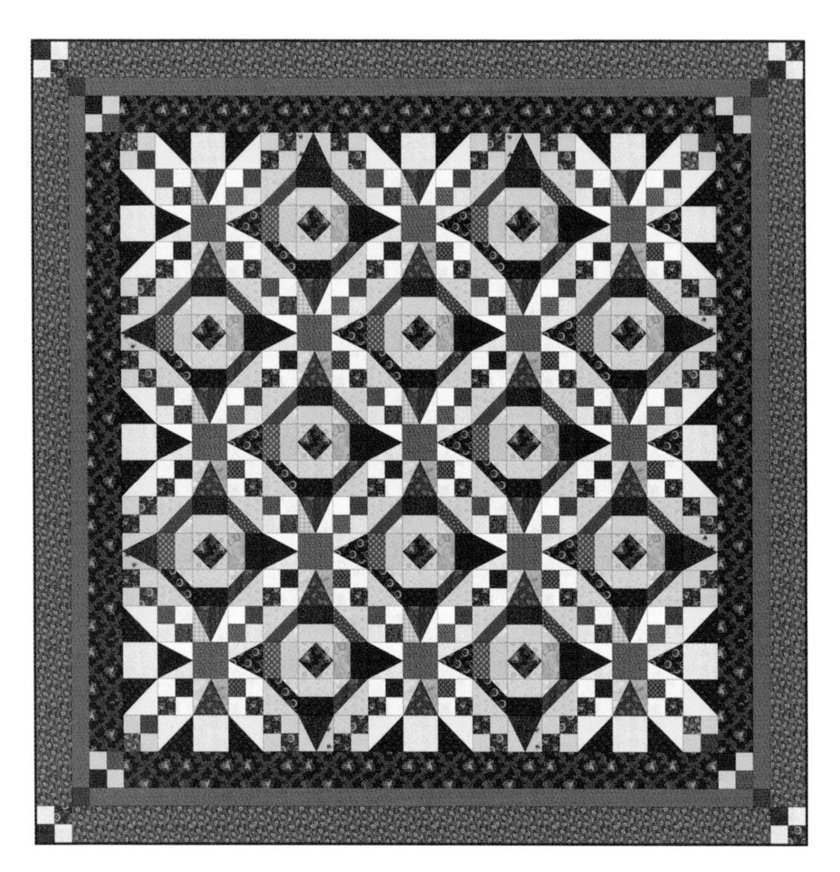

SUGGESTED LAYOUT

For my quilt I have made a total of twelve of block 1 and thirteen of block 2. You will also need to make twenty more four-patch units in brown and cream fabrics, twenty-four large half square triangle (HST) units (4"/10.2cm finished - use 4⅞"/12.4cm) squares and follow the instructions on page 19), eight more triangle in a square units and twelve 4½" (11.4cm) squares in assorted cream prints for the first pieced border. I've added 4" (10.2cm), 2" (5.1cm) and 4" (10.2cm) finished borders to the quilt and added four-patch units as cornerstones (you'll need eight more units) and simple square cornerstones on border 2. The whole quilt finishes at 88" x 88" (223.5 x 223.5cm).

59 SHARDS OF GLASS

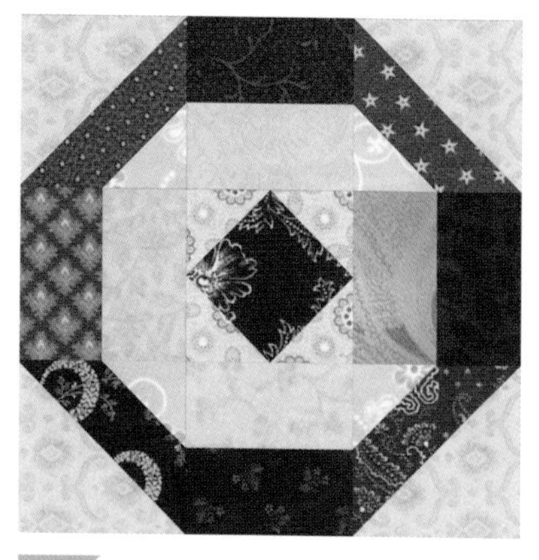

For block 1 you will need:

Finished block size: 12" (30.5cm) square

- Four 2½" x 4½" (6.4 x 11.4cm) rectangles in blue print
- Four 2½" x 4½" (6.4 x 11.4cm) rectangles in tan print
- Four 2⅞" (7.3cm) squares in tan print, cross-cut on both diagonals to yield a total of eight small half square triangles (HSTs)
- One 3⅜" (8.6cm) square in blue print
- Two 4⅞" (12.4cm) squares in tan print, cross-cut on one diagonal to yield four large HSTs Four trapezoid shapes cut in assorted blue prints using the template on page 223

Assembling the block

1. Use one blue and one tan rectangle to make a 'rail fence' unit by joining them along one long edge. Make a total of four.
2. Use four small tan HSTs and the blue square to make one 'square on point' unit for the block centre.
3. Sew a small and a large HST to either side of a blue trapezoid as shown. Make a total of four.
4. Sew the units into rows, then join the rows.

When you're adding plain borders to a pieced quilt top, fold and mark the ¼, ½ and ¾ marks on the border and the quilt top to help you to match your border up perfectly. Pin well and sew with an accurate ¼" (6mm) seam allowance. It's generally a good idea to press seam allowances away from the pieced quilt and onto the plain border.

For block 2 you will need:

Finished block size: 12" (30.5cm) square

- Eight 2½" (6.4cm) squares in assorted brown prints
- Eight 2½" (6.4cm) squares in assorted cream prints
- Four triangles-in-a-square centre pieces in assorted blue prints, cut using template A on page 223
- Four side triangles and four reverse side triangles in assorted cream prints, cut using template B on page 223
- One 4½" (11.4cm) square of large scale blue/brown print

Assembling the block

1. Make four four-patch units using the brown and cream 2½" (6.4cm) squares.
2. Make the 'triangles-in-a-square' units. Make four in total.
3. Arrange the four-patch and 'triangles in a square' units around the centre square.
4. Sew the units into rows, then join the rows.

60 PYRAMIDS

Once you get the hang of cutting patches using a template (see page 14), you'll have this gorgeous modern quilt made in no time. Turquoise prints are contrasted with deep red and just a touch of gold for a quilt that is opulent and striking.

SUGGESTED LAYOUT

If you're making a large quilt don't make 'blocks'. Instead, sew your pyramids into rows, join the rows to make the whole top, and then quilt. Bind the edges, either 'jagged' following the shape of the triangles or trimmed even. My virtual quilt is 36" (91.4cm) square and is made up of twelve rows of twenty-five pyramids.

Vary the placement of the turquoise and red fabrics to create larger 'diamonds'. A design wall (see page 27) is useful for this.

For one block you will need

Finished block size: 9" (22.9cm) square

- 3½" (8.9cm) wide strips of assorted turquoise prints – cut ten pyramid shapes
- 3½" (8.9cm) wide strips of red solid – cut ten pyramid shapes
- Scraps of gold solid or gold print – cut one pyramid

Assembling the block

1. Download and print (see page 220 for link) or photocopy the Pyramids template on page 223. Following the instructions on page 14, cut out the pyramids as listed above.
2. Arrange the pyramids in rows, alternating the red and turquoise fabrics and perhaps adding a gold pyramid for variety. Each row will have seven pyramids.
3. Sew the pyramids in rows, pressing the seams towards the red triangles.
4. Sew the rows together, matching the intersections of the pyramids carefully.
5. Trim the block to 9½" (24.1cm) square.

CURVES

So much of patchwork is based on straight-sided geometric shapes and I love them – every one of them – but add some curves to your quilting and suddenly you're in the major league! Curved piecing is seen by some as a challenge, but trust me on this: getting a beautifully curved seam is no harder than achieving a half square triangle with a really sharp point. Yes, it takes a little practice and a few extra pins. Your first attempt may not be as good as the third or fourth, but don't forget, squares and strips were just as challenging when we started our quilting journey. If you're a beginner, there are tips and techniques here to have you sewing curves like a pro, so dive in and try something different.

SHOW OFF YOUR CURVES!

So why are quilts with curves so exciting? Maybe it's the contrast between the order and precision of sharp-pointed triangles lying next to a curvy swag border, maybe it's the appliquéd flowers that rise from a pieced sash or the optical effects of a curved shaped meeting a straight-sided neighbour – whatever it is, quilts with curves are special. They always seem to me to have that extra something, that star quality that raises them higher and gets that extra-long 'oooh' when they are held up at guild meetings. Curves can be pieced or appliquéd, worked by hand or machine; sometimes the curves are illusions and sometimes they are simply buttons or yo-yos, added after quilting. Feel free to add appliqué to any of the quilts in this book and see what the power of curves can do for your quilting!

61 I LOVE CANDY!

I love candy stripes and although I don't have a massively sweet tooth I can't resist a candy cane at Christmas. This block makes for a very quick and easy baby or child's quilt, with or without the appliqués. I've used 1½" (3.8cm) strips, but you could easily use 2½" (6.4cm) pre-cut strips and double the size of the block to 10½" x 20½" (26.7 x 52cm).

SUGGESTED LAYOUT

For my virtual quilt, I used twenty I Love Candy blocks sewn together in five vertical rows of four. Cut vertical sashing pieces 40½" (102.9cm) long x 3" (7.6cm) wide and sew them between the rows. Add a 1" (2.5cm) finished border to make a 34½" x 42" (87.6 x 106.7cm) quilt. I've added solid pink heart appliqués scattered across the quilt. Use the template on page 223 and your favourite appliqué method (see page 24) to do this. Increase or decrease the size as you see fit.

When deciding on the method of appliqué for a quilt, consider its use. If the quilt is going to be used and washed often, a turned edge method (such as starch and press or interfaced method) will produce a more durable finish than fused raw edge appliqué.

For one block you will need

Finished block size: 5" x 10" (12.7 x 25.4cm)

- Five assorted 1½" x 11" (3.8 x 28cm) strips in pink prints

Assembling the block

1. Sew the strips together, side by side, to create a panel that is 5½" (14cm) wide and approximately 11" (28cm) long. Keep the edges fairly even, but don't sweat this!
2. Trim the length of the pieced unit to 10½" (26.7cm).

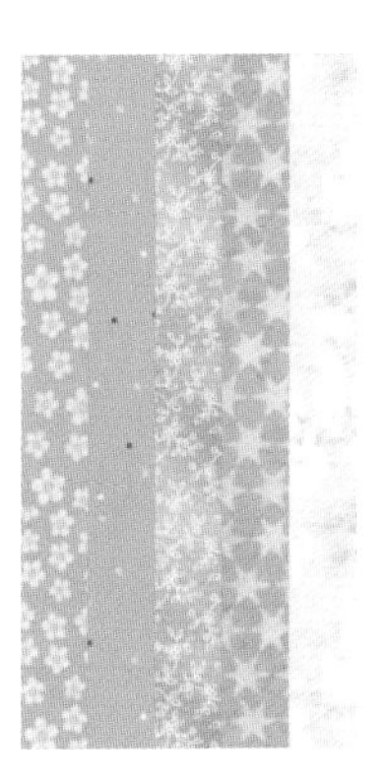

STRING WINDOW

String-pieced backgrounds and an easy machine-stitched cathedral window technique make this quilt a breeze, using nothing but strips and squares!

SUGGESTED LAYOUT

In my virtual quilt, I have set twelve String Window blocks together with four additional blocks for the corners. I made the corner blocks by using 4" (10cm) finished squares of background fabric, 4" (10cm) finished folded blue squares and 4" (10cm) feature squares. These sixteen total blocks make a quilt that is 64" (162.6cm) square.

For one block you will need

Finished block size: 16" (40.7cm) square

- Assorted strips of assorted print fabrics for the background – each strip should be at least 9" (22.9cm) long and between 1" (2.5cm) and 2½" (6.4cm) wide (these can be straight strips or slightly wonky!)
- Four 8½" (21.6cm) squares in medium blue solid
- One 8½" (21.6cm) square in feature print

Layer the quilt top with backing and wadding (batting) and 'tie' the quilt at regular intervals. For example, tie the block intersections and the tips of the 'windows' with cotton perle. Take a big stitch through the quilt sandwich and then knot your thread off several times. Clip the thread ends to leave a 'tuft' of thread on the top of the quilt.

Assembling the block

1. Sew assorted 9" (22.9cm) strips together to make a panel approximately 9" (22.9cm) square. Trim to 8½" x 8½" (21.6 x 21.6cm). Make four in total.
2. Fold each of the 8½" (21.6cm) blue squares in half on the diagonal, wrong sides together, and press.
3. Lay out the four string-pieced background blocks in a two by two arrangement, with the strips alternating in direction as shown.
4. Lay the folded blue 'triangles' on top of the background squares so that all of the raw edges are in the centre and the folded edges form a 'square on point'. Tack (baste) or pin the blue triangles to the backgrounds.
5. Sew the four squares together in the two by two arrangement. Press the seams open.
6. Lay your 8½" (21.6cm) feature print square on top of the 'square on point'.
7. Roll back the edges of the blue triangles to cover the raw edges.
8. Sew in place by hand or machine.

63 SEASIDE WINDMILLS

There's nothing more evocative of childhood seaside holidays in Britain than the sight of a brightly coloured windmill on a stick. We would walk along the seafront holding onto them for dear life, battling against the icy winds, distracted from the cold by the sight of those spinning blades! Ahhh... happy memories!

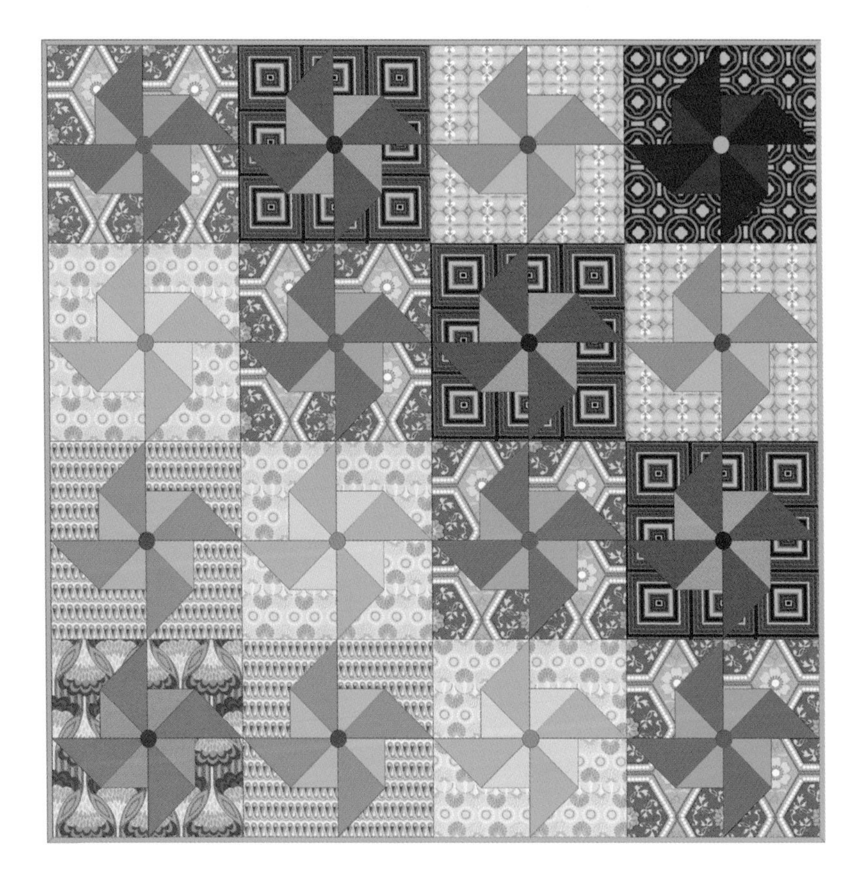

SUGGESTED LAYOUT

For my virtual quilt, I have set sixteen Seaside Windmill blocks in a four by four arrangement, creating diagonal bands of colour with both the backgrounds and the windmills themselves. After layering and quilting, try adding covered buttons, regular buttons or fabric yo-yos over the block centres. The finished wall quilt is 32" (81.2cm) square.

For one block you will need

Finished block size: 8" (20.3cm) square

- Four 2½" x 4½" (6.4 x 11.4cm) rectangles and four 2½" (6.4cm) squares in background fabric – I've picked a large-scale patterned print
- Four 2½" (6.4cm) squares in dark pink solid
- Four 4½" (11.4cm) squares in medium pink solid

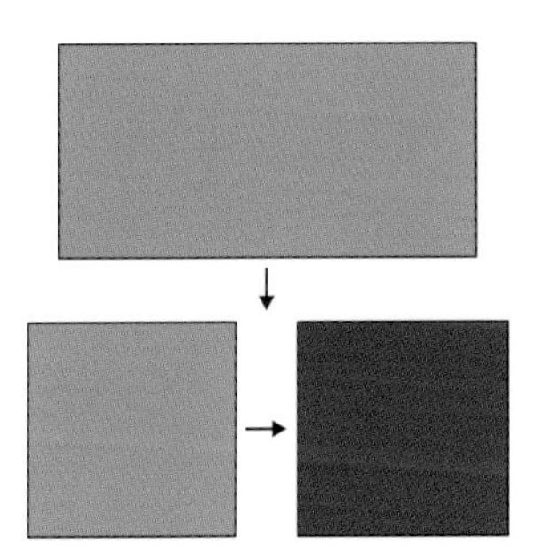

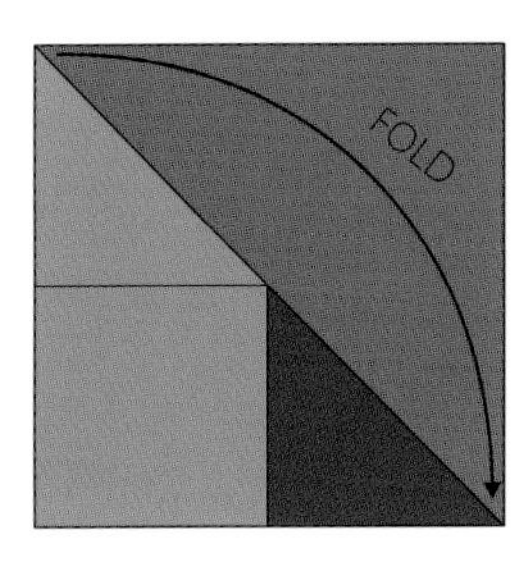

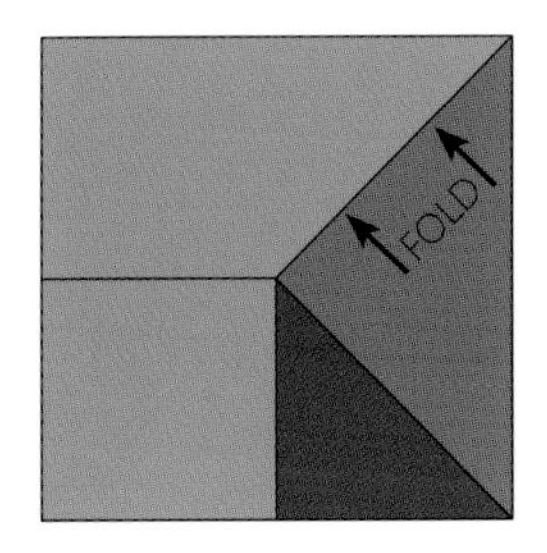

Assembling the block

1. Lay out one rectangle and one square of background fabric and one 2½" (6.4cm) square of dark pink solid. Sew the units together to make a 4½" (11.4cm) square unit. Make four units.
2. Fold each of the 4½" (11.4cm) squares of medium pink solid in half on the diagonal, wrong sides together, and press.
3. Lay one folded square on top of a pieced background unit, with the fold running diagonally across the centre of the square, covering half of the dark pink square, then fold the top corner of the folded square back down on itself, matching the raw edges carefully. Pin or tack (baste) in place. Make four.
4. Arrange the units together to create the windmill , as shown, then sew together. Press the seams open to reduce the bulk.
5. For more 'curve appeal', you could bend the edges of your windmills and stitch the in place.

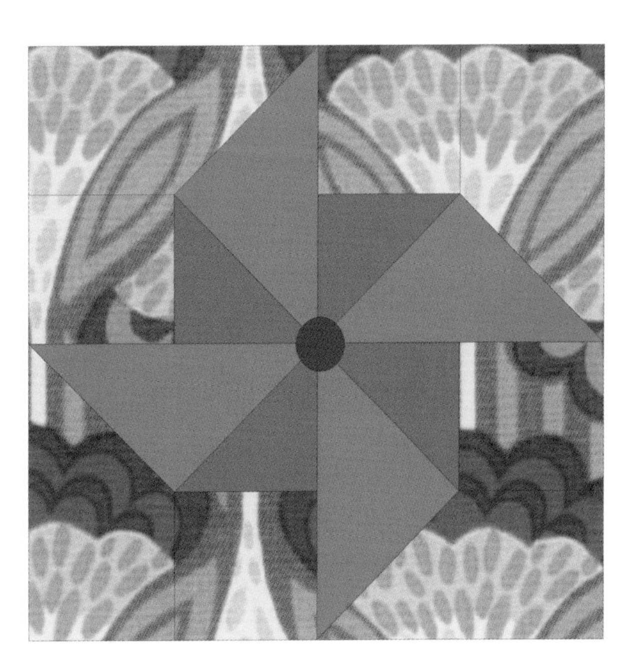

This quilt is three-dimensional and is perfect for a wall quilt. If you want to make it as a quilt to use, consider sewing the edges of the windmills down.

64 PINEAPPLE LOG CABIN

Log cabin blocks never fail to please – they have a fascinating history, endless variations and would you believe this quilt is made with only strips and squares? No triangles at all!

SUGGESTED LAYOUT

I have made nine Pineapple Log Cabin blocks and set them in a three by three arrangement. I've added a 6" (15.2cm) finished border and 6" (15.3cm) finished cornerstones to make a quilt that is 57" x 57" (144.8 x 144.8cm). I've added twelve double swags to the border and 'closed' the gaps with leaves and circles cut from an assortment of copper, rust and black prints. The templates are on page 223. Use your favourite appliqué method (see page 24) to add these.

For one block you will need

Finished block size: 15" (38.1cm) square

- Twenty assorted scraps of various rust and copper brown prints – sixteen of them cut to 3½" (8.9cm) squares, the remaining four cut to 2" (5.1cm) squares
- From an assortment of cream and light tan prints, cut the following:
- One 3½" (8.9cm) square for the block centre

  Round 1: two 2" x 3½" (5.1 x 8.9cm) strips, two 2" x 6½" (5.1 x 16.5cm) strips

  Round 2: two 2" x 6½" (5.1 x 16.5cm) strips, two 2" x 9½" (5.1 x 24.1cm) strips

  Round 3: two 2" x 9½" (5.1 x 24.1cm) strips, two 2" x 12½" (5.1 x 31.7cm) strips

  Round 4: two 2" x 12½" (5.1 x 31.7cm) strips, two 2" x 15½" (5.1 x 39.4cm) strips

Anchor the corners of your quilts by creating focal points. It might be as subtle as using a different print in the corners or adding appliqués to draw the eye outwards. This keeps the viewer's eyes moving over your whole quilt.

Assembling the block

1. Mark the diagonal on the back of all twenty rust and copper squares lightly in pencil.
2. Use the 2" (5.1cm) copper and rust squares and the 3½" (8.9cm) cream centre square to make one square in a square unit, following the instructions for stitch and flip on page 20. Press.
3. Round 1: Sew the 3½" (8.9cm) cream/tan strips to opposite sides of the unit, press them back, then sew the 6½" (16.5cm) strips to the remaining two sides. Press.
4. Lay one of the 3½" (8.9cm) copper/rust squares right side down over the corner of your unit, with the marked diagonal line 'cutting' across the corner. Sew on this line, flip it back and press, then trim the background away from underneath the copper square, leaving a ¼" (6mm) seam allowance. Repeat on the remaining three corners.
5. Repeat steps 2 and 3, using the strips and squares for rounds 2, 3 and 4. Your finished block should measure 15½" x 15½" (39.4 x 39.4cm), raw edge to raw edge.

65 CLAMSHELLS

Clamshell quilts are classic 1970s fare, but a collection of favourite prints or jewel-bright solids can bring this gorgeous design right up to date. The blocks are big and the curves are gentle so even a confident beginner can tackle this design. Breaking the clamshell down into half and quarter circles makes the piecing even easier!

For one block you will need

Finished block size: 12" (30.5cm) square

- Five 13" (33cm) squares in assorted prints or solids

Assembling the block

1. Download and print (see page 220 for link) or photocopy the Clamshells templates on page 224. Following the instructions on page 14, from one of the squares of fabric cut one half circle (template A) and two backgrounds (template B). You will need to flip the background template for one of the backgrounds.
2. From the remaining four fabrics cut a total of two more backgrounds (template B), flipping the template for one of them, and two quarter circles (template C), again, flipping the template for one of them.
3. Arrange the patches to form the block, as shown. Sew the two matching backgrounds to the two quarter circles. Join the resulting units.
4. Sew the remaining backgrounds together, then sew in the half circle piece, matching the centres carefully.
5. Join the two units to complete the block.

Careful placement of your fabrics is essential for this quilt to make sure that fabrics match up. Use a design wall (see page 27) or lay your patches out carefully on a bed, and work systematically in rows. When sewing curves, match the centres and ends, then pin really well. Take your time and clip the seam allowances a little to help the block lie flat.

SUGGESTED LAYOUT

My quilt uses thirty-six Clamshells blocks set in a six by six arrangement to make a 72" (182.8cm) square quilt.

66 SPLIT LEAVES

I love the simplicity of this leaf shape – it's modern, sleek and the strong diagonal gives plenty of setting opportunities once your blocks are made. Have fun playing with the layout of this quilt or add extra rows for even more options!

For one block you will need

Finished block size: 9" (22.9cm) square

- Two 9⅞" (25cm) squares in assorted bright leaf green prints
- Two 4" x 14" (10.2 x 35.6cm) rectangles in assorted lilac/purple prints

Assembling the block

1. On the back of one of the 9⅞" (25cm) leaf green squares, mark the diagonal lightly in pencil. Layer this square with the other, right sides together, and pin.
2. Sew ¼" (6mm) either side of the drawn line, then cut apart on the line to yield two half square triangle (HST) units, which should each measure 9½" (24.1cm) square.
3. Sew the two purple rectangles together down one long side to create a larger rectangle approximately 7½" x 14" (19 x 35.6cm).
4. Download and print (see page 220 for link) or photocopy the Split Leaves template on page 224, ensuring that you transfer the centre line.
5. Use the starch and press appliqué method (see page 24) to cut out and turn the edges of your leaf, centring the seam with the centre line on your template.
6. Appliqué the leaf over the centre seam of the background square, as shown.

For an easier quilt, trace the large leaf template onto the paper side of fusible web. Fuse to the wrong side of the pieced rectangle, lining up the centre mark on the template with the centre seam on your rectangles. Cut out the leaf shape along the line and then fuse it to the background squares. Finish the edges of your leaf shapes with a small zigzag or blanket stitch, using toning or contrasting thread.

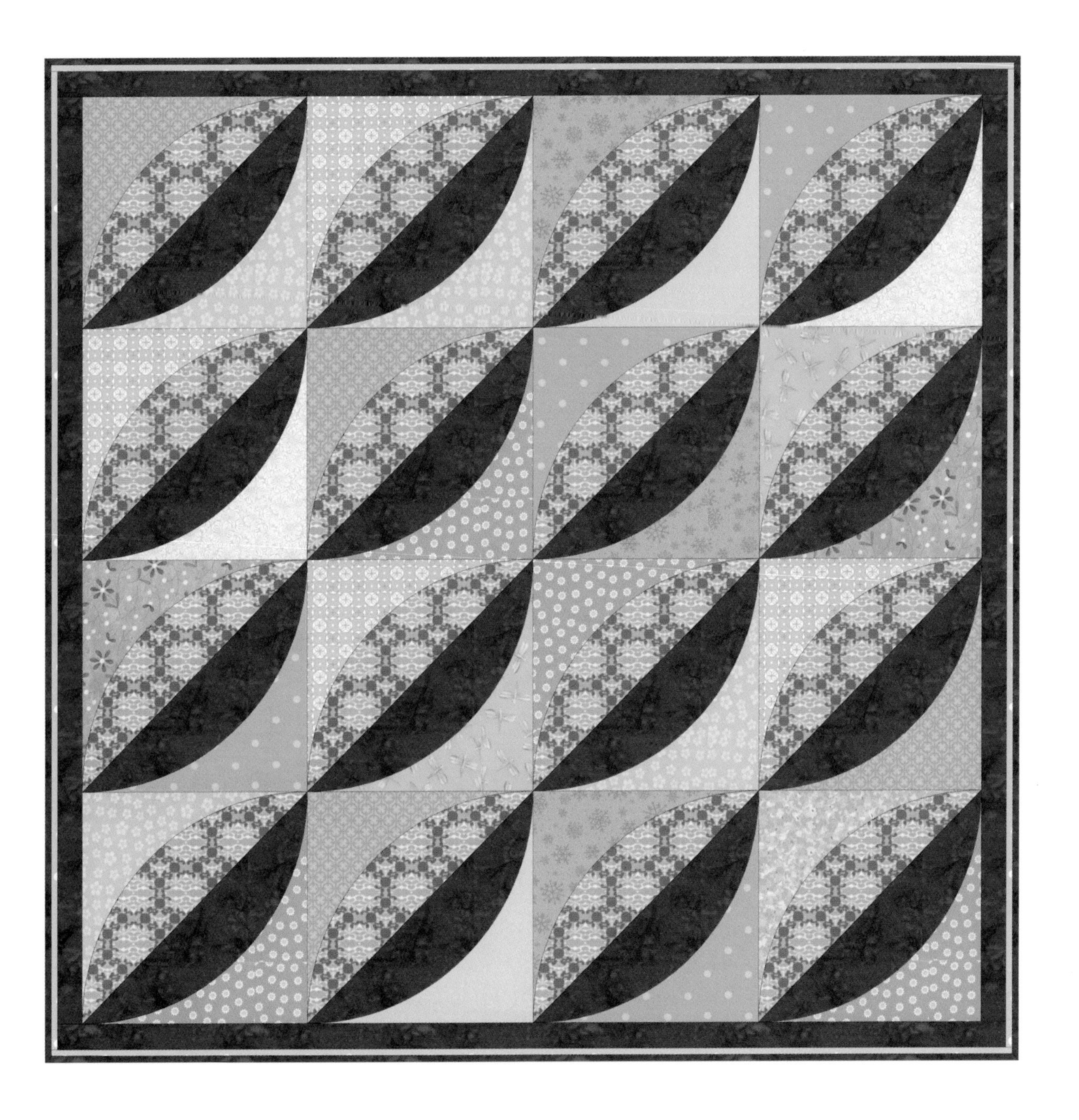

SUGGESTED LAYOUT

For my quilt I have set sixteen blocks in a four by four arrangement, with all the leaves pointing one way, but there are many possible layouts – have fun with it! I've added a 1" (2.5cm) finished border in dark purple and inserted a ¼" (6mm) bright green flange between this border and the binding. My quilt finishes at 38" x 38" (96.5 x 96.5cm).

67 RIC RAC

I've used an Accuquilt die cutter for this quilt, but I have included the templates (see page 224) so you can cut your own ric rac if you prefer.

SUGGESTED LAYOUT

For my quilt I made twenty-five Ric Rac blocks and set them in a five by five arrangement, rotating half of them through 90 degrees. The quilt finishes at 47" x 47" x (119.4 x 119.4cm).

For one block you will need

Finished block size: 9½" (24.1cm) square

- Fusible web
- Two assorted print fabrics in toning colours
- One 10" (25.4cm) square of white solid
- Accuquilt Ric Rac die 401572 (optional)

Assembling the block

1. Download and print (see page 220 for link) or photocopy the Ric Rac templates on page 224. Following the instructions on page 14, trace the 4" (10.2cm) wide ric rac once and the 2" (5.1cm) ric rac twice onto the paper side of your fusible web. Cut the shapes out roughly.
2. Iron the wider tracing to the wrong side of one of your chosen print fabrics and the two narrow tracings to the wrong side of the other print fabric.
3. Cut your ric rac out neatly on the lines.
4. Alternatively, iron fusible web to the back of both print fabrics. Layer one fabric over the wider ric rac on the Accuquilt Ric Rac die, wrong side up, and then cut the other fabric into two pieces, at least 10" (25.4cm) long and 2½" (6.4cm) wide. Layer both of these pieces, wrong side up, over the narrow ric rac. Cut your ric rac pieces with your die cutter.
5. Peel the paper off the fused ric racs and arrange the pieces on your white fabric square. Make sure that the wide ric rac runs through the centre of the block and place a narrow strip either side, approximately ¾" (19mm) apart. Fuse in place.
6. Sew the edges of the fused ric racs with a zigzag or machine blanket stitch. Trim the edges of the block is there is any 'over-hang'.

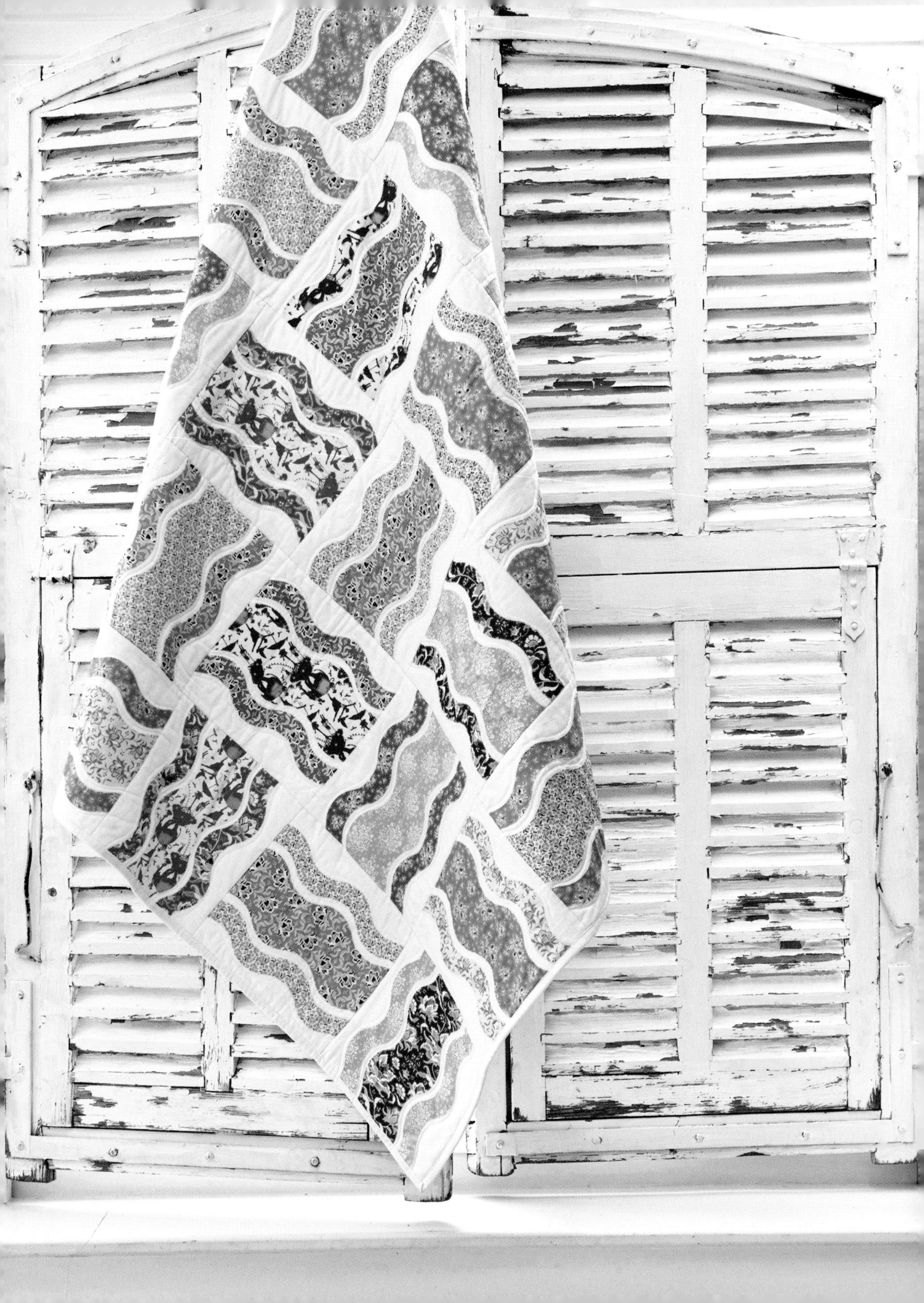

68 SHOWCASE

Sometimes we buy fabrics that are simply too beautiful to cut up - here is the perfect pattern to showcase your favourite prints. It's ideal for an Asian fabric collection, large-scale bright florals or a prized collection of batiks. Or do as I have and show off a beautiful assortment of black and white prints on an ombre-effect coloured background.

For one block you will need

Finished block size: 9" (22.9cm) square

- One 8" (20.3cm) square of feature print
- One 9½" (24.1cm) background square of green solid
- One 8" (20.3cm) square of lightweight fusible interfacing

Assembling the block

1. Download and print (see page 220 for link) or photocopy the Showcase circle template on page 224. Following the instructions on page 14, cut out an equal number of shapes in light and dark fabrics. Use this template to draw a circle lightly in pencil on the wrong side of your feature fabric. Alternatively, draw around a 7" (17.8cm) bowl or plate.
2. Layer the interfacing, glue side against the right side of the fabric, and pin well.
3. Using a shorter than normal stitch on your sewing machine, sew all around the circle, right on the drawn line. Cut the circle out, leaving a very skinny ¼" (6mm) seam allowance around the edge.
4. Carefully pull the fabric and interfacing circles apart and cut a 2" (5.1cm) cross through the interfacing. Turn the circle through to the right side and finger press the edges. Do not use an iron!
5. Lay your prepared circle on top of your background square, centring it - fold light creases in both the background and the circle to help you do this.
6. Fuse the circle in place with an iron following the interfacing manufacturer's instructions.
7. Appliqué the circle in place with a zigzag or blanket stitch and matching thread.

Use the starch and press appliqué method if you prefer (see page 24). Circles are very easy to do with either method and both give great results!

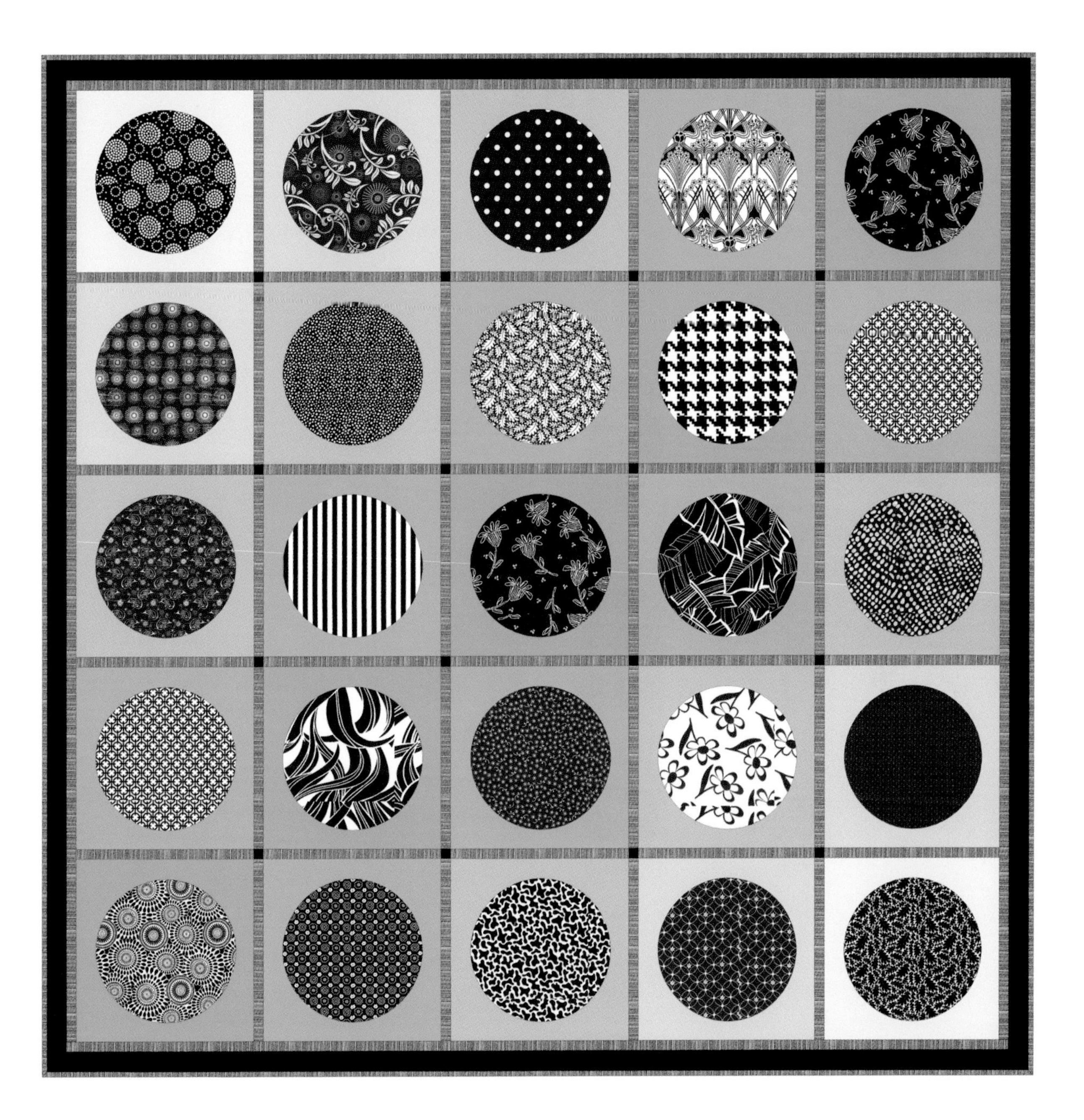

SUGGESTED LAYOUT

For my virtual quilt, I have made twenty-five Showcase blocks, with monochrome circles appliquéd to green solids. I've set them, arranged in a fade from the centre out, in a five by five arrangement, separated by ½" (12mm) finished sashing and cornerstones. I've added a ½" (12mm) and a 1" (2.5cm) finished border to complete this 50"x 50" (127 x 127cm) quilt.

69 STAR BAKER

I love to bake but in my home the star baker is most definitely my husband, Charlie. His cupcakes are a sight to behold and a delight to eat. These cakes, rendered in fabric, are guaranteed to add no inches to your waistline - so whip up a whole batch!

For one block you will need

Finished block size: 9" (22.9cm) square

- One 5" x 9½" (14 x 24.1cm) rectangle in bright geometric print
- One 5" x 9½" (14 x 24.1cm) rectangle in mustard yellow solid
- Scraps of assorted bright prints for the cupcake wrapper, icing (frosting) and a small solid red scrap for the cherry
- Fusible web

Assembling the block

1. Download and print (see page 220 for link) or photocopy the Star Baker templates on page 225. Following the instructions on page 14, trace one cupcake wrapper (cut as one large rhomboid shape), one cupcake centre (the 'flowerpot' shape in the middle of the large rhomboid), one icing and one cherry shape onto the paper side of your fusible web. Cut each shape out roughly.
2. Fuse the web to the wrong side of your chosen fabrics following the manufacturer's instructions. Leave to cool, then cut the shapes out neatly along the lines.
3. Sew both 5" x 9 ½" (14 x 24.1cm) rectangles together down one long side to create a 9½" (24.1cm) square. Press the seams to one side.
4. Arrange your cupcake shapes on the background - wrapper first, with the flowerpot-shaped cupcake centre on top, followed by the icing and finally the cherry. Fuse in place.
5. Sew around the edges of your appliqués with a zigzag or blanket stitch.

Keep an eye out for fun novelty prints to use for the icing - anything white or pink with a geometric print will look like sprinkle-covered icing!

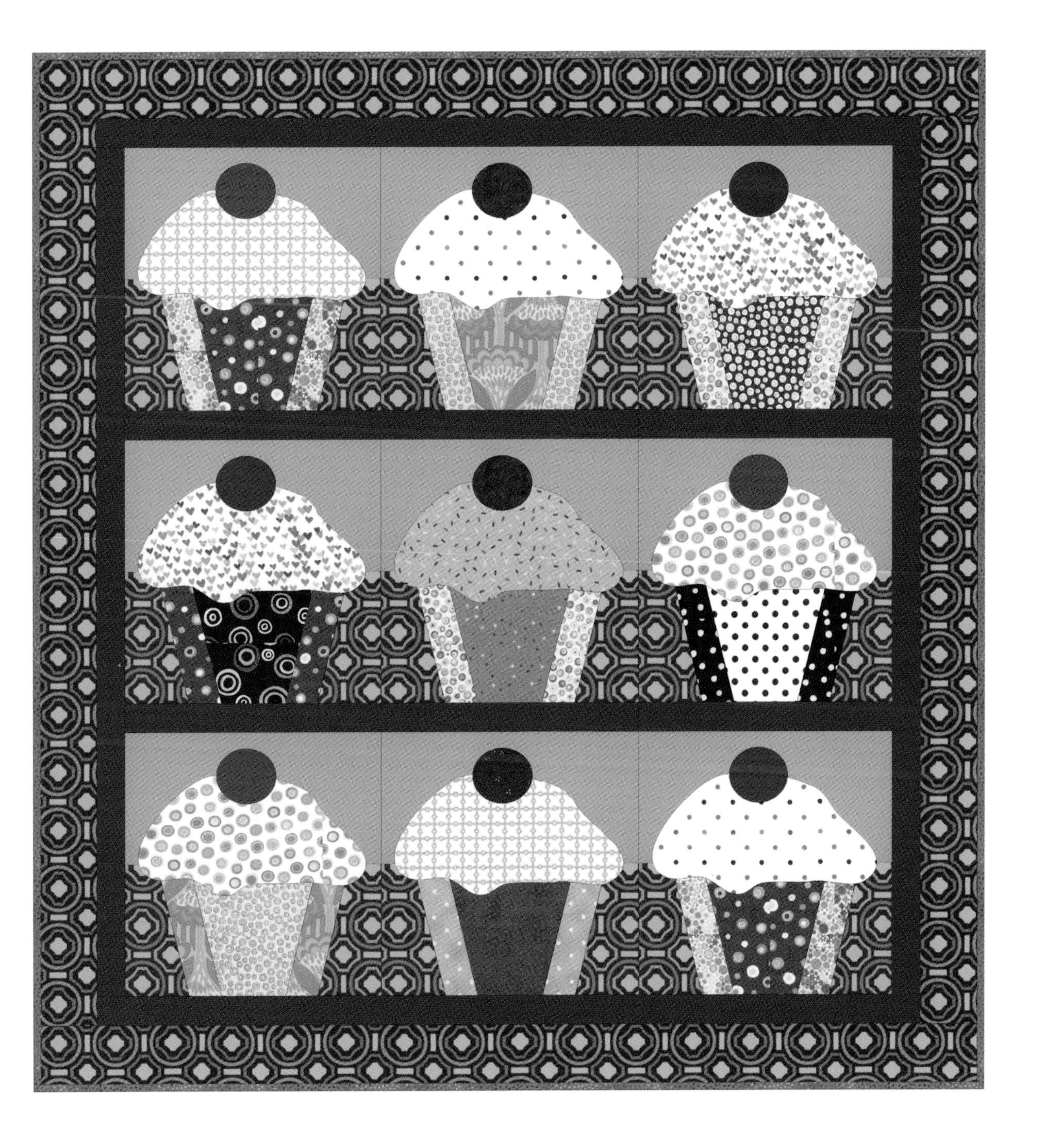

SUGGESTED LAYOUT

My virtual quilt sets nine Star Baker blocks in a three by three arrangement. I've added a 1" (2.5cm) finished sash between the horizontal rows to create bakery 'shelves' and then added a 1" (2.5cm) finished border around the cupcakes in the same brown solid. A final 2" (5.1cm) finished border in a different bright geometric completes this fun 33" x 35" (83.8 x 89cm) quilt.

70 POLKA

Be bold and be beautiful! Circles take centre stage in this fun quilt, where a simple abstract polka dot pattern comes to life in all your favourite brightly hued fabrics.

SUGGESTED LAYOUT

For my virtual quilt I sewed sixteen Polka blocks together in four rows of four to make a 48" (122cm) square quilt. Twist and turn the blocks to create movement in your quilt.

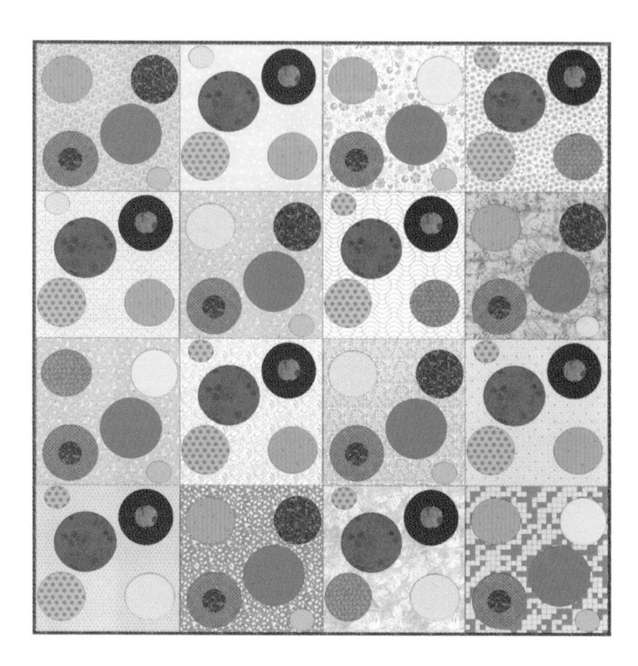

Experiment with the various decorative and embroidery stitches on your sewing machine and use your favourites to sew down the circles.

For one block you will need

Finished block size: 12" (30.5cm) square

- Six scraps of brightly coloured fabrics for the polka dots
- One 12½" (31.7cm) square in blue/aqua for the block background

Assembling the block

1. Download and print (see page 220 for link) or photocopy the Polka templates on page 225. Following the instructions on page 14, make templates of the six polka dot circles.
2. Use your favourite method of appliqué to prepare the circles (see page 24).
3. Arrange the circles on your background square and pin or fuse in place.
4. Sew the circles in place with a straight stitch, zigzag or blanket stitch.

BUTTONS

My mum keeps buttons in a tin, and sometimes I'd open the tin and make patterns with the contents. I've always thought buttons were things of beauty and this little wall quilt would be perfect to brighten up a corner of your sewing room.

SUGGESTED LAYOUT

For my virtual mini quilt, I have made four button blocks and joined them with 1" (2.5cm) finished sashing and cornerstones and a couple of 1" (2.5cm) finished borders. The quilt measures 14" x 41" (35.6 x 104.1cm), but can easily made longer or shorter by adding or subtracting blocks.

If you find cutting the thread holes out fiddly, you could trace the four small circles onto web, fuse to fabric that matches the background and then fuse the holes on top of the button. Finish the edges neatly with a zigzag or blanket stitch.

For one block you will need

Finished block size: 8" (20.3cm) square

- One 8½" (21.6cm) background square in bright solid
- One 8" (20.3cm) square in medium solid
- One 7" (17.8cm) square in dark solid
- Fusible web

Assembling the block

1. Download and print (see page 220 for link) or photocopy the Buttons templates on page 225. Following the instructions on page 14, make templates of the outer button (which is shown as a ring) and the inner button (with four holes). Draw the shapes on the fusible web. Cut out roughly.
2. Fuse the web to the wrong side of your chosen fabrics.
3. Cut out the shapes neatly. Layer the button appliqués on your background square and fuse in place.
4. Sew the edges of the button and the holes with matching thread and a small zigzag or blanket stitch.

HALF CIRCLES

Appliqué circles mimic the look of curved piecing but in a fraction of the time. This is oh so much easier to achieve!

SUGGESTED LAYOUT

For my quilt I have arranged twelve rows of Half Circles in alternating 'A' and 'B' rows. A rows have five Half Circle blocks sewn end to end and B rows have four Half Circle blocks and a 5" x 5¼" (12.7 x 13.3cm) rectangle of background fabric added to either end to offset the half circles. My finished quilt is 47½" x 54" (120.7 x 137.2cm).

For one block you will need

Finished block size: 4½" x 9½" (11.4 x 24.1cm)

- One 9" (22.9cm) square in print fabric
- One 10" (25.4cm) square in light-coloured background fabric
- Fusible web

Assembling the block

1. Download and print (see page 220 for link) or photocopy the Half Circles template on page 225. Following the instructions on page 14, trace this onto the back of the fusible web. Cut out roughly. Alternatively, draw around an 8" (20.3cm) round plate or bowl.
2. Fuse the roughly cut circle of fusible web to the wrong side of the print fabric. Allow to cool, then cut the circle out neatly.
3. Fold the 10" (25.4cm) square of light-coloured background fabric into quarters. Do the same (lightly!) with the circle.
4. Use the creases to centre the circle on the background block. Fuse in place.
5. Appliqué the circle by stitching around it with a zigzag or small blanket stitch. Press the block.
6. Use a rotary cutter to cut the block into two 5" x 10" (12.7 x 25.4cm) rectangles.

To keep your fused appliqués soft and flexible, use the 'doughnut' method when using web – draw the outer circle and cut out roughly, then cut the centre section of the fusible away, leaving a ½" (12mm) ring or 'doughnut' of web. Fuse this to your fabric, then cut out on the outer line. The absence of fusible web in the centre of the circles keeps the fabrics soft.

73 FLOWERING SNOWBALL

These gentle curves are easy to piece and there are only nine pieces of fabric per block - so take your time, pin well and make this gorgeous quilt, which gives such a lot of bang for your buck!

SUGGESTED LAYOUT

My virtual quilt sets sixteen Flowering Snowball blocks in a four by four arrangement - see how the blocks join up to make circles! This quilt has a similar look and feel to a double wedding ring, but is much easier and quicker to piece. Add a ¼" (6mm) black flange border and a final 1" (2.5cm) finished border to complete this 42" x 42" (106.7 x 106.7cm) wallhanging.

Look out for the 'curve master' foot for your sewing machine - this is a brilliant foot that allows you to sew curves perfectly without pinning!

For one block you will need

Finished block size: 10" (25.4cm) square

- Four 5½" (14cm) squares in assorted black prints
- One 9" (22.9cm) square in white solid
- One 2" (5.1cm) square in red solid

Assembling the block

1. Download and print (see page 220 for link) or photocopy the Flowering Snowball templates on page 225. Following the instructions on page 14, cut four pieces in black prints using template A, four pieces in white solid using template B and one piece in red solid using template 3.
2. Matching the ends and centre point, pin then sew a template B shape to either curved side of a template A shape. This is unit 1. Make two.
3. Sew the remaining two template A shapes to either side of the centre red square (template C). This is unit 2.
4. Matching the centres carefully, sew one of the unit 1s to unit 2, as shown. Repeat with the remaining unit 1.

LOLLIPOP FLOWERS #1

A simple cross spray of bright golden lollipop flowers set on a black print background seems to glow, but bright or pastel blooms on a white or cream background would look wonderful, too. An easy-to-piece alternate chain block frames each appliqué beautifully.

For one block you will need

Finished block size: 16" (40.7cm) square

- ¾" (19mm) wide strip of bright green fabric for the stem, approximately 30" (76.2cm) in length
- One small scrap of bright green print for the centre circle
- Twenty-four small scraps of assorted bright green prints, batiks and solids for the leaves
- Assorted scraps of bright gold, copper and yellow prints, batiks and solids for the flowers
- One 16½" (42cm) square of black print fabric for the background
- ⅜" (10mm) bias tape maker

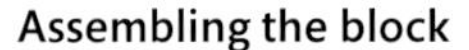

Assembling the block

1. Download and print (see page 220 for link) or photocopy the Lollipop Flowers #1 templates on page 225. Following the instructions on page 14, and your favourite method of appliqué (see page 24), prepare the flowers, leaves and centre. Use the flower centre template for the green central piece.
2. Use a ⅜" (10mm) bias tape maker to make a folded stem about 30" (76.2cm) in length, then cut it in half to make two stems each 15" x ⅜" (38.1 x 10mm).
3. Fold the background square lightly on both diagonals and use these creases to help you position the stems. Appliqué the stems in place by hand or machine. Sew the small green circle over the centre.
4. Place six leaves on either side of the stem pieces, as shown, and appliqué them in place. Add the flowers, covering the raw ends of the stems. Ensure that you have left ¼" (6mm) seam allowance all around the outside of the block. Press.

Spray starch and iron your stem fabrics before you cut them into strips. When you make your bias tape, the starch already in the fabric will help to ensure a really crisp professional finish to your stems.

SUGGESTED LAYOUT

For my virtual quilt I have set twelve Lollipop Flower blocks with thirteen simple chain blocks. The chain blocks are made from a 4½" (11.4cm) cut gold print centre square, surrounded by 2½" (6.4cm) cut strips in black print and 2½" (6.4cm) cut gold print cornerstones. The quilt has two 1" (2.5cm) finished borders of the same fabric, separated by a ¼" (6mm) folded flange border to add a fine pop of colour. The finished quilt is 84" x 84" (213.3 x 213.3cm).

75 ALL OF MY HEART

The Christmas holidays always brings out my most romantic and sentimental side. It's a time for love and peace and joy and nothing really says that to me like a heart. But just imagine if the hearts were all in green and the nine-patch blocks, too - what a lovely quilt to celebrate Saint Patrick's Day!

For one block you will need

Finished block size: 12" (30.5cm) square

- Four scraps of assorted red prints, each approximately 6" (15.2cm) square
- One 12½" (31.7cm) background square in a light cream or white print
- Fusible web

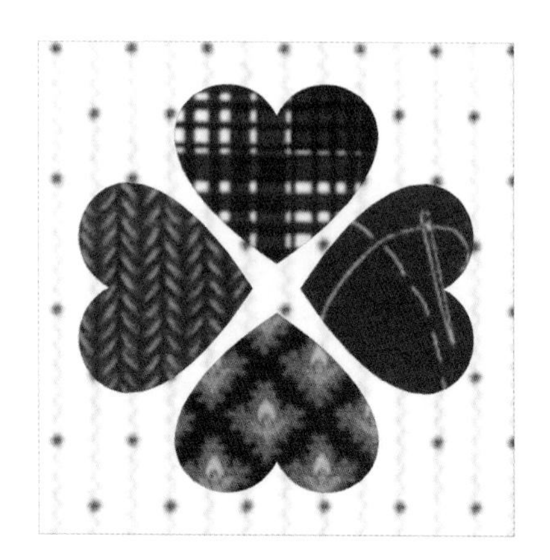

Assembling the block

1. Download and print (see page 220 for link) or photocopy the All of My Heart template on page 225 four times. Following the instructions on page 14, trace them onto the paper side of the fusible web and then fuse them to the wrong side of the red fabric scraps. Cut the fabrics out neatly along the drawn lines.
2. Lightly crease the background square into four quarters and use the creases to position the hearts, as shown. Ensure there is at least 1" (2.5cm) margin around the outside edges of the block.
3. Fuse the hearts in place, following the manufacturer's instructions.
4. Sew around the outside edges of the hearts with a zigzag or blanket stitch and matching thread.

Cover your pressing surface with baking parchment when using fusible web. Cover your project in the same way, then press through the paper; this will help prevent you from getting glue on your iron or ironing board.

SUGGESTED LAYOUT

For my virtual Christmas quilt, I have set nine All of My Heart blocks on point with four nine-patch blocks – these are quickly made using 4½" (11.4cm) squares of assorted greens and a light grey print. A jolly holly print fabric is perfect for the setting triangles. Cut two 18¼" (46.3cm) squares of holly print fabric, then cross-cut each one on both diagonals to yield eight setting triangles. The corner triangles are cut from two 9 ⅜" (23.8cm) squares, cut on one diagonal to yield four triangles. There is a final 1" (2.5cm) finished border in bright green. The finished quilt is approximately 40" x 40" (102 x 102cm) and would look wonderful as a sofa throw or wallhanging.

76 LOLLIPOP FLOWERS #2

From the most sophisticated arrangement to a wild flower growing by the side of the road, flowers always make me happy - and they inspire many of my quilt designs and colour schemes. The simplicity of shape and repetition of the block allow me to go completely crazy with colours in this quilt. Bright turquoise prints make for an exciting 'neutral' background and, to top it off, I've used raindrop quilting! Always remember, 'No showers... no flowers!'

SUGGESTED LAYOUT

I made sixteen Lollipop Flower blocks and joined them in four rows of four. I made strip-pieced sashing made of a 1" (5.1cm) finished strip of light turquoise batik sewn either side of a 1½" (3.8cm) finished strip of orange print fabric to make 3½" (8.9cm) finished sashing strips. I also added 3½" (8.9cm) finished cornerstones. The quilt is 58" (147.3cm) square.

For one block you will need

Finished block size: 10" (25.4cm) square

- Four 5½" (14cm) squares in assorted turquoise prints for the background
- Three assorted bright scraps for the flower
- Two assorted green scraps for the leaves
- One ¾" (19mm) wide bias-cut strip of fabric for the stem
- A ⅜" (10mm) bias tape maker

Assembling the block

1. Sew the four background squares together to make a 10½" (26.7cm) square. Press.
2. Prepare your assorted bright scraps and green scraps for your chosen method of appliqué (see page 24).
3. Download and print (see page 220 for link) or photocopy the Lollipop Flowers #2 templates on page 225. Following the instructions on page 14, cut out the shapes.
4. Make the stem by passing the ¾" (19mm) wide strip of fabric through the ⅜" (10mm) bias tape maker and pressing it. You will need approximately 10" (25.4cm) of 'stem'.
5. Using the picture as a guide, appliqué the stem first, followed by the large circle, then the medium-sized circle and finally the flower centre. Appliqué the leaves either side of the stem. Press.

77 ROSE PETALS

Whisper-soft backgrounds of lilac and dove grey lend a restful air to this baby quilt, while appliquéd petals in deep rose pinks add movement and delectable curves to this lovely scrap buster. Use a turned-edge appliqué technique to keep the quilt soft and easy to launder.

For one block you will need

Finished block size: 4" (10.2cm) square

- One 5" (12.7cm) square in rose print
- One 4½" (11.4cm) square in pale lilac or dove grey print for the background

Assembling the block

1. Download and print (see page 220 for link) or photocopy the Rose Petals template on page 226. Following the instructions on page 14, cut out a petal shape in rose print fabric. Remember to add a turn-under allowance if you are using a turned edge appliqué technique.
2. Appliqué the petal to the background using your preferred method (see page 24). Remember to leave an even ¼" (6mm) seam allowance on all edges of the background square.
3. Press your block carefully from the back.

For speedier construction of a quilt like the one opposite, you could appliqué and quilt the rose petals in one step. Sew the sixty-four background squares together first, layer with wadding (batting) and backing, then tack (baste) or pin the rose petals on top. Appliqué and quilt the edges of the petals with a straight stitch, sewn very close to the appliqué edge.

SUGGESTED LAYOUT

For my virtual quilt, I have used forty-eight Rose Petals blocks and sixteen squares of assorted lilac and dove grey fabric cut at 4½" x 4½" (11.4 x 11.4cm) and set them in an eight by eight arrangement. The quilt finishes at 32" x 32" (81.2 x 81.2cm).

78 RACING TRACK

When I was young, my brother had an electric racing car set for Christmas one year. I remember us playing with it for many years – we loved sending the cars careering off the edges by running them too fast and were always frustrated by how hard it was to snap the tracks together. My quilt reminds me of those ill-matched tracks, but this time, the offset tracks are a virtue!

For one block you will need

Finished block size: 16" (40.7cm) square

- Assorted red, brown, golden brown, grey and gold scraps
- White solid scraps

Assembling the block

1. Download and print (see page 220 for link) or photocopy the Racing Track templates on page 226. Following the instructions on page 14, cut out one background (template A) in deep red, two of each thin arc (templates B and D) in white, two tracks (template C) – one brown and one gold – and two quarter circles (template E) – one golden brown and one grey.
2. Start by sewing a thin white arc to both of the quarter circles. Before sewing, match the centre and ends carefully and pin, then pin in between these points.
3. Add the 'track' and the remaining white arc to each quarter circle section. Make two and press carefully.
4. Sew one pieced arc to the side of the background piece. Press carefully, then sew the other pieced arc to the opposite side.

When piecing curves, fold the patches in half and find the midpoint. Mark with a crease or a pin. Use these midpoints to help you line your patches up accurately.

SUGGESTED LAYOUT

My virtual quilt uses sixteen blocks. Once you have made the blocks, it's a good idea to use a design wall to arrange them (see page 27). Play with your arrangement until you are happy, then sew the blocks into rows and finally sew the rows together. The finished quilt is 64" x 64" (162.6 x 162.6cm).

79 ROB PETER TO PAY PAUL

I love the old-fashioned names of quilt blocks and this one, 'Rob Peter to pay Paul', is a classic! It's sometimes called the Sugar Bowl block; perhaps Paul had a particularly sweet tooth? I've coloured this for Halloween and it would make a great table runner for a spooky party!

For one block you will need

Finished block size: 9" (22.9cm) square

- Assorted orange scraps
- Assorted black print scraps
- Assorted white print scraps

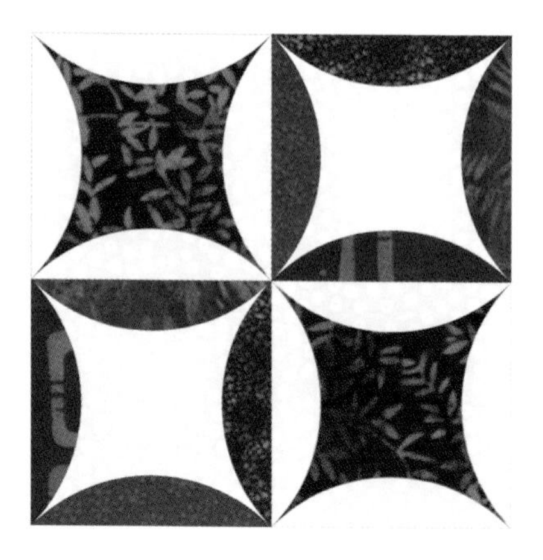

Assembling the block

1. Download and print (see page 220 for link) or photocopy the Rob Peter to Pay Paul templates on page 226. Following the instructions on page 14, cut the following pieces: two centres (template A) in black (or orange) and two in white, eight curved edges (template B) in orange and eight in white.
2. Piece one unit at a time. Find the centres of each of the curved edges by folding the patches lightly in half and creasing.
3. Using these creases to line up your patches, sew each curved edge to one side of a centre patch, then press back before adding the next patch. Make four units in total, sewing the orange curved edges to the white centres and the white curved edges to the black or orange centres.
4. Sew your four units together into a four-patch.

Add small black buttons at some of the block intersections and then hand embroider 'spiders legs' for even more Halloween charm!

SUGGESTED LAYOUT

My virtual table runner uses a total of twelve Rob Peter to Pay Paul blocks, set in a two by six arrangement. The runner finishes at 18" x 54" (45.7 x 137.2cm).

80 CROMER CRABS

This block is a 'pickle dish' variation, but as soon as I started playing with colours, all I could see were crabs! The best crabs in the world, in my humble opinion, come from Cromer, on the North Norfolk coast.

For one block you will need

Finished block size: 16" (40.7cm) square

- Assorted bright orange and orange-red scraps
- Mid and light grey print scraps for the background

Assembling the block

Make the 'legs' first

1. Download and print (see page 220 for link) or photocopy four copies of Cromer Crabs foundation A (page 227) and paper piece the blocks following the instructions on page 21. Trim your units to 4½" x 4½" (11.4 x 11.4cm) along the outer line. Make four units in total.
2. Cut two 4½" (11.4cm) squares of assorted grey prints and set aside. Cut two 4½" (11.4cm) squares in assorted orange and orange-red prints.
3. Sew the 'legs' and background squares together as shown. Make 2 units.

Make the 'bodies'

1. Use the Cromer Crabs templates provided on page 227 to cut two quarter circles (template B) in orange prints and two backgrounds (template C) in assorted grey prints.
2. Sew the quarter circle to the background, then press. Make two.
3. Arrange the leg and body units as shown and sew together. Finally, remove the foundation paper. Add appliqué or button eyes if you like!

SUGGESTED LAYOUT

For my virtual quilt, I have arranged four blocks together to make a 32" x 32" (81.2 x 81.2cm) wallhanging.

If you don't enjoy curved piecing, you could always appliqué the quarter circles to background squares instead: cut the grey print background squares for the 'body' sections at 8½" x 8½" (21.6 x 21.6cm) and then appliqué the quarter circles to one corner.

FOUNDATION PIECING

Foundation piecing is a technique I learned many years ago in my search for patchwork perfection. I'd been quilting for a few years and just wasn't getting the precision I craved. Sewing your fabrics to a foundation (whether it's paper, calico, interfacing or even a piece of quilt wadding/batting), using printed or drawn lines as a guide, means that the trickiest -looking blocks are just a hop, skip and a jump away from anyone who can sew a straight line! It's definitely a technique I would encourage you to learn, make friends with and use. Once you've added this technique to your tool box, you'll see that a world of opportunities opens up and quilts you thought were way too hard will be easily within your reach.

FOUNDATION PIECED PERFECTION!

There's a detailed explanation of paper foundation piecing in the techniques chapter (see page 21) and I've included a bonus easy Square in a Square block to practise on (see page 220). It's well worth making this block as a test run, even if you've had a go at foundation piecing before, just to familiarize yourself with my easy techniques. Once you have boosted your skills it's time to pick your pattern! I've included some striking modern quilts, like Quiver and Whirl, a couple of re-worked classics, like Wild Goose Chase and Kaleidoscope, added some brand new blocks, including Kogin (based on Japanese embroidery) and a smattering of fun novelty quilts – so if you're looking for something just a little bit different, then look no further!

QUIVER

Strikingly modern, made in a collection of warm or cool solids, this was inspired by a close-up of a bird's feather. Easy to piece, this block would make a gorgeous quilt - or simply make two blocks for a pair of cushions.

SUGGESTED LAYOUT

My virtual quilt uses forty-two blocks set in a six by seven arrangement. I've added 2" (5.1cm) finished vertical sashing to match the 'spines' of the feathers and a final 2" (5.1cm) finished border all around to make a quilt that is 110" x 116" (279.4 x 294.6cm). Just one block with a 2" (5.1cm) border makes a perfect 20" (50.8cm) square pillow - just add a simple envelope back.

Try out new techniques by making smaller projects - cushions and pillows are ideal. If you enjoy the results, you can always make the larger quilt project, too!

For one block you will need

Finished block size: 16" (40.7cm) square

- Twelve 2½" x 40" (6.4 x 101.6cm) strips in assorted solid fabrics
- One 2½" x 16½" (6.4 x 42cm) strip for the spine of the 'feather'

Assembling the block

1. Download and print (see page 220 for link) or photocopy two copies of the Quiver foundation (page 227).
2. Use the 40" (101.6cm) strips to piece each foundation in numerical order, following the instructions on page 21. Trim each unit to 7½" x 16½" (19 x 42cm).
3. Sew the foundations to either side of the 'spine', turning one foundation through 180° so that the quilts of the feather form a V-shape.

82 KOGIN

This design is inspired by Japanese Kogin embroidery. I'm always seeing inspiration in other needle arts (and crafts in general). There's a huge amount of crossover, and this dynamic block would be equally at home made into a bag front, cushion or runner.

SUGGESTED LAYOUT

My quilt uses thirteen Kogin blocks set on point. The setting triangles are cut from two 21⅜" (53.6cm) squares cut on both diagonals to yield a total of eight setting triangles and two 10⅞" (27.6cm) squares cut once on the diagonal to yield a total of four corner triangles. The quilt finishes at almost 60" (152cm) square.

For one block you will need

Finished block size: 14" (35.6cm) square

- Two 2½" x 42" (6.4 x 106.7cm) strips in navy/blue print fabric
- One 1½" x 60" (3.8 x 152.4cm) strip in white tone-on-tone fabric

Assembling the block

1. Download and print (see page 220 for link) or photocopy one copy each of Kogin foundations A and B (page 228).
2. Use the strips of fabric to foundation piece the block in numerical order, following the instructions on page 21.
3. Trim each unit along the dotted outer line, then join the two sections.

You can use pre-cut 2½" (6.4cm) strips for this pattern, but they will only just fit! I don't recommend washing pre-cut strips and squares before you use them – all fabric shrinks a little and you need every ⅛" (3mm)!

BUNTING

These half rectangle triangles are easiest to piece with a paper foundation and can be whipped up in no time. Twisting the blocks creates movement and is the perfect showcase for a collection of favourite fabrics.

SUGGESTED LAYOUT

For my virtual quilt, I have set twenty-four blocks in a four by six arrangement to create a quilt centre that measures 48½" x 72½" (123.2 x 184.2cm). Borders 1 and 3 are 1" (2.5cm) finished in red and the middle border in blue finishes at 3" (7.6cm). The whole quilt finishes at 58" x 82" (147.3 x 208.3cm).

Use a shorter than normal stitch length when paper piecing. Try a length of 1.5–1.8 on your machine. The paper should tear easily when pulled, but not disintegrate as you sew.

For one block you will need

Finished block size: 12" (30.5cm) square

- Six 5" x 7" (12.7 x 17.8cm) rectangles in assorted printed fabrics, each cross-cut once on the diagonal
- Six 5" x 7" (12.7 x 17.8cm) rectangles in cream or white solid or print, each cross-cut once on the diagonal

(You'll have enough fabric here to make two blocks)

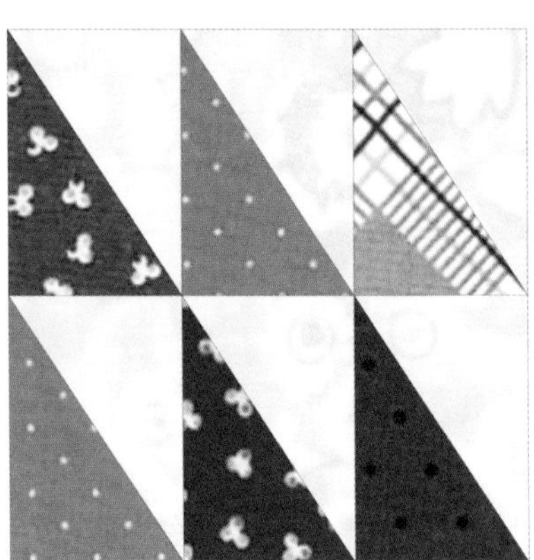

Assembling the block

1. Download and print (see page 220 for link) or photocopy two copies of the Bunting foundation (page 228).
2. Following the instructions on page 21, piece both foundations in numerical order. Make sure you use the assorted printed fabrics for patches 1, 3 and 5 and your cream/white fabrics for patches 2, 4 and 6 throughout.
3. Trim each foundation along the dotted outer line. Join the two foundations.

84 STAINED GLASS ROSE WINDOW

I love the look of stained glass and it's easy to reproduce in patchwork using paper foundation piecing. I prefer to use a light pewter-coloured 'lead' rather than the more usual charcoal or black – it produces a softer effect.

SUGGESTED LAYOUT

For my virtual quilt, I have sewn sixteen blocks into a four by four arrangement, turning each set of four blocks so that the pink fabrics come together. I have added ½" (12mm) finished sashing between all of the blocks and completed the quilt with a 1" (2.5cm) finished border in the same light pewter solid fabric. The quilt measures 51½" x 51½" (130.8 x 130.8cm).

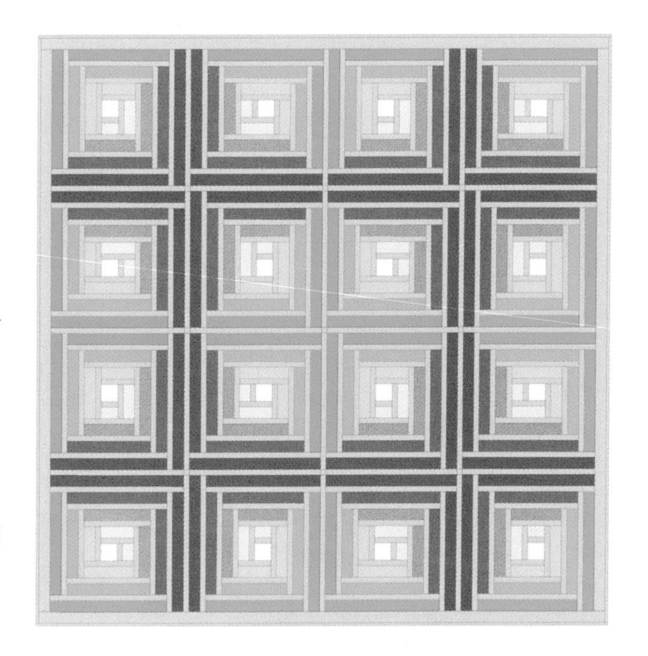

Leave foundation papers in place until your blocks are joined to sashing strips – this will keep your blocks square and prevent distortion.

For one block you will need

Finished block size: 12" (30.5cm) square

- 1½" (3.8cm) strips of light pewter solid, approximately 120" (305cm) in length (this doesn't have to be a continuous length)
- One 2" (5.1cm) square of white solid
- Four shades of rose pink fabric shaded from light to dark: 2" (5.1cm) strips of each, up to 24" (61cm) in length
- Three shades of leaf green fabric from light to dark: 2" (5.1cm) strips of each, up to 24" (61cm) in length

Assembling the block

1. Download and print (see page 220 for link) or photocopy one copy of the Stained Glass Rose Window foundation (page 229).
2. Following the instructions on page 21, piece the block in numerical order.
3. Trim your block along the dotted outer dotted line.

85 ZEBRA

Who says zebras have to be black and white? Although wouldn't this quilt look lovely in a collection of black on white and white on black prints - yummy! Easy-to-piece using foundations, a simple A and B colourway keeps it fun but fast and simple.

SUGGESTED LAYOUT

For my virtual quilt, I made a total of thirty-six blocks: eighteen of block 1 (starting and ending with white) and eighteen of block 2 (same foundation, but start and finish with purple strips). I sewed the blocks in six rows of six and turned every other row around. The finished quilt is 60" x 60" (152.4 x 152.4cm).

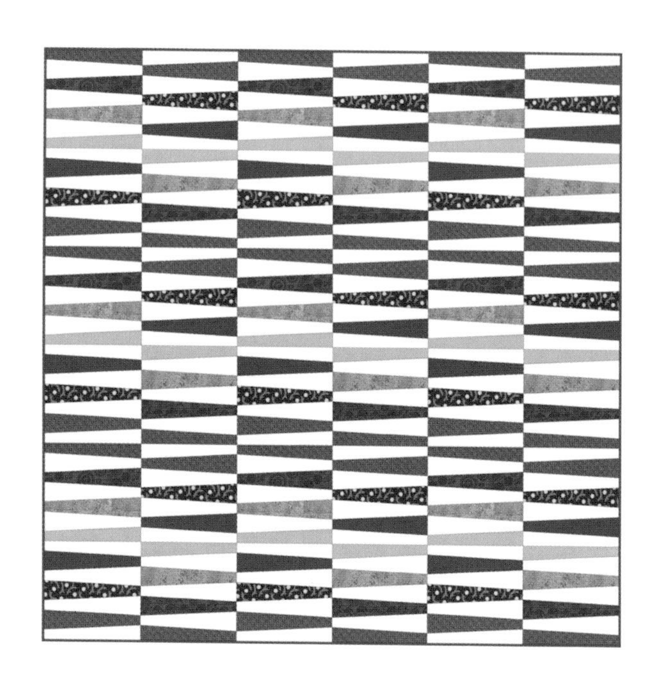

If you have trouble getting the paper out from foundation-pieced blocks, try spritzing the back of the block lightly with water. Leave for 30 seconds, then the softened paper should be easy to remove.

For one block you will need

Finished block size: 10" (25.4cm) square

- Assorted 2½" x 11" (6.4 x 28cm) strips of purple fabrics
- Assorted 2½" x 11" (6.4 x 28cm) strips of white-on-white prints

Assembling the block

1. Download and print (see page 220 for link) or photocopy one copy of the Zebra foundation (page 230).
2. Piece the block in numerical order, alternating the strips,starting and ending with a white strip. (The diagram right is block 1; for block 2, start and end with a purple strip.) Trim the unit along the dotted outer line.

BEST IN SHOW

When you want to let someone know they are the best of the best, here is the perfect quilt!

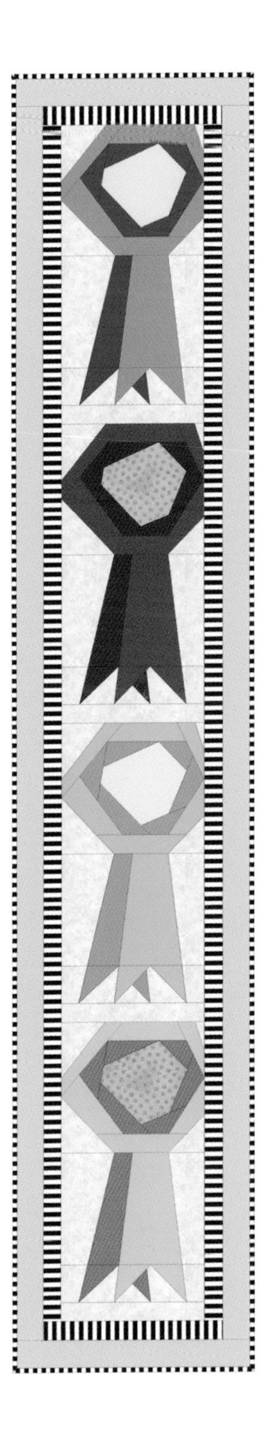

SUGGESTED LAYOUT

For my virtual mini quilt, I made four blocks using various solid fabrics. I've added a 1" (2.5cm) finished black-and-white striped border and a 1½" (3.8cm) finished yellow outer border to make a quilt that is 11" by 53" (28 x 134.6cm) – perfect for tucking into a tiny nook.

Embroider 'Best in Show' or some other special message or award in the centre of the rosettes before you piece them, either by hand or machine, for a truly personalized quilt.

For one block you will need

Finished block size: 6" x 12" (15.2 x 30.5cm)

- Scraps of light solid
- Scraps of medium solid
- A scrap of gold print
- Scraps of very pale mottled print for the background

Assembling the block

1. Download and print (see page 220 for link) or photocopy one copy each of Best In Show foundations A, B and C (page 231).
2. Piece each foundation in numerical order, following the instructions on page 21.
3. Sew the three sections together. Trim the units along the dotted outer lines.

87 ICE LOLLY

I am a child of the 1970s and for me, summer will absolutely be forever connected with ice lollies, licked till my tongue matched the colour of the lolly. Modern lollies just don't have that kind of lurid colouring in them (which is a good thing), but half the fun of eating one was sticking out my tongue at anyone I passed!

SUGGESTED LAYOUT

My quilt is made using sixteen Ice Lolly blocks set in a four by four arrangement. I've added a 1" (2.5cm) finished border to complete this 38" x 46" (96.5 x 116.8cm) quilt.

For one block you will need

Finished block size: 9" x 11" (22.9 x 28cm)

- One 5½" x 8½" (14 x 21.6cm) rectangle in bright solid for the lolly
- One 2" x 4" (5.1 x 10.2cm) rectangle in brown solid for the lolly stick
- Bright blue, turquoise or green fabric for the background; a fat quarter is more than enough - from this, cut two 2¾" x 11½" (7 x 29.2cm) rectangles for the block sides and use the rest for foundation piecing the block

Assembling the block

1. Download and print (see page 220 for link) or photocopy one copy each of Ice Lolly foundations A and B (page 232).
2. Piece each foundation in numerical order, following the instructions on page 21. Trim the units along the dotted outer lines, then join the two sections together.
3. Sew each of the 2¾" x 11½" (7 x 29.2cm) background rectangles to the sides of your lolly. Finally, remove the foundation papers.

Clip your threads as you piece your blocks so that no big 'haircuts' are needed at the end!

NOW VOYAGER

This is a really fun quilt to plan, gather fabrics for, piece and quilt for your very own tiny sailor! Easily made using foundation piecing and with optional stars appliquéd onto the finished quilt top.

SUGGESTED LAYOUT

For my virtual quilt, I used fifteen Now Voyager blocks set in a three by five arrangement. I also added a 1"(2.5cm) and a 2" (5.1cm) finished border to make a quilt that is 42" x 66" (106.7 x 167.6cm). Once the quilt top is complete, add star appliqués if you wish – use the Old Glory star template on page 221 at a variety of sizes. Use the fusible web method (page 24) to add the appliqués and stitch them in place before layering and quilting.

To increase the variety of 'sky' prints, take a look at the wrong side of your fabrics. The reverse is often a paler and perfectly useable version of the fabric. Two for the price of one!

For one block you will need

Finished block size: 12" (30.5cm) square

- One 7½" (19cm) square in white or pastel solid for the sails, cross-cut on the diagonal to yield two triangles
- One 5" x 12" (12.7 x 30.5cm) rectangle in bright print for the hull
- One 2" x 13" (5.1 x 33cm) rectangle in deep blue print for the sea
- One fat quarter of background 'sky' fabric (this should be enough for two blocks depending on how generously you cut your patches)

Assembling the block

1. Download and print (see page 220 for link) or photocopy one copy of each of Now Voyager foundations A and B (sails) and C (hull) on page 233.
2. Piece each foundation in numerical order, following the instructions on page 21. Trim the units along the dotted outer lines.
3. Join the sail sections A and B together first, then sew the hull (C) to the bottom.

FRESH CARROTS

I love the bright beauty of fresh fruits and vegetables - their colours and shapes inspire me in so many ways, particularly when I'm working out my colour schemes. A friend brought me a bunch of fresh carrots from his garden and I couldn't help but sit down and design this fun block to celebrate the humble but glorious carrot. Traditionally carrots are white, purple, gold as well as orange - so don't hold back when you colour your quilt!

SUGGESTED LAYOUT

For my wall quilt, I have made sixteen Fresh Carrots blocks and joined them in a four by four setting. I love the secondary patterns that appear when four blocks are set together! I've added a 1" (2.5cm) finished border, a ¼" (6mm) folded flange and a final 1" (2.5cm) finished outer border to complete this 40" x 40" (101.6 x 101.6cm) quilt.

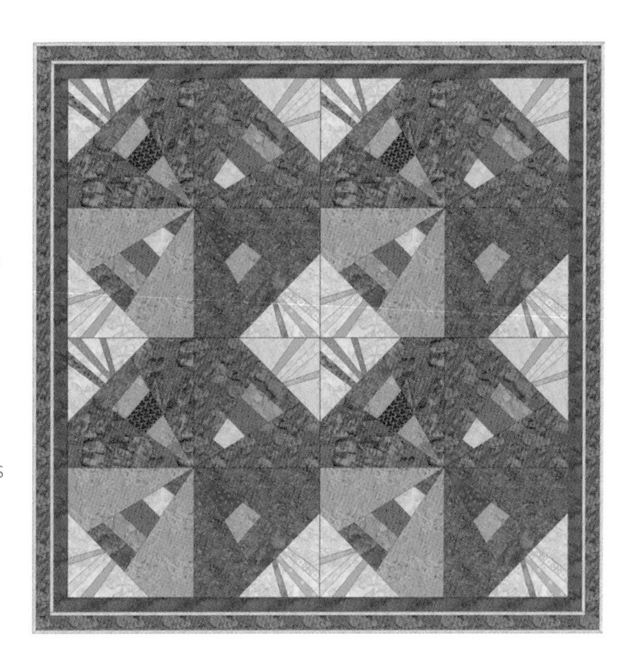

Quilters usually press seam allowances to one side but in foundation piecing, when I'm joining several units together, I like to press those seams open. It helps to distribute bulky seams and prevents lumps and bumps in my quilt.

For one block you will need

Finished block size: 9" (22.9cm) square

- Five assorted small scraps of bright orange print fabrics
- Three assorted small scraps of bright green print fabrics
- One 10" (25.4cm) square in 'earth' brown batik
- One 6" (15.2cm) square in light 'sky' blue batik

Assembling the block

1. Download and print (see page 220 for link) or photocopy one copy of each of Fresh Carrots foundations A and B (page 232).
2. Piece the foundations in numerical order, following the instructions on page 21. Trim the units along the dotted outer lines.
3. Join the units together as shown.

90 KHUFU

Named after the ancient Egyptian pharaoh who had the Great Pyramid of Giza built, these blocks will take significantly less time to build!

SUGGESTED LAYOUT

For my virtual quilt, I have set twenty-five Khufu blocks on point with twelve setting triangles cross-cut on both diagonal from 12⅝" (32cm) squares. The four corner triangles are cut from two 6⅝" (16.2cm) squares, cut on one diagonal. I've added a ½" (12mm) and a 4" (10.2cm) finished border to make a 54" (137.2cm) square quilt.

Make sure your strips hang off the edges of the foundation as you sew. Better to trim extra off than find one of your strips is ½" (12mm) too short!

For one block you will need

Finished block size: 8" (20.3cm) square

- One 8½" (21.6cm) square of quilter's calico or light-coloured cotton solid
- One 9" (22.9cm) square in black print, cross-cut on one diagonal (use the other half for a second block)
- Four or five strips of assorted gold coloured print strips, between 1½" (3.8cm) and 3½" (8.9cm) wide and 4" (10.2cm) and 12" (30.5cm) long

Assembling the block

1. Draw a diagonal line on the calico square from corner to corner, then draw a second line ¼" (6mm) away from this.
2. Lay the black print triangle on top of the calico square, right side facing up and the raw diagonal edge lined up with the second line you drew.
3. Lay your first strip of gold print on top, right sides together with the black print, raw edges aligned. Sew a ¼" (6mm) seam to join the fabrics.
4. Flip the gold strip back against the calico foundation and press. Add another strip, on top of the first, right sides together, and sew a ¼" (6mm) seam.
5. Continue to stitch and flip the strips until the foundation is covered. Trim the square. using the calico foundation square as a guide.

HASHTAG

When I first joined Instagram (@stuarthillardsews), my friend and fellow quilt author Bonnie K. Hunter told me, 'It's all about the hashtag!' She was so right, so in her honour, here is my hashtag quilt!

SUGGESTED LAYOUT

For my virtual quilt, I have set sixteen Hashtag blocks together in a four by four arrangement. I've added 1" (2.5cm) finished sashing (or should that be 'hashing'?!) and a 1" (2.5cm) finished border. The quilt finishes at 45" x 45" (114.3 x 114.3cm).

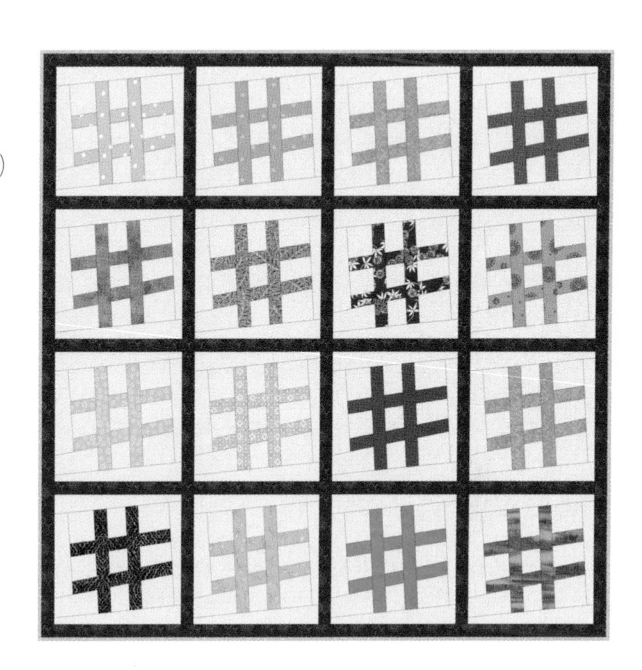

Enlarge or reduce blocks and make other projects, like a cushion, using four 7" (17.8cm) finished hashtag blocks.

For one block you will need

Finished block size: 10" (25.4cm) square

- One 2-2½" (5.1-6.4cm) wide strip of main fabric, approximately 42" (106.7cm) long
- Background fabric - a fat quarter is plenty

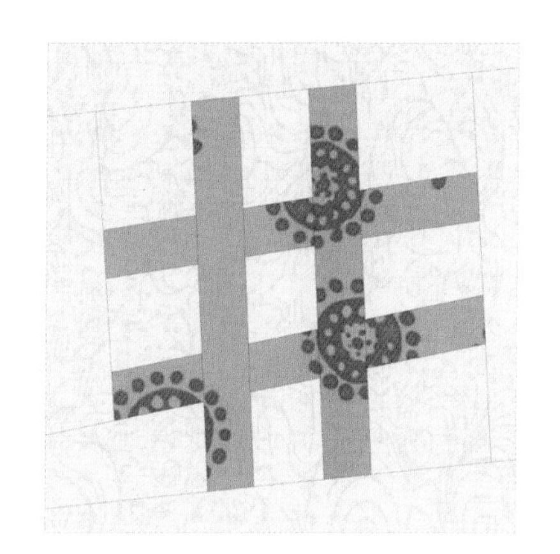

Assembling the block

1. Download and print (see page 220 for link) or photocopy one copy each of Hashtag foundations A, B, C, D and E (page 234).
2. Paper piece sections A, B and C in numerical order, following the instructions on page 21, and machine baste the background fabric to foundations D and E.
3. Trim all foundations along the dotted outer lines.
4. Join A, B and C together, then add D and E.

92 MONDRIAN

This quilt is named after the painter, Mondrian, who is best known for his bold blocks of colour separated by bands. I'm sure given the chance he would have made quilts!

SUGGESTED LAYOUT

For my virtual quilt, I have made sixteen Mondrian blocks, added ½" (12mm) finished sashing between the blocks and added finished borders at 1" (2.5cm), 2" (5.1cm) and 1" (2.5cm). The finished quilt is 48" x 48" (122 x 122cm). I love the way this quilt looks like stained glass; using batiks is a great way to achieve this.

Any hand-dyed fabrics would work well for this project and still give you a 'stained-glass' effect. For a totally different look, use rich holiday fabrics and replace the dark grey strips with shiny gold lamé for a very glitzy Christmas quilt!

For one block you will need

Finished block size: 10" (25.4cm) square

- Nine 5" (12.7cm) squares in brightly coloured batiks
- Dark grey or black solid fabric, cut into strips 1½" (3.8cm) wide

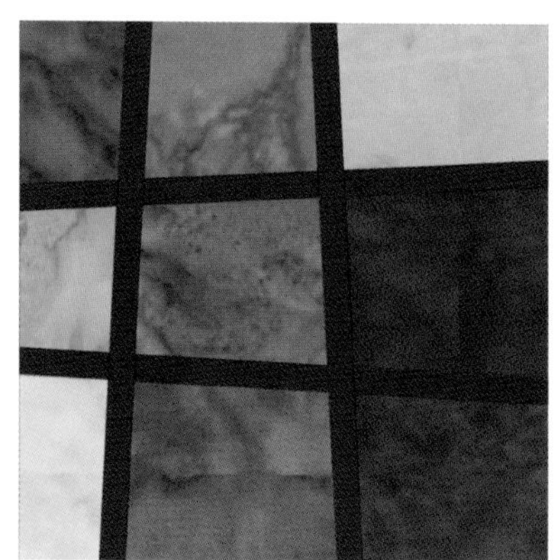

Assembling the block

1. Download and print (see page 220 for link) or photocopy one copy each of Mondrian foundations A, B and C (page 234).
2. Use your bright batik prints and dark grey or black strips to piece each foundation, following the instructions on page 21.
3. Trim your completed units along the dotted outer line.
4. Sew the sections together, being careful to match the 'sashings'.

93 SHOAL

Like a shoal of golden fish swimming across your quilt! These spiky triangles are easy to achieve with foundation piecing and the results are dazzling.

SUGGESTED LAYOUT

For my virtual quilt, I have used sixty-six Shoal blocks in eleven vertical columns of six blocks. A 1" (2.5cm) finished border brings the quilt up to 51½" x 62" (130.8 x 157.4cm).

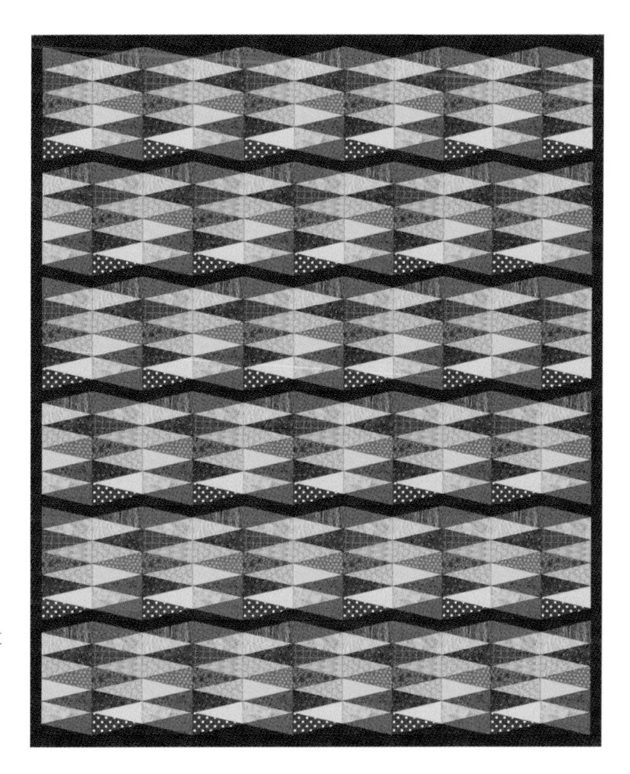

Add a dash of colour to your 'neutral' backgrounds – light yellow here, instead of cream or tan, adds sparkle and visual interest. It keeps the viewer's eyes darting over your quilt and it's an easy way to make your quilt stand out!

For one block you will need

Finished block size: 10" x 4½" (25.4 x 11.4cm)

- Five 3" x 6" (7.6 x 15.2cm) scraps of assorted orange and gold prints
- Four 3" x 6" (7.6 x 15.2cm) scraps of assorted cream, tan and light yellow
- Two 2" x 6" (5.1 x 15.2cm) rectangles in dark brown print

Assembling the block

1. Download and print (see page 220 for link) or photocopy one copy of the Shoal foundation (page 235).
2. Piece the block in numerical order, following the instructions on page 21.
3. Trim the block along the dotted outer lines, so that it measures 5" x 10½" (12.7 x 26.7cm).

94 WHIRL

This quilt looks super advanced and tricky to piece, but it's not! Foundation piecing makes sewing the blocks a cinch, and although the setting looks complex it's just a simple block setting with straight rows - nothing fancy!

SUGGESTED LAYOUT

For my quilt, I set thirty-six blocks in a six by six arrangement, rotating them to create the 'whirl', as shown. The finished wall quilt is 42" x 42" (106.7 x 106.7cm).

Before assembling your quilt top, lay out your blocks and take some photographs. You'll spot if a block is turned the wrong way far more easily in a photograph than with your naked eye.

For one block you will need

Finished block size: 7" (17.8cm) square

- Four 2½" x 7½" (6.4 x 19cm) scraps of assorted yellow print fabric
- Five 2½" x 7½" (6.4 x 19cm) scraps of assorted grey print fabrics
- Two 1½" x 8" (3.8 x 20.3cm) strips of darker grey print fabric

Assembling the block

1. Download and print (see page 220 for link) or photocopy one copy of the Whirl foundation (page 235).
2. Use your grey and yellow fabrics to piece the foundation in numerical order, following the instructions on page 21.
3. Trim the block along the dotted outer line.

HENRY MOORE
LE UNIVERSITÀ DELL'EUROPA
NATIONAL GEOGRAPHIC THE PHOTOGRAPHS

ABSTRACT ROSE

This is a wonderfully liberated (and liberating) block to make. It's organic - just like the roses I love so much - and is a joy to make. The results are always different, but you can be sure that every one will be lovely!

For one block you will need

Finished block size: 9" (22.9cm) square

- One 10" (25.4cm) square of calico
- A variety of green, purple, pink and red fabrics cut into strips of varying widths - 1"-2" (2.5-5.1cm) is good. The strips need not be straight and actually it's better if they are a little wonky!

Assembling the block

1. From a scrap of green or yellow cut a 'wonky' square approximately 1½" x 1½" (3.8 x 3.8cm) and pin it near the centre of your calico foundation square, right side facing up.
2. Lay a strip of purple on top of the square, right sides together, and sew along the edge of the strip to join it to both the square and the calico underneath. Trim the strip even with the centre square.
3. Working anti-clockwise, sew strips around the centre square until you have completed one full round.
4. Using a different colour, repeat the process. Keep going in this way until the calico square is completely covered. It's nice to include a few pieces of green at the outer edges for 'leaves'.
5. Press your block from the back and then trim to 9½" x 9½" (24.1 x 24.1cm).

Experiment with other starting shapes in the centre. A wonky pentagon (five sides) will create a lovely block, too!

SUGGESTED LAYOUT

For my quilt I have made sixteen Abstract Rose blocks and joined them in a four by four setting. A ¼" (6mm) flange border and a 1" (2.5cm) finished border bring the quilt up to 38" x 38" (96.5 x 96.5cm).

96 FISHBONES

This whimsical quilt would make the most wonderful gift for a cat lover or even your beloved kitty herself!

SUGGESTED LAYOUT

My virtual quilt uses nine Fishbones blocks separated by 3" (7.6cm) finished sashing and 3" (7.6cm) finished cornerstones each made from nine 1½" (3.8cm) squares sewn together. The outer border is 3" (7.6cm) finished and the quilt measures 66" (167.6cm) square.

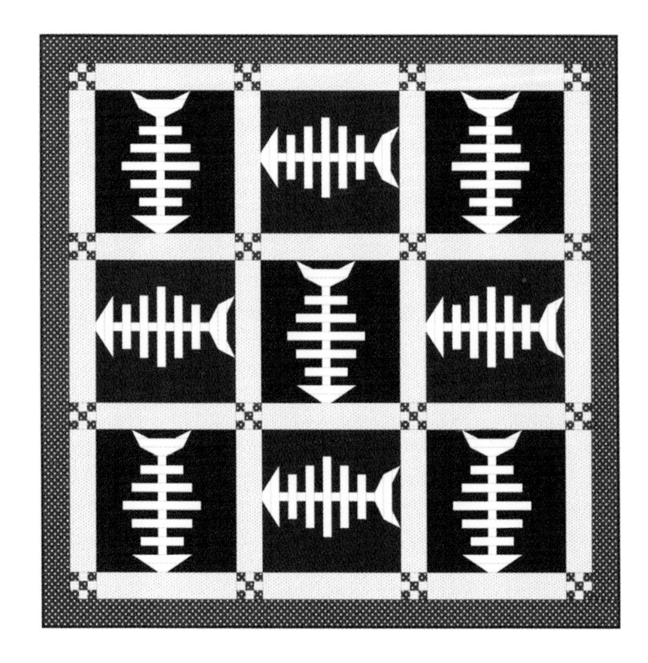

Add fabric yo-yos or button eyes to the quilt for even more fishy personality!

For one block you will need

Finished block size: 16" (40.7cm) square

- One fat quarter of white solid or tonal print cut into 1½" (3.8cm) strips
- One fat quarter of red mottled print cut into 1½" (3.8cm) strips

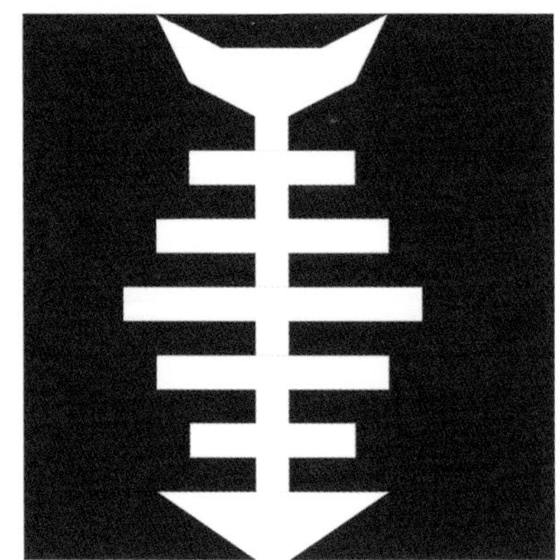

Assembling the block

1. Download and print (see page 220 for link) or photocopy one copy each of Fishbones foundations A to P (page 236).
2. Foundation piece the sections in numerical order, following the instructions on page 21. Trim each section along the dotted outer lines.
3. Join the foundations together.

97 WILD GOOSE CHASE

This is a great quilt for showing off a fabric collection, whether it's one amassed over years or from a fabric collection you have fallen in love with and bought in its entirety! Small- and medium-scale prints work best for this pattern.

SUGGESTED LAYOUT

My virtual quilt uses sixteen blocks, separated by 1" (2.5cm) finished sashing and cornerstones. I've added a 5" (12.7cm) finished border to make a 75" x 75" (190.5 x 190.5cm) quilt.

When paper foundation piecing, it's a really good idea to trim the seam allowances as you go. Keep a paper bag taped to the table next to you to collect all your tiny trimmings and thread waste, then at the end of the day simply toss the bag away for a super-quick clean-up!

For one block you will need

Finished block size: 15" (38.1cm) square

- Gold print: six 3½" (8.9cm) squares, each cross-cut on one diagonal to yield twelve half square triangles (HSTs), and one 4½" (11.4cm) square
- Sixteen 2½" (6.4cm) squares of light cream print, each cross-cut on one diagonal to yield thirty-two small HSTs
- Two 3½" (8.9cm) squares of medium/dark pink print, each cross-cut on one diagonal to yield four HSTs
- Two 3½" (8.9cm) squares of black print, each cross-cut on one diagonal to yield four HSTs
- One 12" (30.5cm) square of medium pink larger-scale print, cross-cut on both diagonals to yield four quarter square triangles (QSTs)

Assembling the block

1. Download and print (see page 220 for link) or photocopy two copies of Wild Goose Chase foundation A, and one copy each of foundations B and C (page 237).
2. Piece each foundation in numerical order, following the instructions on page 21.
3. Trim each of the units along the dotted outer lines. Join the units together as shown.

98 KALEIDOSCOPE

Some of the best-loved quilt patterns are those that contain secondary designs, which appear – as if by magic – when multiple blocks are set together. I love the circles that appear when A and B Kaleidoscope blocks meet. Simply reverse the colouring of your blocks to make the magic happen.

For one block you will need

Finished block size: 12" (30.5cm) square

- Assorted strips of red print and solid fabrics, from 1" (2.5cm) to 2" (5.1cm) wide and 15" (38.1cm) or more long
- Two 4½" (11.4cm) squares in red/ white plaid, each cross-cut on one diagonal to yield four half square triangles (HSTs)
- 10" (25.4cm) length of turquoise polka dot print

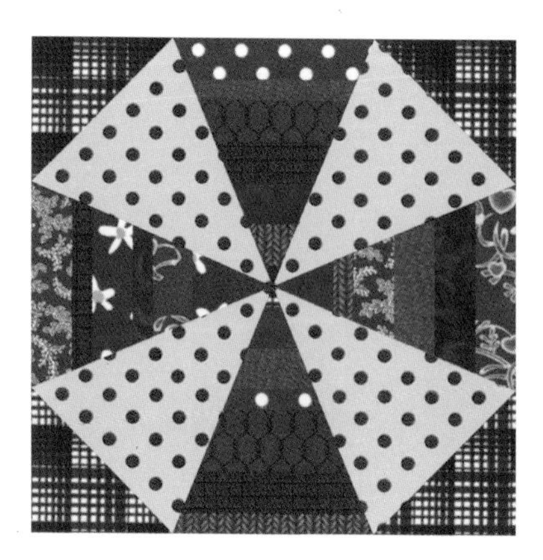

Assembling the block

1. Download and print (see page 220 for link) or photocopy one full copy each of Kaleidoscope foundations A and B (page 237) and one extra copy to use as a triangle template.
2. Sew the assorted red strips together to make a strip-pieced panel about 15" x 7" (38.1 x 17.8cm). Press the seams one way.
3. Make a template of the large triangle and use this to roughly cut out four triangles from the strip-pieced unit. Make sure you add a generous ½" (12mm) seam allowance on all sides.
4. Use the strip-pieced triangles and the remaining patches to foundation piece your block as shown, following the instructions on page 21.
5. Trim the units along to the dotted outer lines.
6. Sew the units together, as shown.

Look for other quilt blocks with large patches in them (like the triangles in this block) and substitute strip-pieced units. It's a great way to use up scraps and bring even more scrap appeal to your favourite quilt patterns.

SUGGESTED LAYOUT

For my virtual quilt, I have made sixteen blocks: eight A blocks with the strip-pieced triangles in red prints and eight B blocks with the colours reversed and the strip-pieced blocks made in assorted turquoise prints. I joined the blocks alternately in a four by four setting. The finished quilt is 48" x 48" (122 x 122cm).

RADIANT STAR

Foundation paper piecing makes this gorgeous quilt a whole lot easier to piece accurately. Choose your favourite two colour combination or go scrappy and divide your fabrics into lights and darks.

SUGGESTED LAYOUT

For my virtual quilt, I have made fifteen String Star blocks and 15 Star Chain blocks and set them together in a five by six arrangement. I've added borders 1 and 3 at 1" (2.5cm) finished, while border 2 finishes at 4" (10.2cm). The final quilt is 72" x 84" (182.8 x 213.3cm).

For one String Star block you will need

Finished block size: 12" (30.5cm) square

- A variety of light cream and tan strips, 1½" (3.8cm) wide, in various lengths
- Cream print scraps for the foundation piecing
- Red print scraps for the foundation piecing
- One 4½" (11.4cm) red print square for the block centre.

Pre-cut patches of fabric for foundation piecing to minimize the trimming later. I like to cut my patches approximately ½" (12mm) bigger on all sides than the finished patch.

Assembling the block

1. Download and print (see page 220 for link) or photocopy four copies each of Radiant Star foundations A and B (page 237).
2. Piece the units in numerical order, following the instructions on page 21.
3. Trim the units along the dotted outer lines.
4. Arrange the foundation pieced units around the red print centre square.
5. Join the units into rows, then join the rows.

For one Star Chain block you will need

Finished block size: 12" (30.5cm) square

- Two 5¼" (13.3cm) squares in dark red print, each cross-cut on both diagonals to yield eight quarter square triangles (QSTs)
- Two 5¼" (13.3cm) squares in light tan print, each cross-cut on both diagonals to yield eight QSTs

Corner units

- Sixteen 1½" (3.8cm) squares in dark red print
- Twenty-four 1½" (3.8cm) squares in medium red print
- Sixteen 1½" (3.8cm) squares in light tan
- Eight 1½" (3.8cm) squares in medium tan

Central square

- Four 1½" (3.8cm) squares in dark red for the corners
- Four 1½" (3.8cm) squares in medium red for the centre
- Eight 1½" (3.8cm) squares in light red for the sides

Assembling the block

1. Use the dark red and tan QSTs to piece four QST units, using two tan and two red triangles for each.
2. Arrange the small squares to create the four corner units, as shown. Sew into rows, then join the rows together. Press the seams in opposite directions so that the seams are 'nested'.
3. Arrange the remaining squares to make the centre of the block.
4. Sew the units together, in rows, then sew the rows together.

100 STRAIGHT TO THE POINT

This is a very modern quilt that utilizes the negative spaces - that expanse of open space to either side of the piecing - to accentuate and frame the design, but also to allow space for wonderful quilting if you choose. I've chosen to foundation piece this block, as it gives the most accurate piecing ever - and with only three blocks to make a stunning quilt, it's worth the extra effort!

For one block you will need

Finished block size: 20" (50.8cm) square

- 2½" (6.4cm) strips in an assortment of gold, blue, turquoise and green fabrics
- Two 2½" x 42" (6.4 x 106.7cm) strips of darker gold fabric for the vertical 'bars'

Assembling the block

1. Download and print (see page 220 for link) or photocopy one copy each of Straight to the Point foundations A, B, C, D, E and F (page 238).
2. Piece the units in numerical order, following the instructions on page 21. Pay careful attention to colour placement and note that the top and bottom fabrics in each unit must match so that, when you join your blocks, the 'arrows' will continue smoothly.
3. Trim each unit along the dotted outer lines. Join the units to make your block as shown.

Sometimes the simplest quilting patterns look the best. 'Matchstick' quilting - straight lines quilted with a walking foot - would suit this quilt beautifully. Quilt your lines horizontally, from side to side, approximately ⅜" (10mm) apart. It takes a while, but it's easy to do and the effect is spectacular and very modern!

SUGGESTED LAYOUT

For my virtual quilt, I have made three Straight to the Point blocks and joined them to make a panel 20½" x 60½" (52 x 153.7cm). I have added a 20½" x 60½" (52 x 153.7cm) solid panel to either side and then a 1" (2.5cm) finished border all around to complete this 62" x 62" (157.4 x 157.4cm) quilt.

TEMPLATES

Photocopy the templates you need at the size indicated, or go to www.pavilionbooks.com/book/simple-shapes-stunning-quilts to download and print full-size templates. Make a test block before embarking on a whole quilt: measure the text block to make sure it has the dimensions indicated in the instructions.

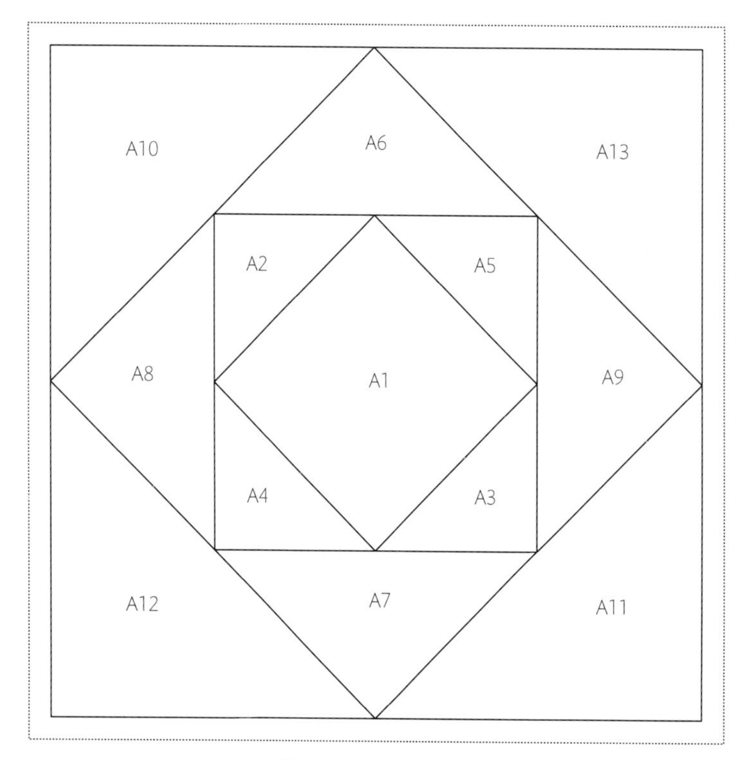

Square in a Square
Enlarge by 200%

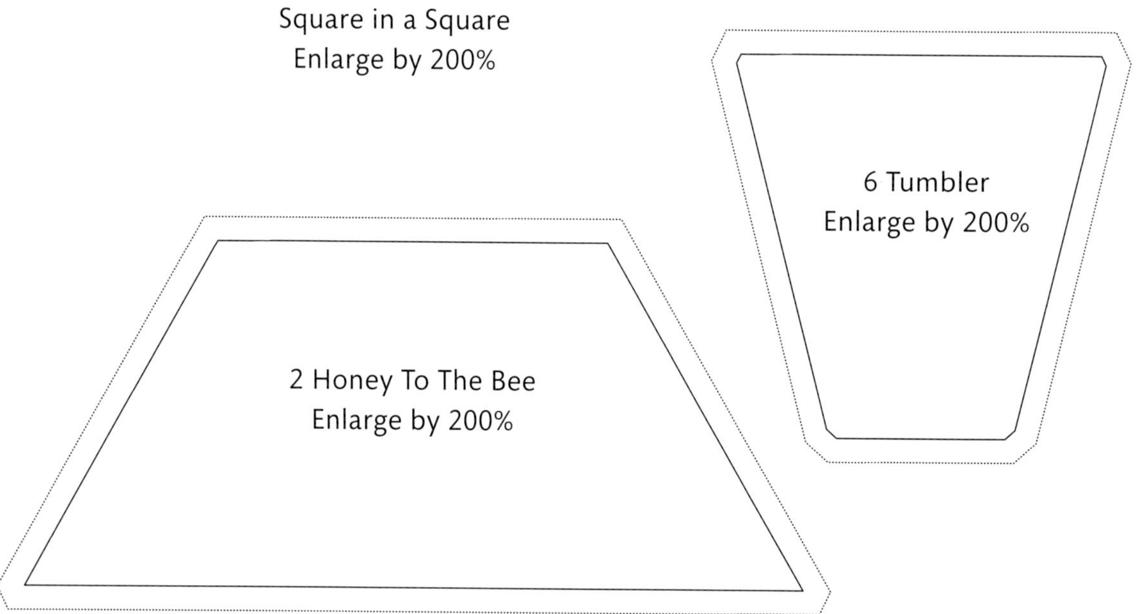

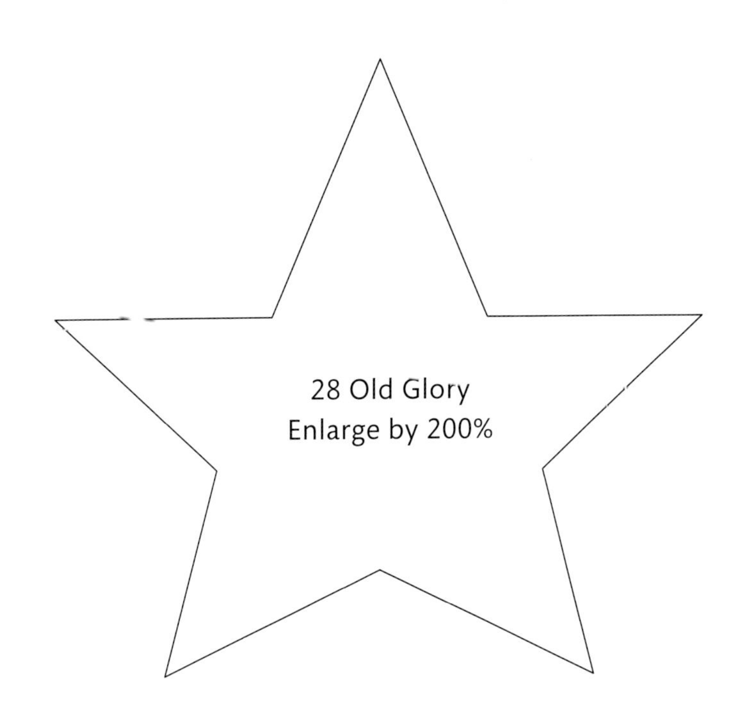

28 Old Glory
Enlarge by 200%

21 Save Your Kisses
Enlarge by 200%

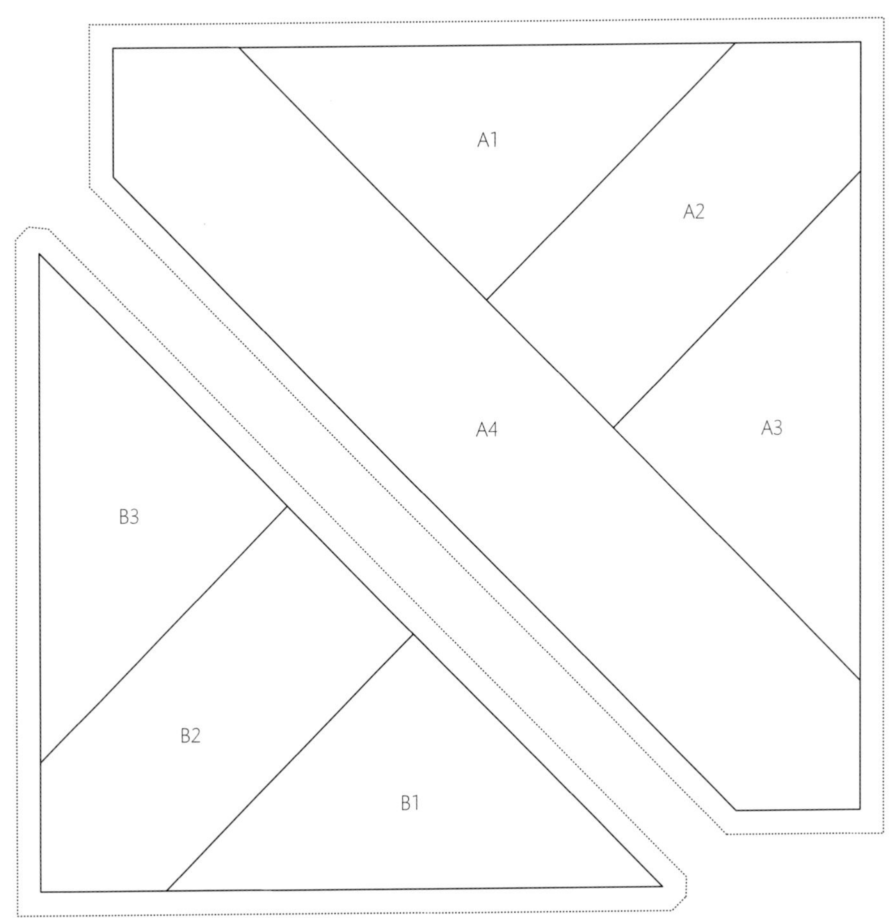

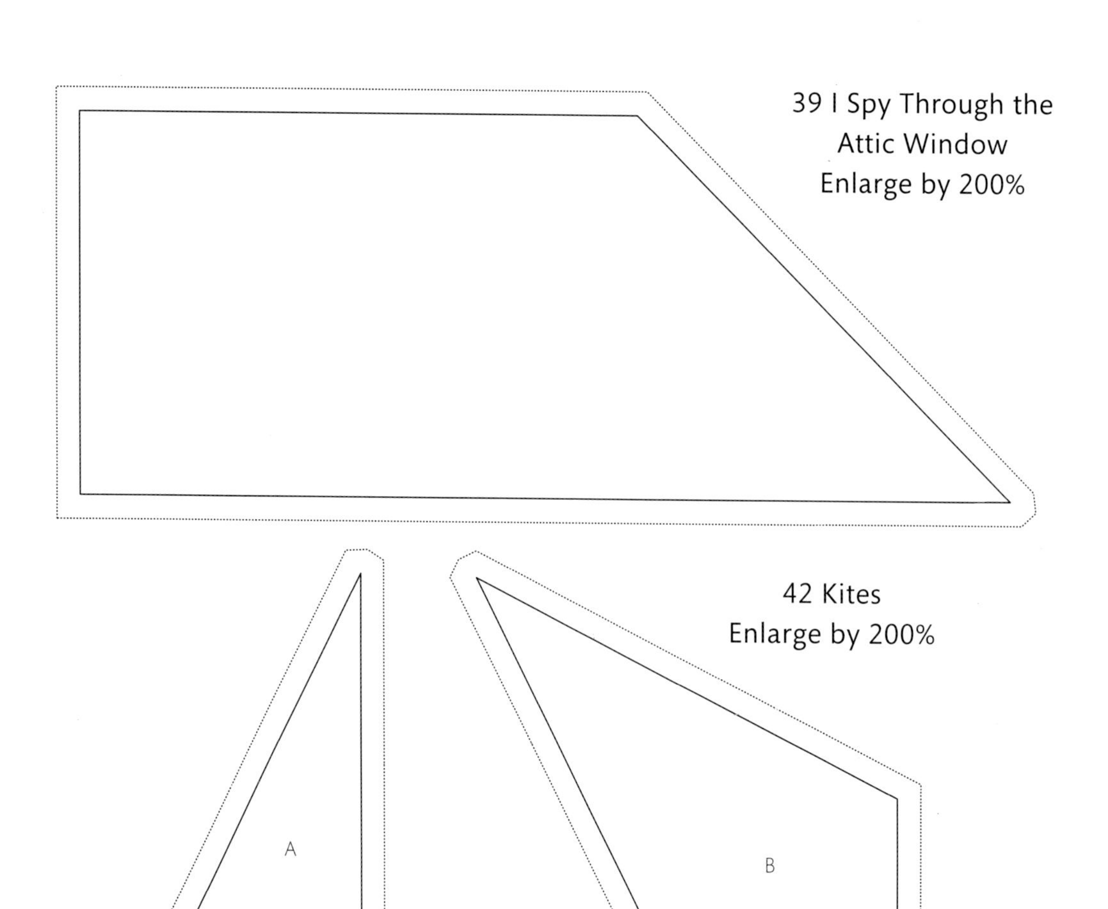

42 Kites
Enlarge by 200%

A

B

48 Ice Crystals
Enlarge by 200%

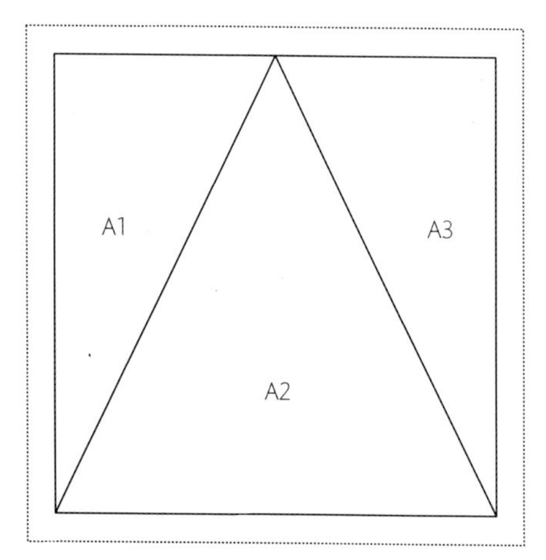

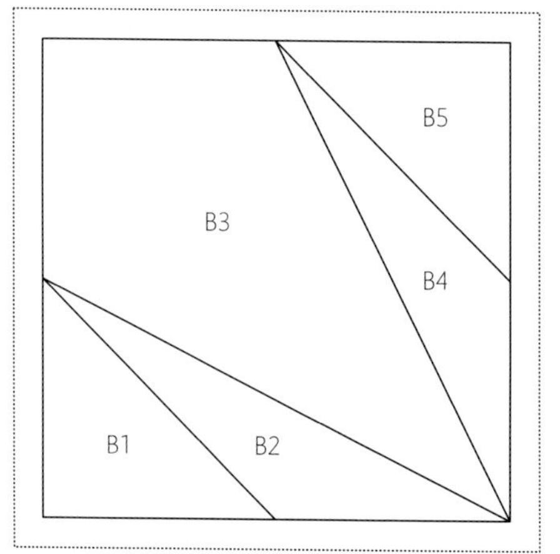

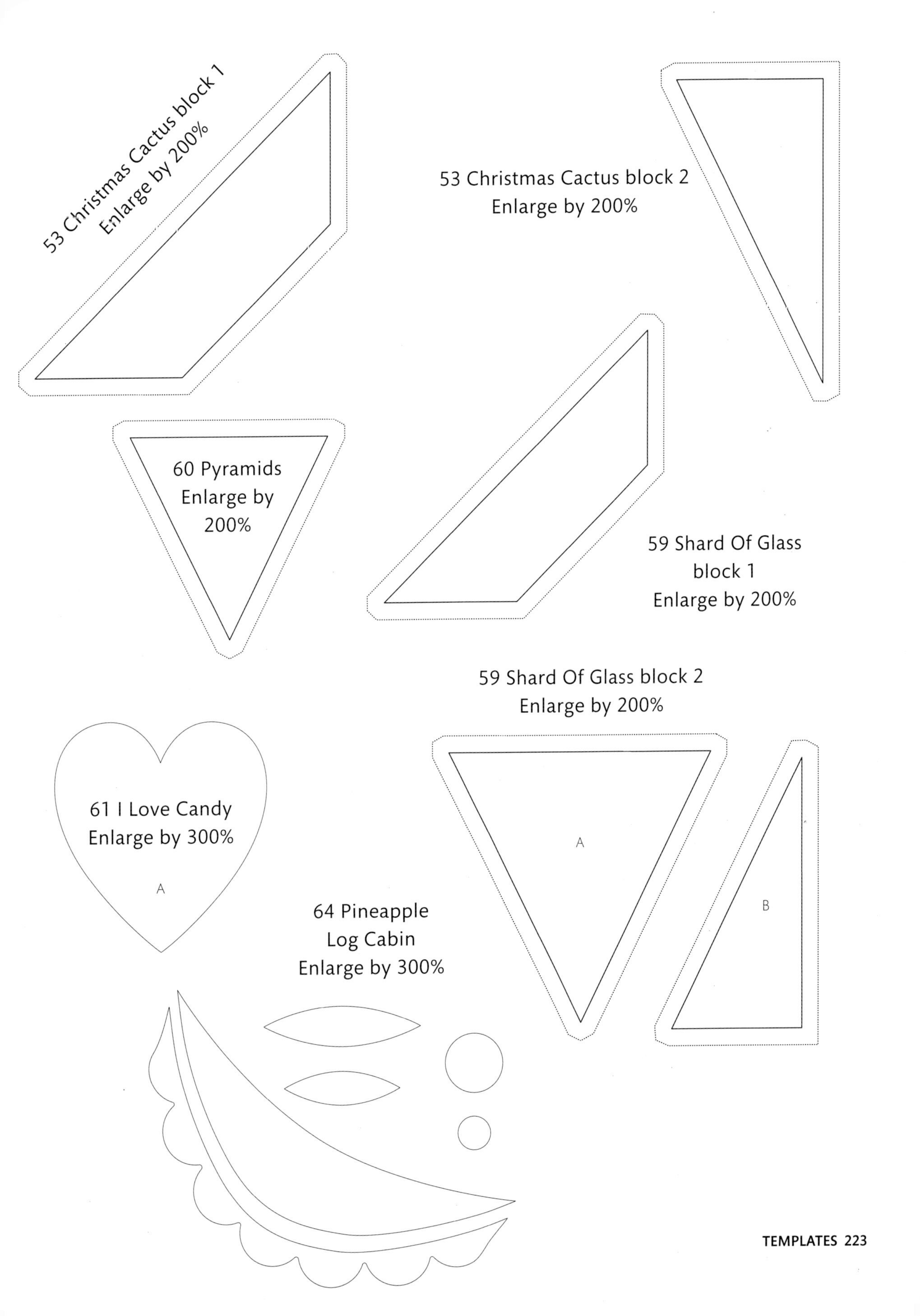
53 Christmas Cactus block 1
Enlarge by 200%
53 Christmas Cactus block 2
Enlarge by 200%
60 Pyramids
Enlarge by
200%
59 Shard Of Glass
block 1
Enlarge by 200%
59 Shard Of Glass block 2
Enlarge by 200%
61 I Love Candy
Enlarge by 300%
A
A
B
64 Pineapple
Log Cabin
Enlarge by 300%

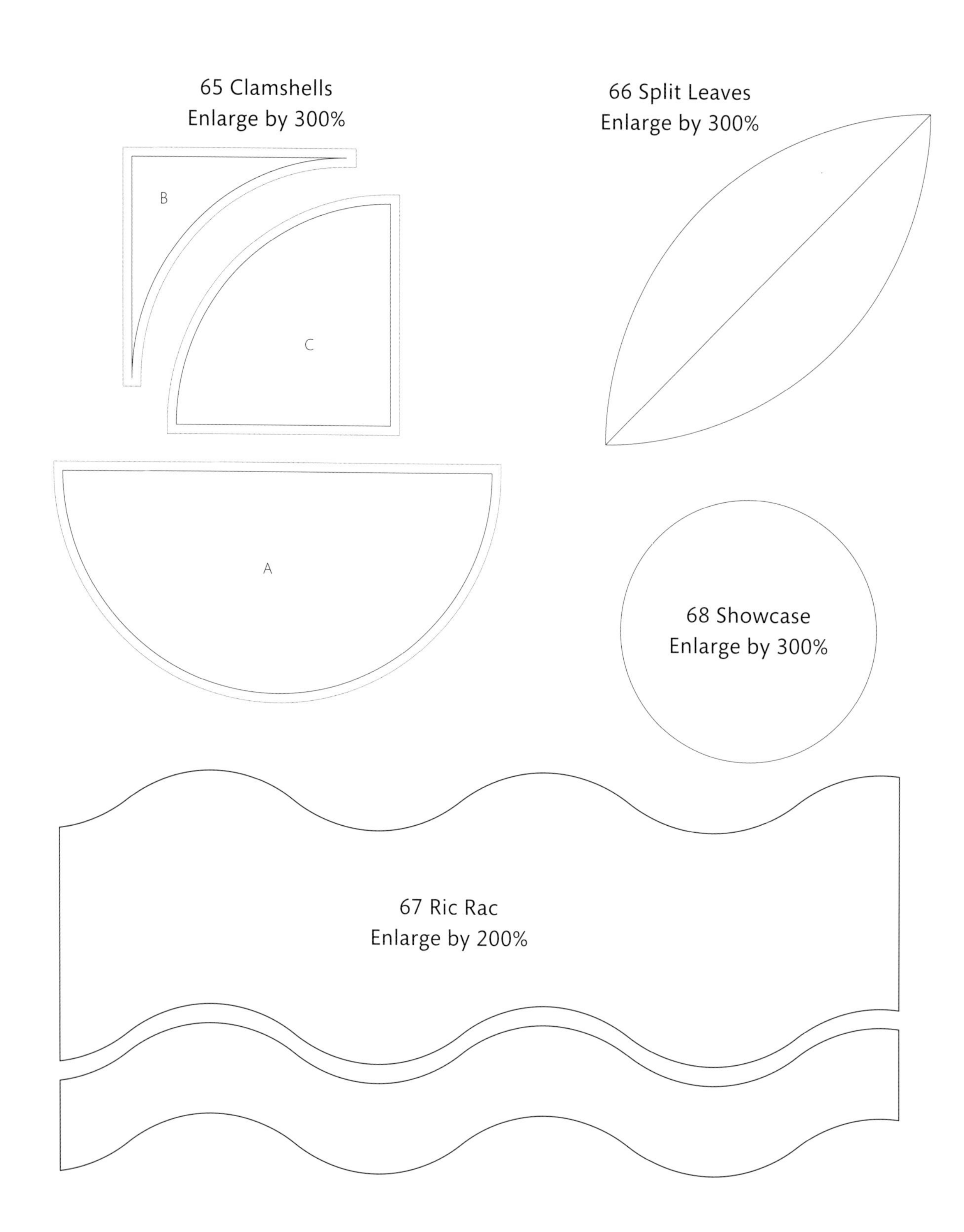
65 Clamshells
Enlarge by 300%
B
C
A
66 Split Leaves
Enlarge by 300%
68 Showcase
Enlarge by 300%
67 Ric Rac
Enlarge by 200%

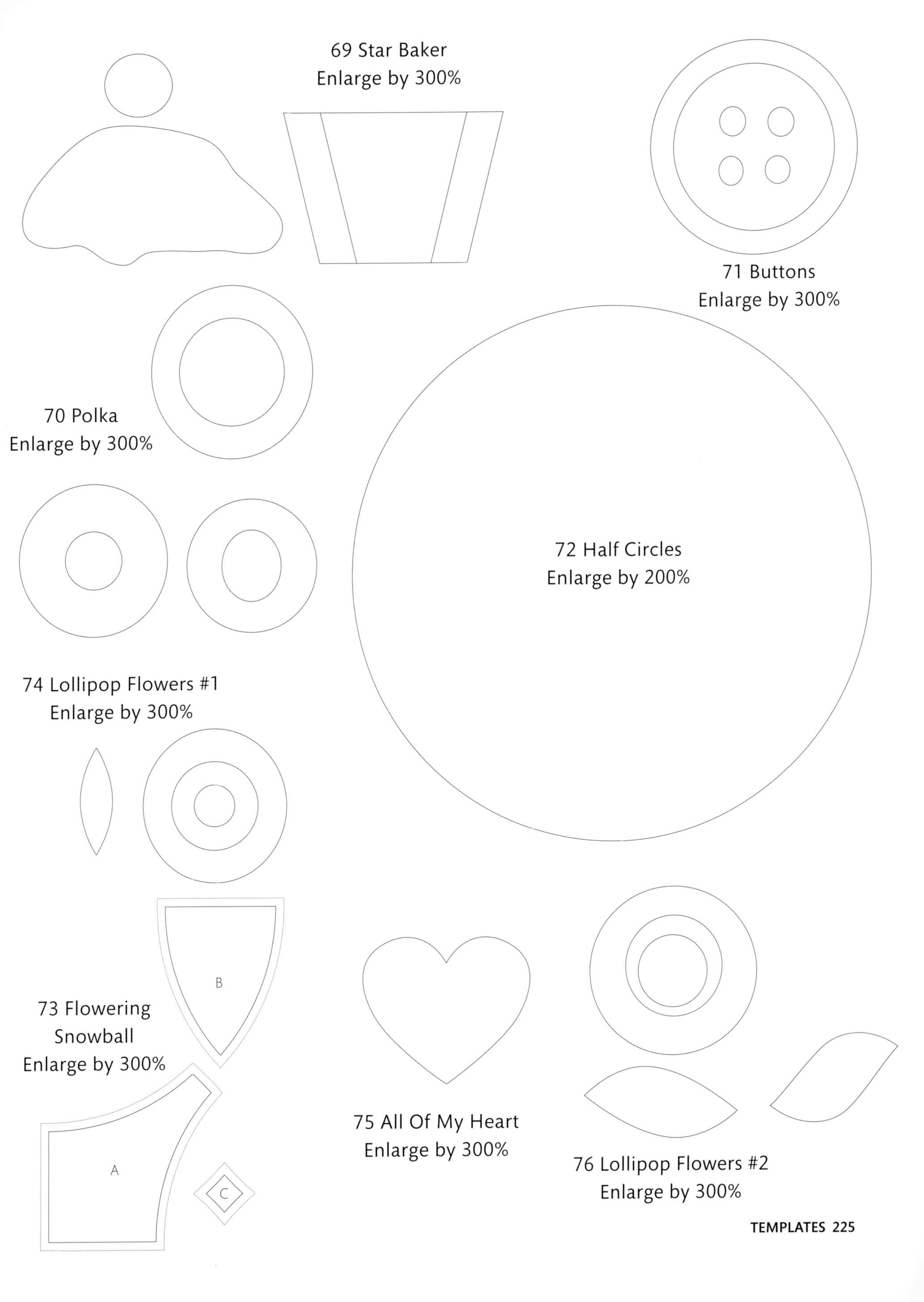
69 Star Baker
Enlarge by 300%
71 Buttons
Enlarge by 300%
70 Polka
Enlarge by 300%
72 Half Circles
Enlarge by 200%
74 Lollipop Flowers #1
Enlarge by 300%
B
73 Flowering
Snowball
Enlarge by 300%
A
C
75 All Of My Heart
Enlarge by 300%
76 Lollipop Flowers #2
Enlarge by 300%

78 Racing Track
Enlarge by 300%

77 Rose Petals
Enlarge by 300%

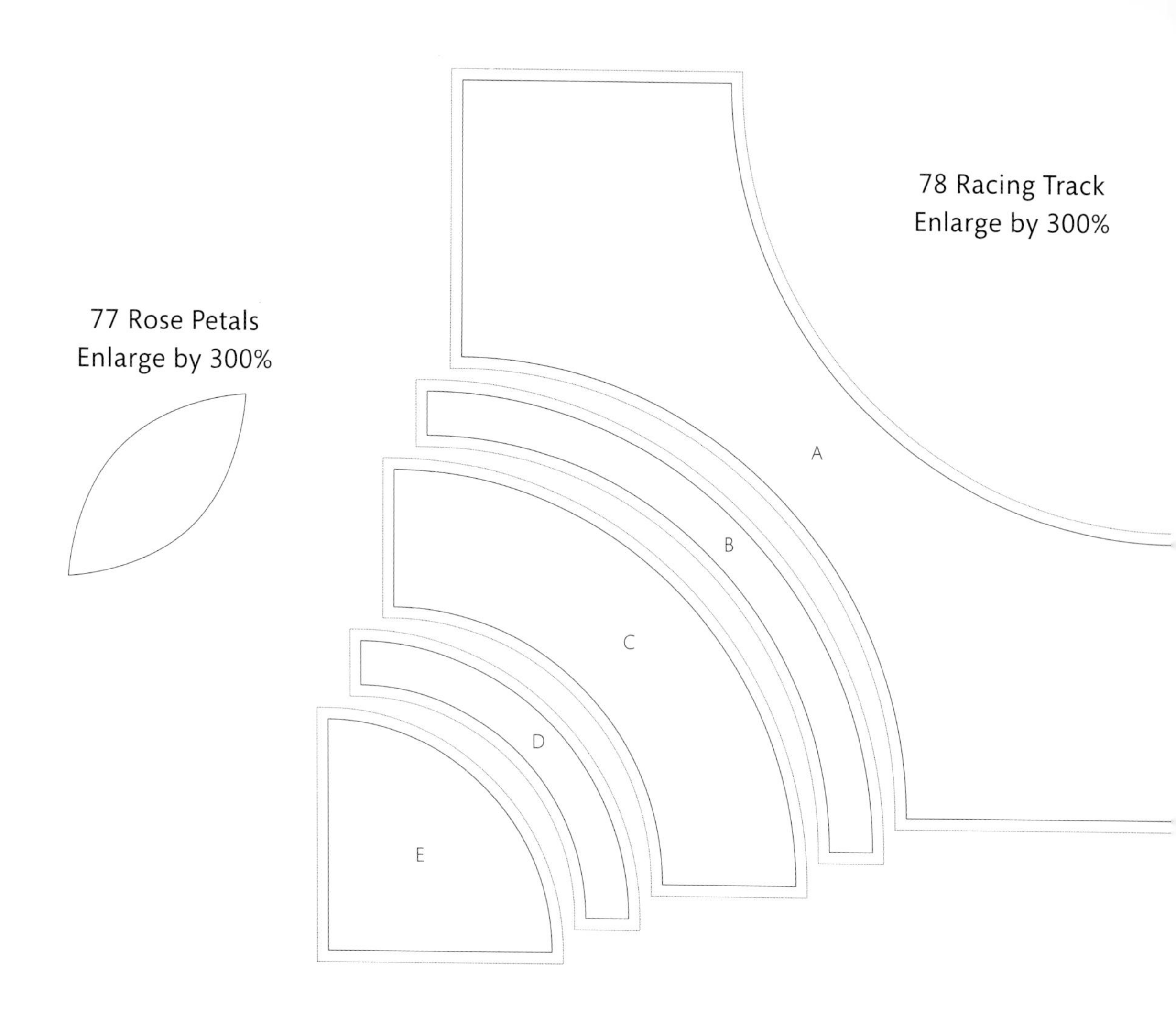

79 Rob Peter Pay Paul
Enlarge by 200%

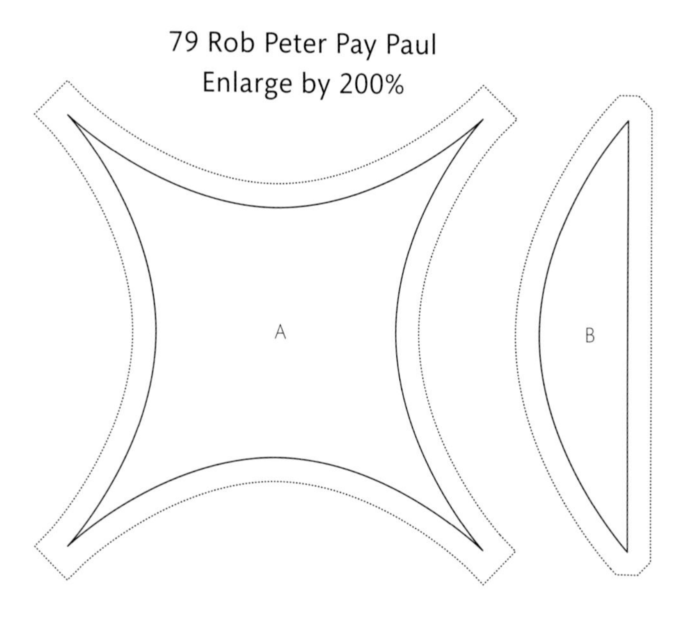

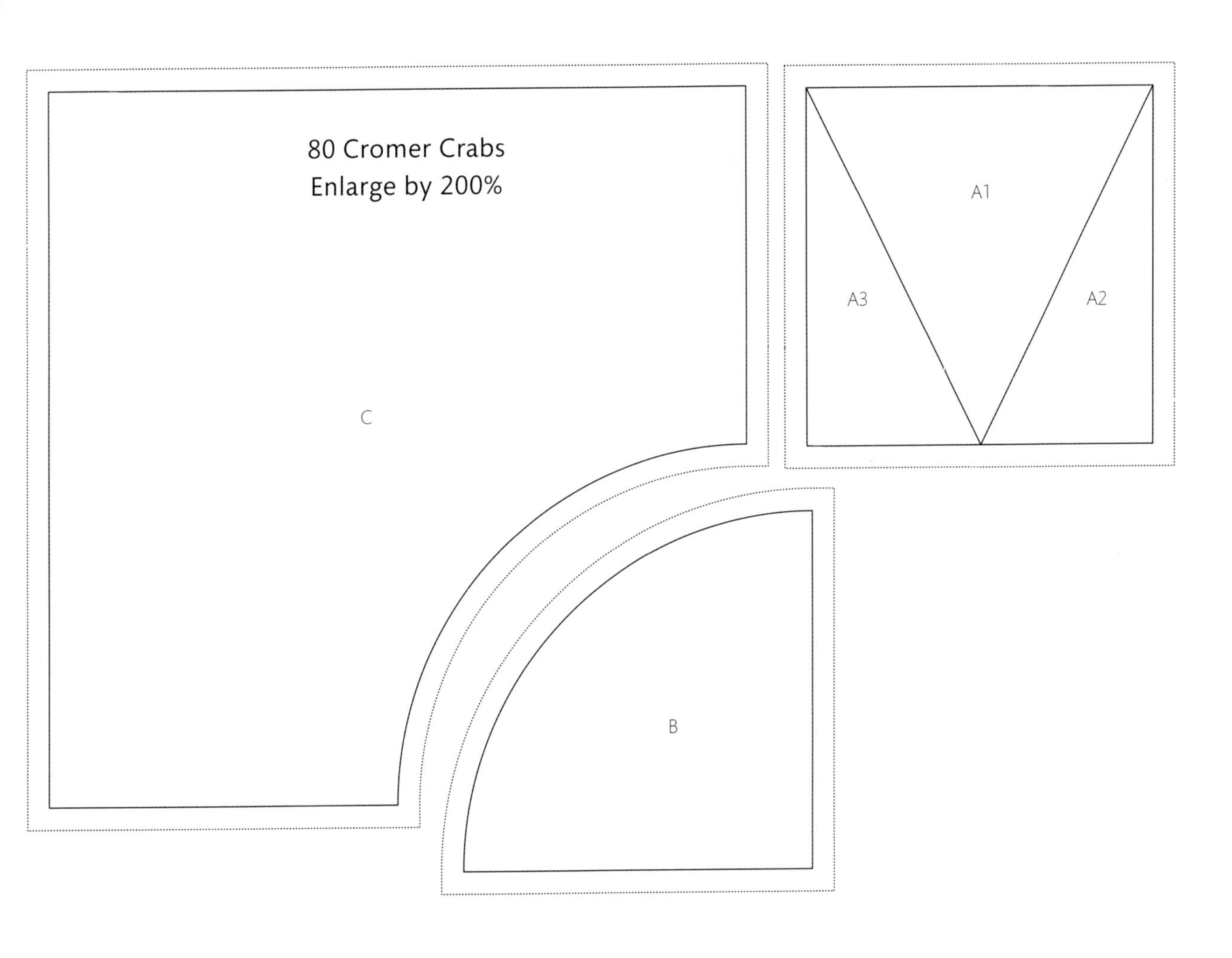
80 Cromer Crabs
Enlarge by 200%
C
B
A1
A3
A2

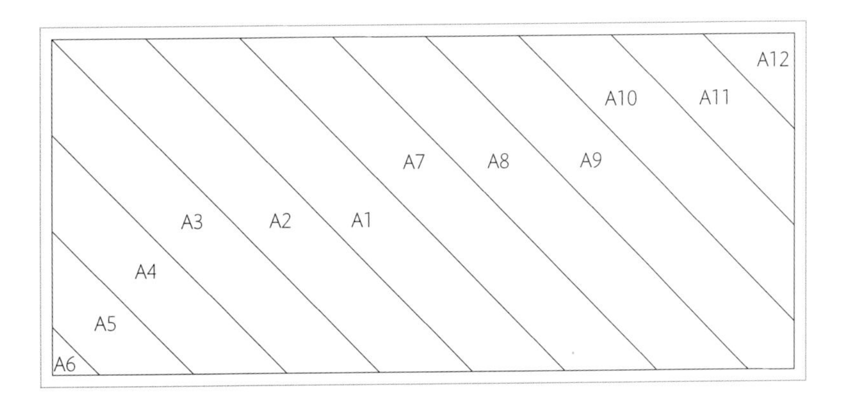
81 Quiver
Enlarge by 300%
A12
A10
A11
A7
A8
A9
A3
A2
A1
A4
A5
A6

82 Kogin
Enlarge by 300%

A7 A8
A2 A1 A6
A5 A4 A3
A10
B9
B8
B7
B6
B5
B1
B2
B3
B4

83 Bunting
Enlarge by 200%

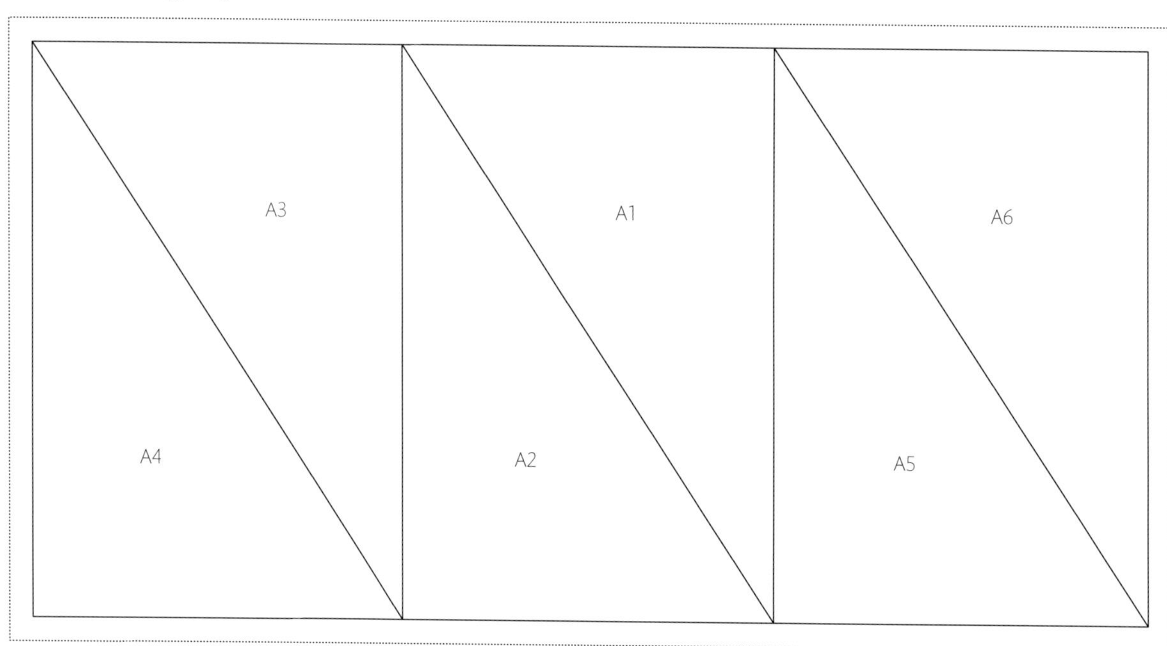

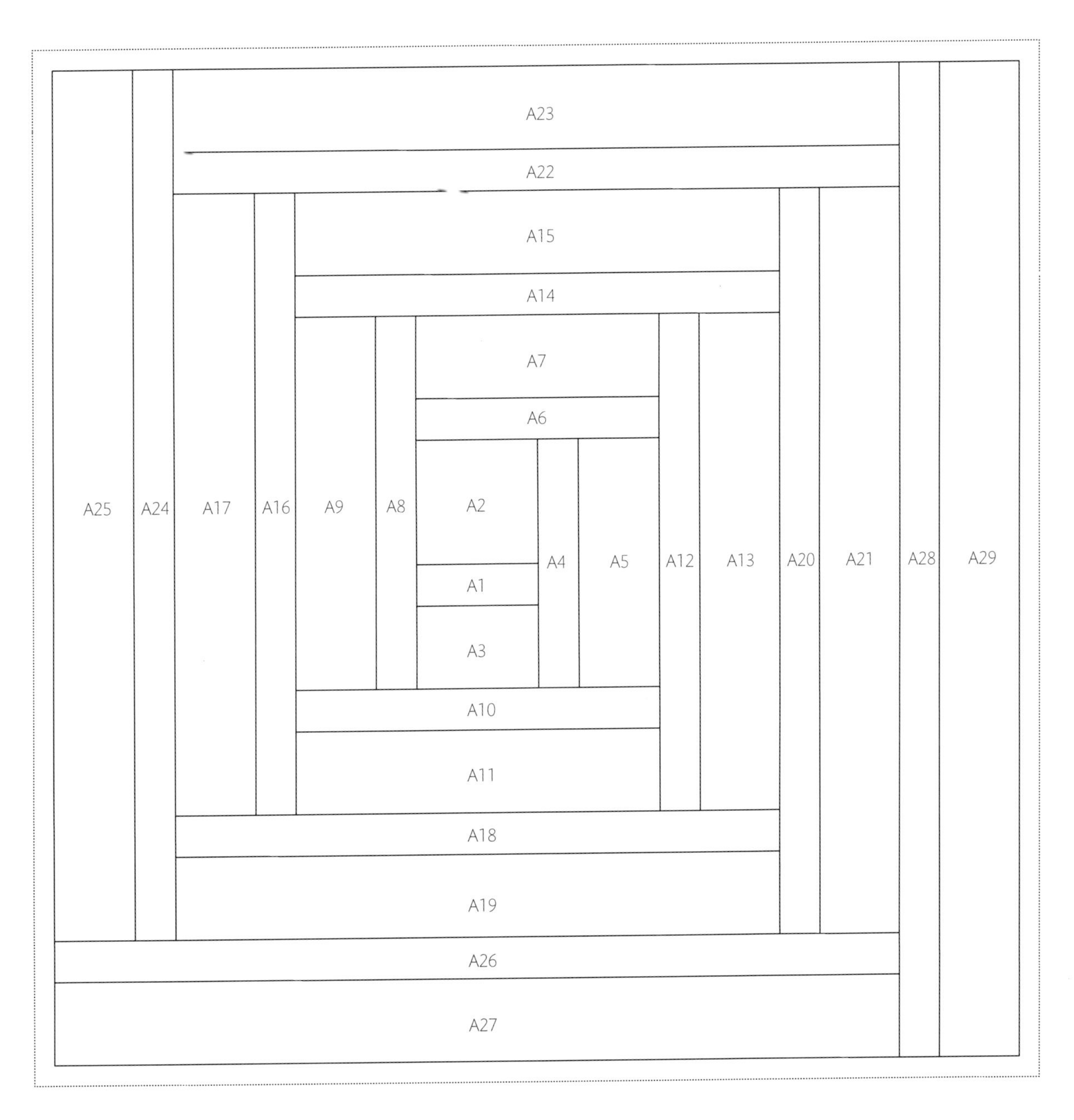

84 Stained Glass Rose Window
Enlarge by 200%

85 Zebra
Enlarge by 200%

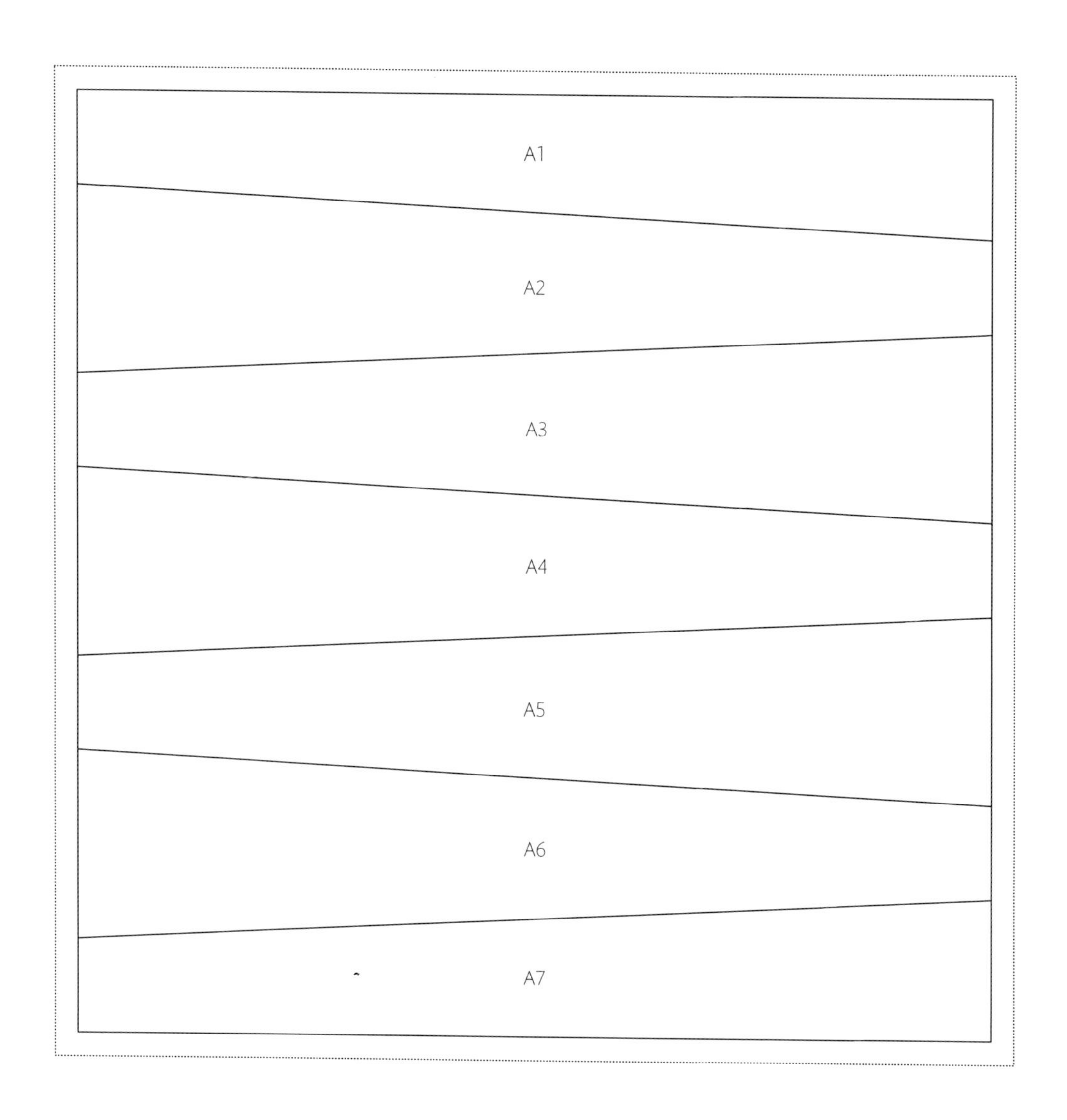

86 Best in Show
Enlarge by 200%

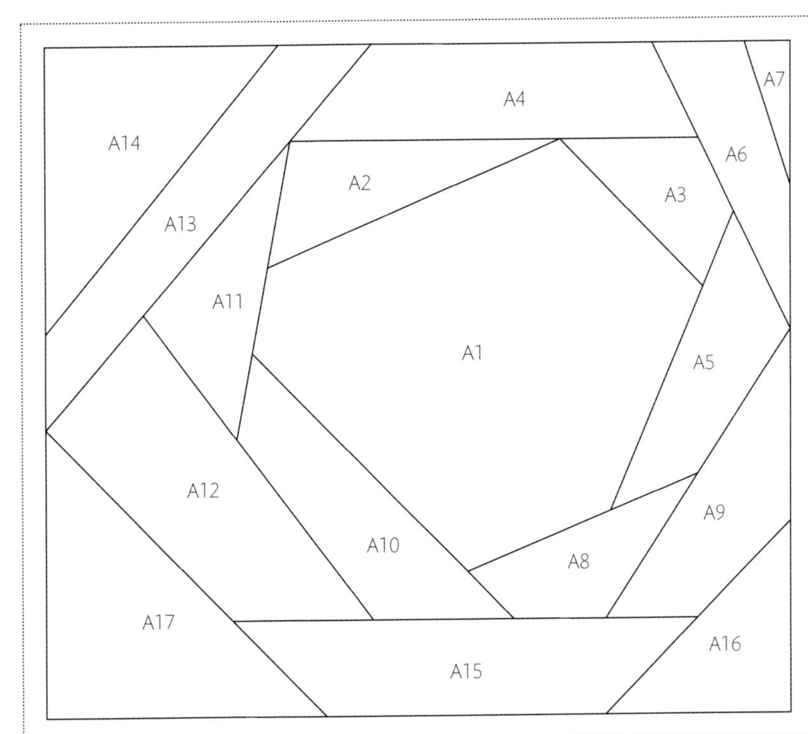

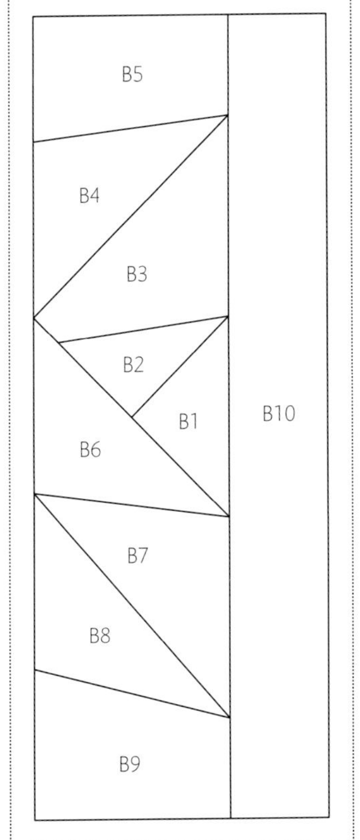

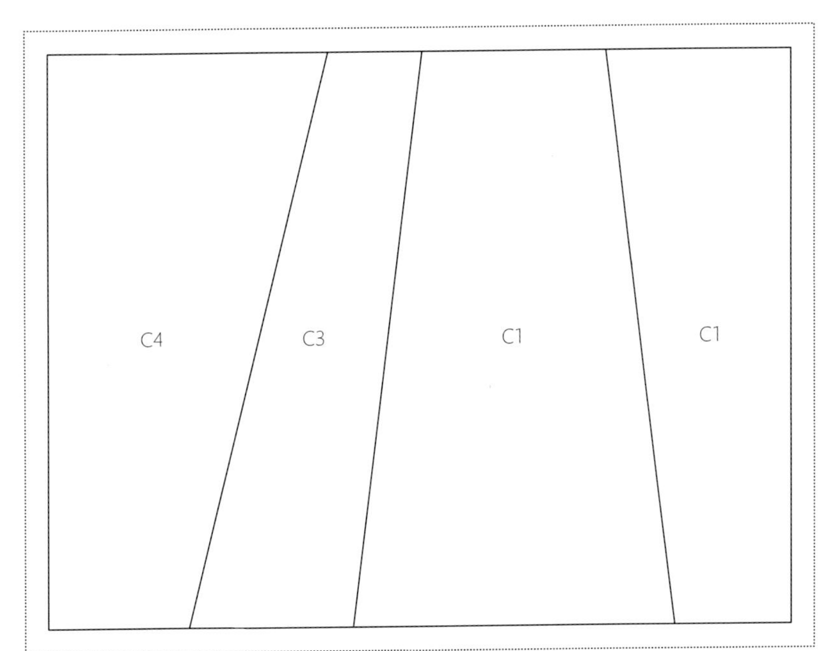

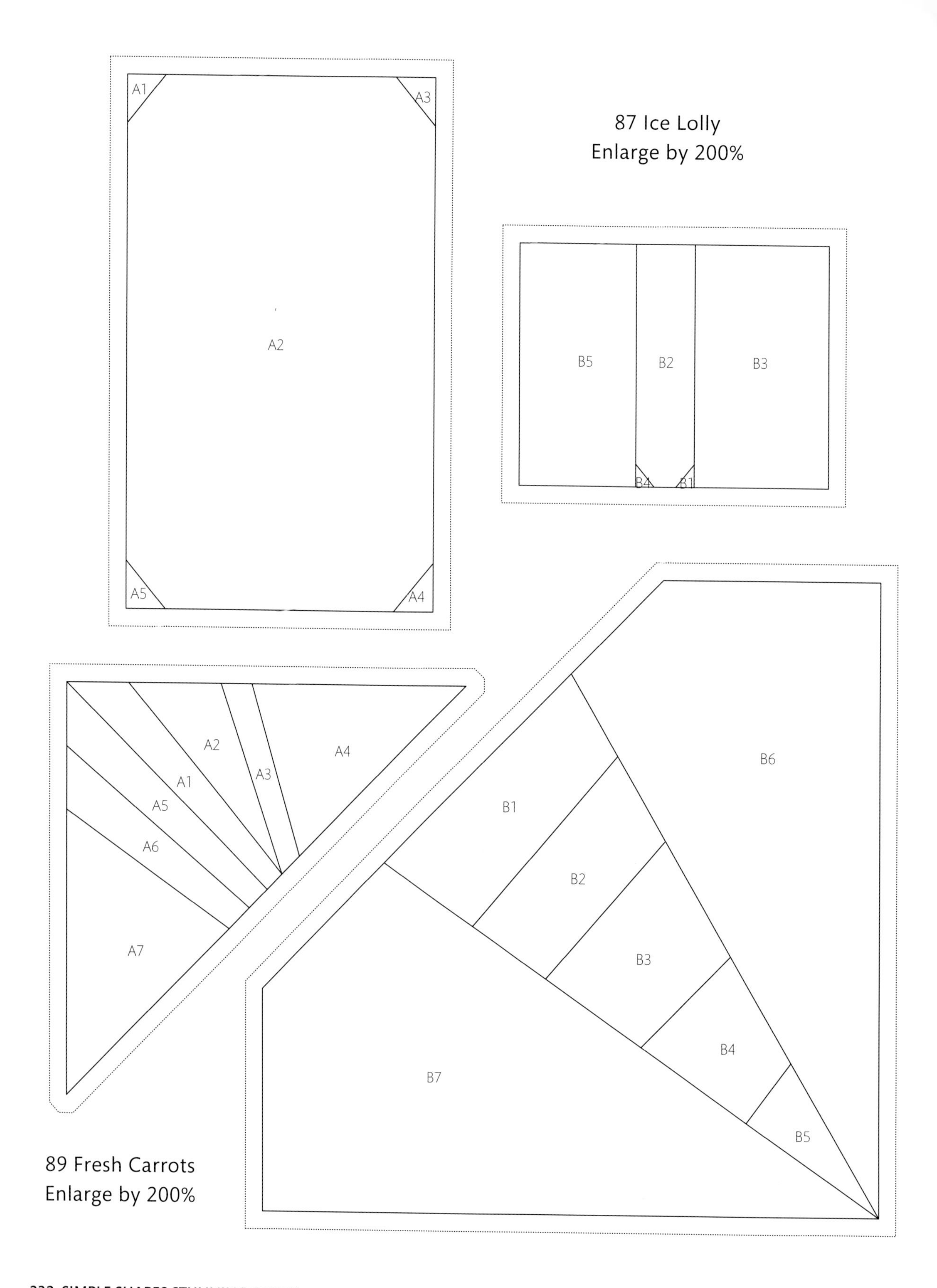

87 Ice Lolly
Enlarge by 200%

89 Fresh Carrots
Enlarge by 200%

88 Now Voyager
Enlarge by 200%

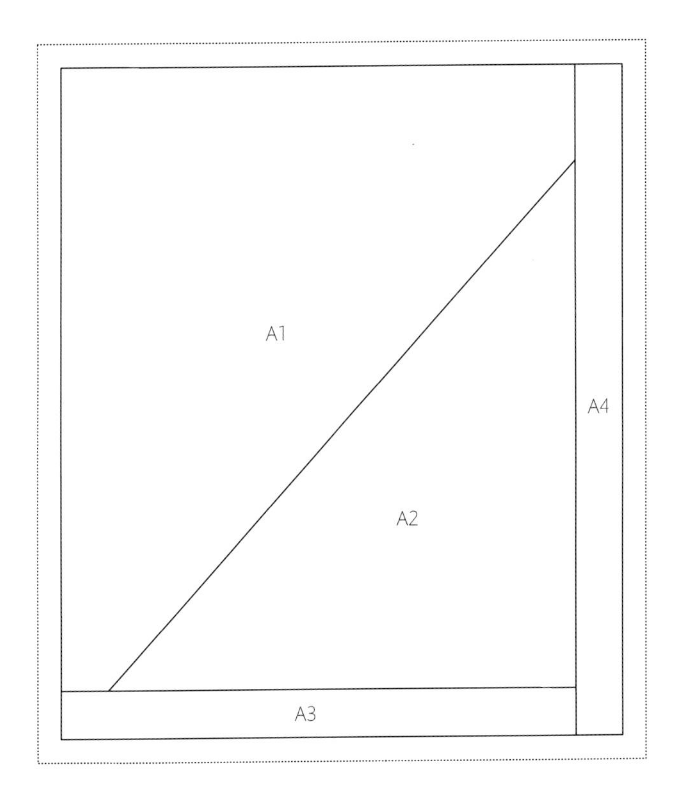

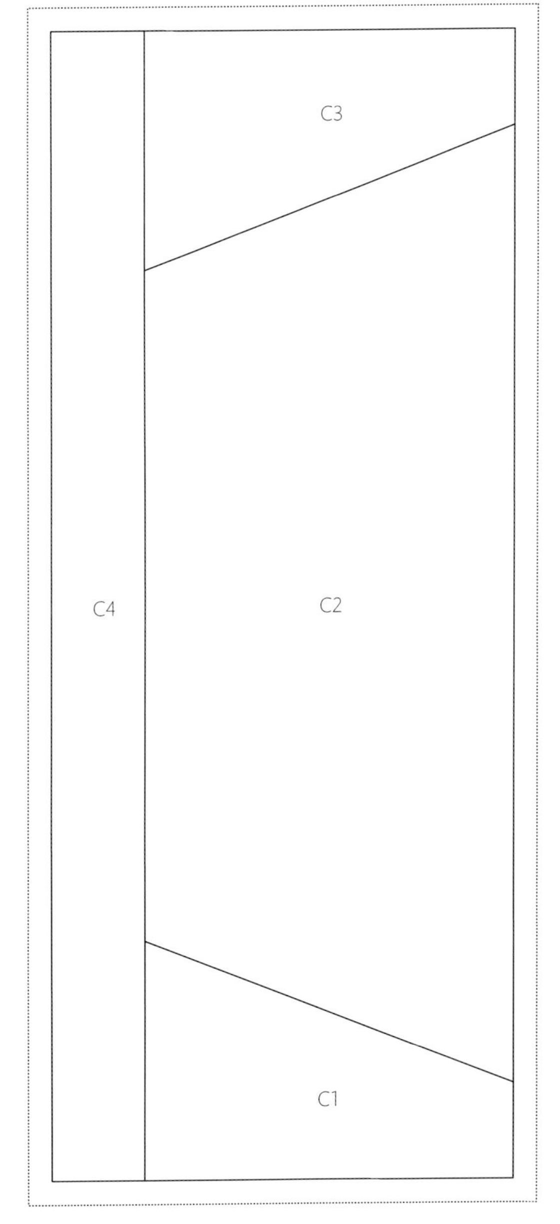

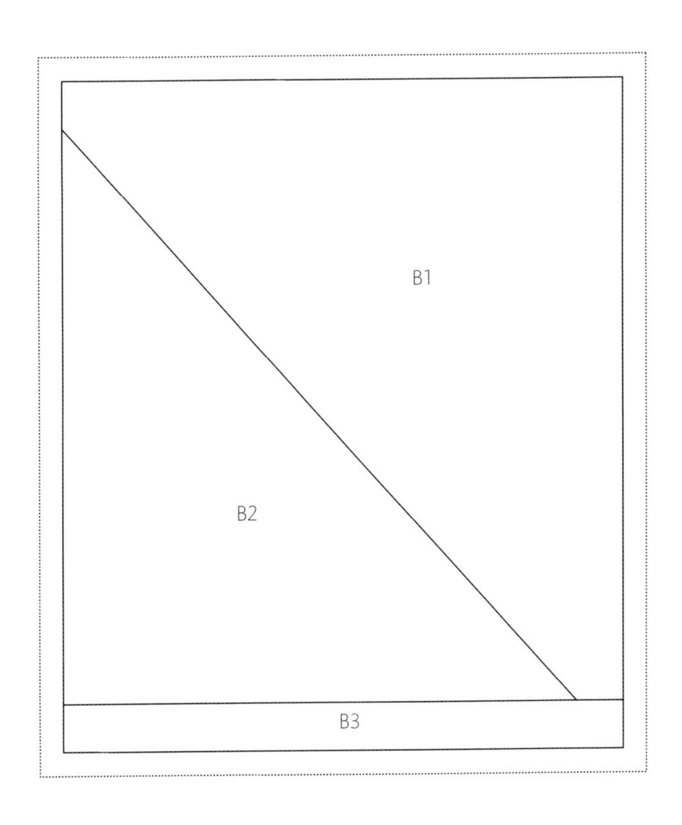

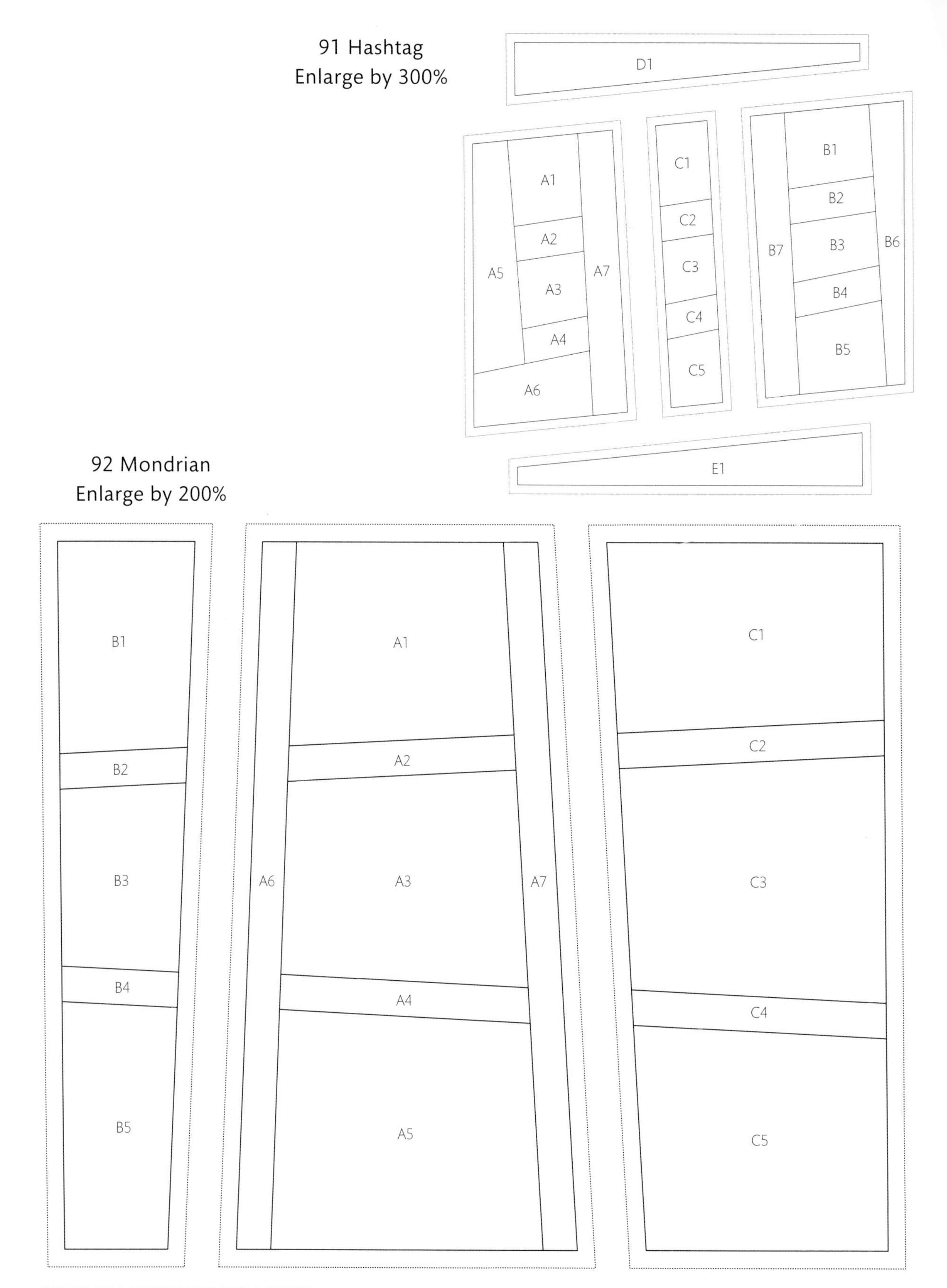
91 Hashtag
Enlarge by 300%
D1
A1
A2
A3
A4
A5
A6
A7
C1
C2
C3
C4
C5
B1
B2
B3
B4
B5
B6
B7
E1
92 Mondrian
Enlarge by 200%
B1
B2
B3
B4
B5
A1
A2
A3
A4
A5
A6
A7
C1
C2
C3
C4
C5

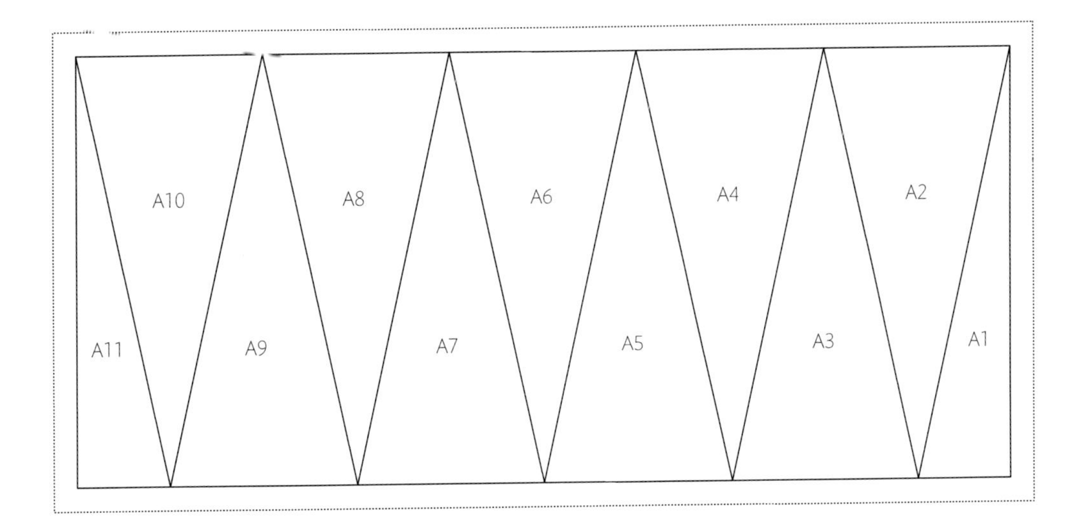

93 Shoal
Enlarge by 200%

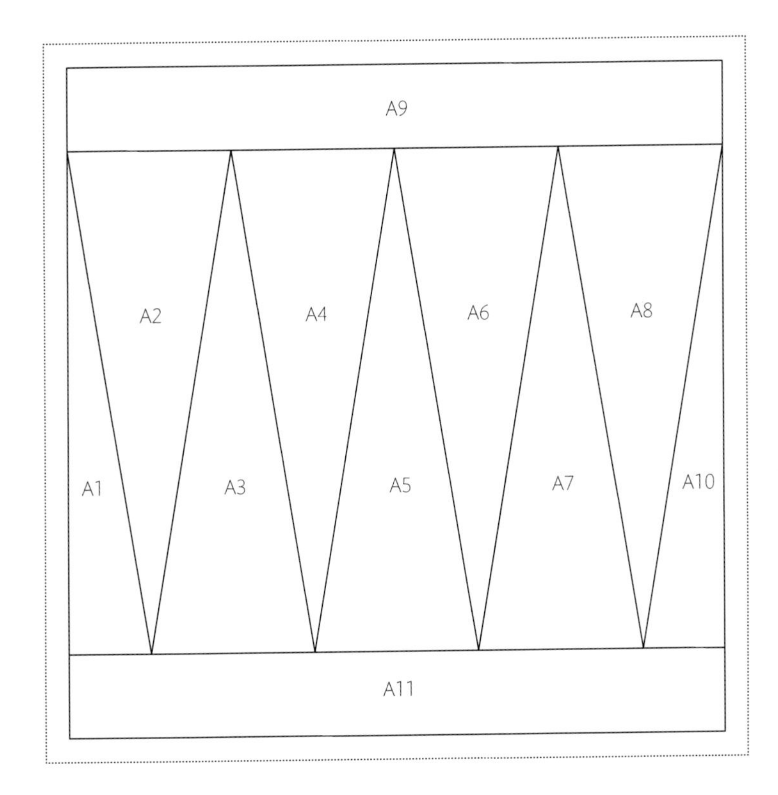

94 Whirl
Enlarge by 200%

96 Fishbones
Enlarge by 300%

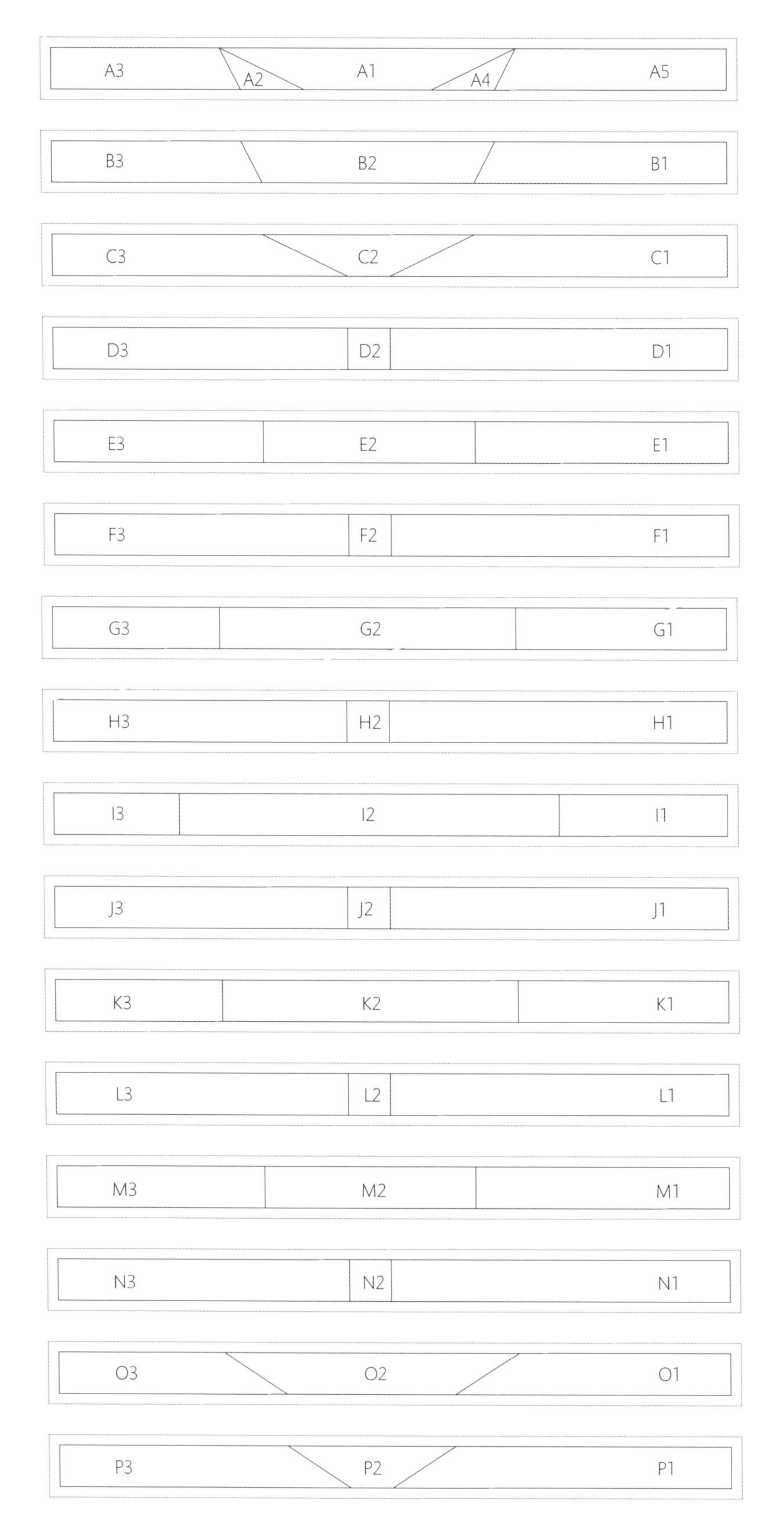

97 Wild Goose Chase
Enlarge by 300%

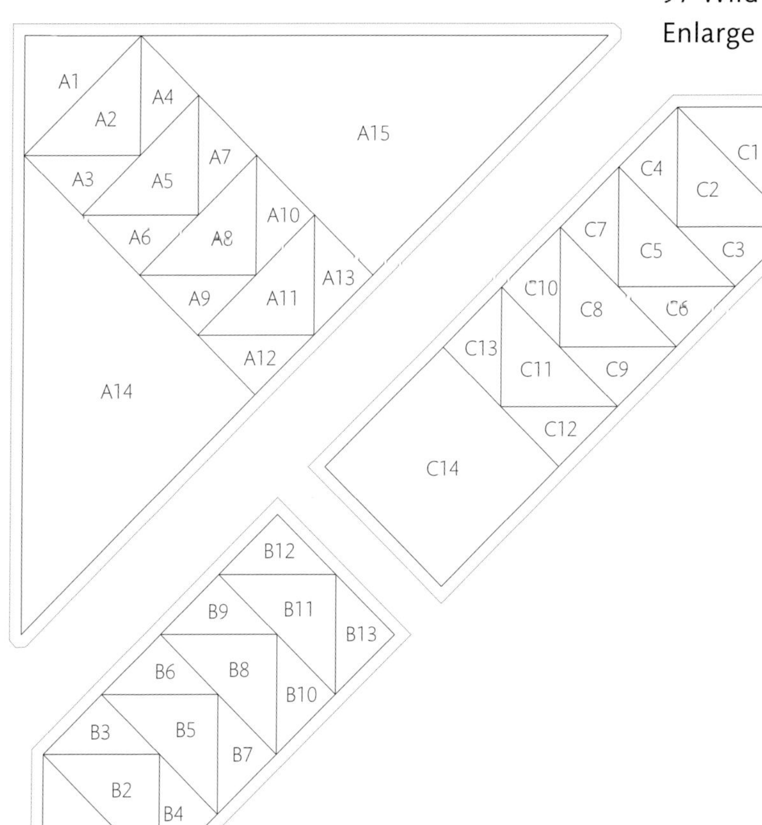

99 Radiant Star
Enlarge by 200%

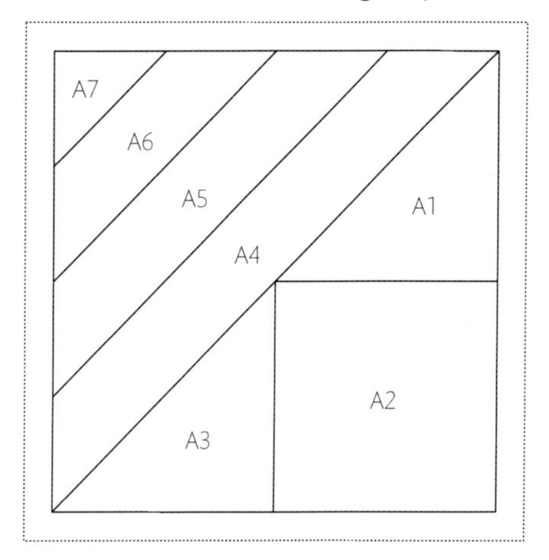

98 Kaleidoscope
Enlarge by 300%

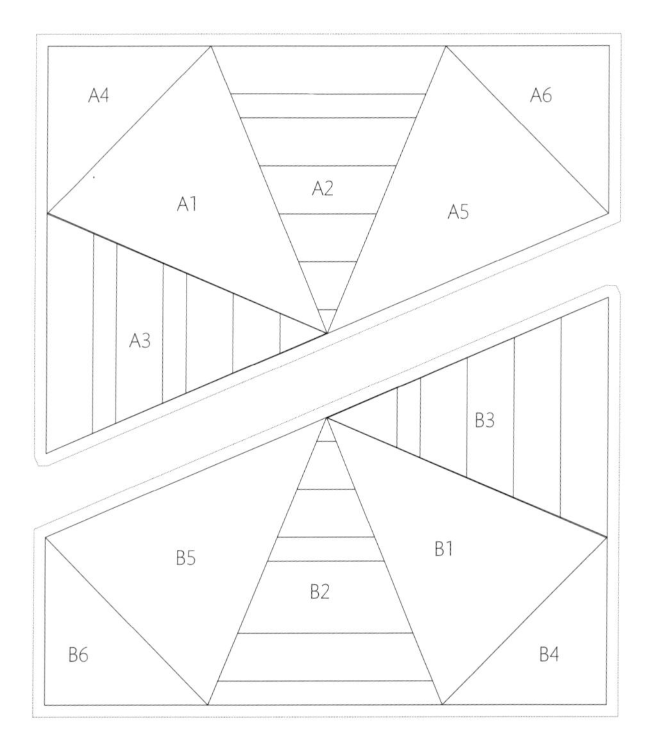

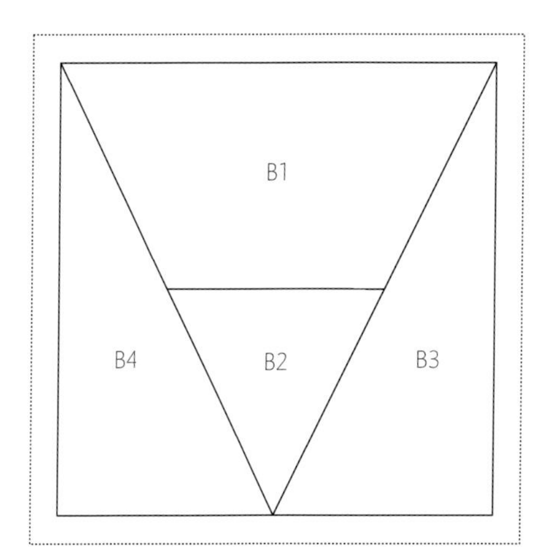

100 Straight To The Point
Enlarge by 300%

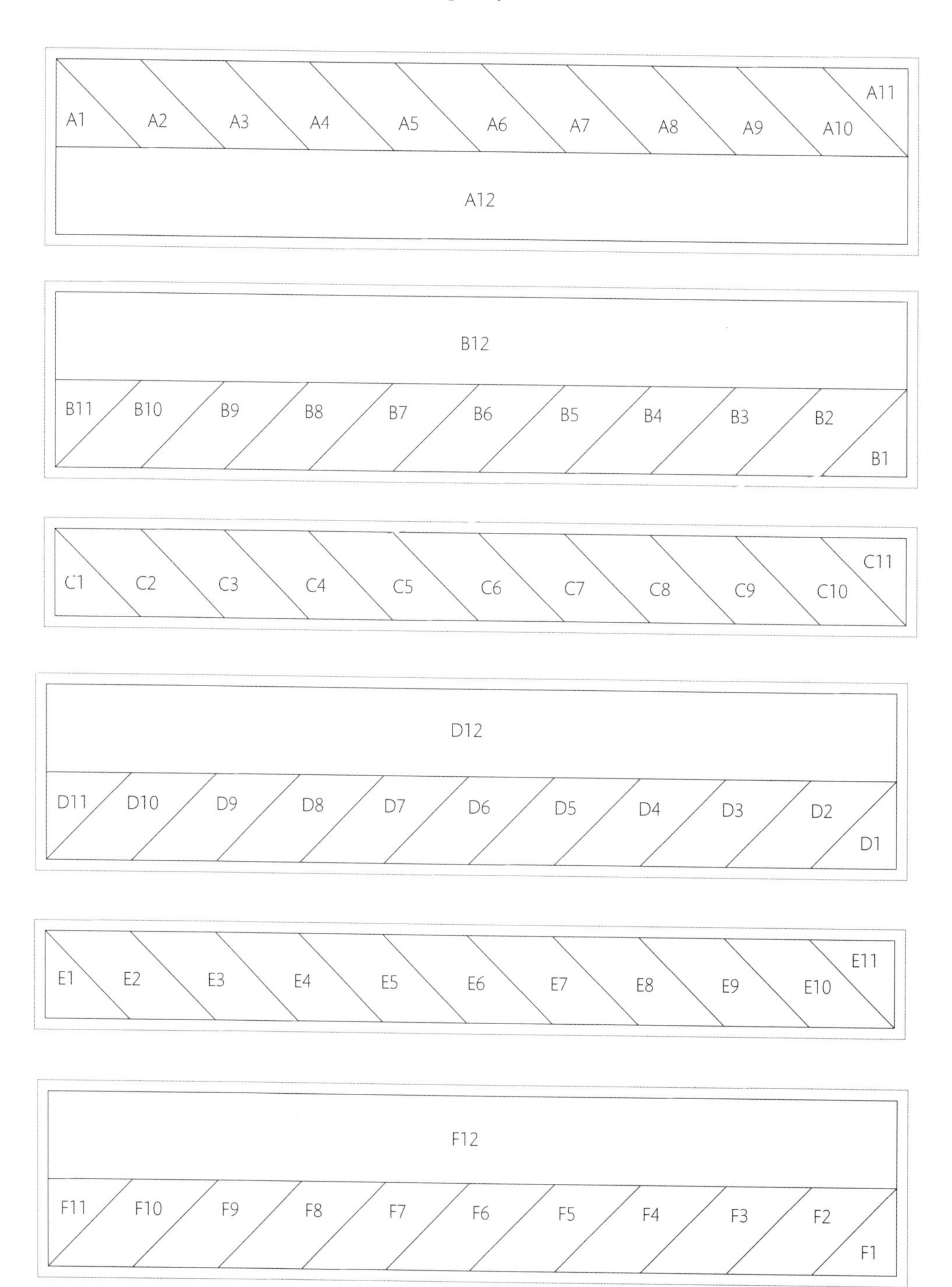

SUPPLIERS

Sewing machines
Bernina
www.bernina.com

Quilting machines
Handi Quilter
For longarm quilting machines
www.pinholequilting.co.uk
www.handiquilter.com

Die cutting supplies
For Go! Cutting machines, strip dies, piecing and appliqué dies
AccuQuilt
www.accuquilt.com

Machine sewing needles
www.schmetzneedles.com

Haberdashery (notions)
John Lewis
For general haberdashery, thread, template plastic, scissors and rotary cutting equipment
www.johnlewis.com

Hobbycraft
For general quilt supplies, including fabric and haberdashery
www.hobbycraft.co.uk

Dunelm
For quilt waddings (battings), threads, general supplies
www.dunelm.com

Coats Thread
www.coats.com

Groves
For general haberdashery, 505 quilt basting spray, cotton quilt wadding), fusible web, Sew Easy rulers and general cutting equipment
www.grovesltd.co.uk

Vliesofix
For fusible web, interfacings and waddings
www.vlieseline.com

Visage Textiles
For general haberdashery, cotton quilt waddings
www.visagetextiles.com

Barnyarns
For general haberdashery and quilting supplies
www.barnyarns.co.uk

Fabrics
Patchwork and quilting supplies, cutting equipment, longarm quilting machines and supplies

The Cotton Patch
www.cottonpatch.co.uk

Lady Sew and Sew Fabrics
www.ladysewandsew.co.uk

Makower UK
www.makoweruk.com

The Craft Cotton Company
www.craftcotton.com

The Cosy Cabin
For general quilting supplies and quilting fabrics
www.thecosycabin.co.uk

ACKNOWLEDGEMENTS

A huge thank you is owed to the many people who have helped and supported me in producing this book: to Charlie, my husband, who makes me believe that I am capable of anything; to my agent and friend Heather and to Cara at HHB Agency; to Katie, Krissy, Amy, Bella and Michelle at Pavilion; and to Rachel, my incredible photographer, and her assistant, Emma. I also want to say massive thanks to everyone at Create and Craft TV, who give me such a wonderful platform to share my books, my designs and my love of quilting with an even wider audience, and to AccuQuilt who have helped me 'cut time so I can quilt more!'

To friends at The Craft Cotton Company, and in particular to Dani and Vicki for their love and support as I grow as a fabric designer, and to Liz and Pete at Pinhole Quilting and all at HandiQuilter in the US who have brought the utter joy of longarm quilting to my life and craft. A very special thank you to Joan and Mel, who both contributed many hours and enormous skill to make several of the samples in this book. You are both incredible quilters and beautiful friends. Finally, thanks must go to the many people who give me such love and friendship through the many quilt shows I attend, the groups I visit and through social media... I couldn't do this without you!

DEDICATION

This book is dedicated to Charlie, my husband and partner in all things, for his constant and unwavering support, his complete faith in my abilities and for loving me just the way I am.

Photography by Rachel Whiting

First published in the United Kingdom in 2019 by
Pavilion
43 Great Ormond Street
London
WC1N 3HZ

ISBN 978-1-911624-39-4

A CIP catalogue record for this book is available from the British Library.

10 9 8 7 6 5 4 3 2 1

Reproduction by Mission Productions Ltd, Hong Kong
Printed and bound by 1010 Printing International Ltd, China

www.pavilionbooks.com